ALSO IN THIS SERIES

LAO-TZU: TE-TAO CHING
A NEW TRANSLATION BASED
ON THE RECENTLY DISCOVERED
MA-WANG-TUI TEXTS.
TRANSLATED, WITH AN
INTRODUCTION AND COMMENTARY,
BY ROBERT G. HENRICKS

SUN-TZU: THE ART OF WARFARE
THE FIRST ENGLISH TRANSLATION
INCORPORATING THE
RECENTLY DISCOVERED
YIN-CH'ÜEH-SHAN TEXTS.
TRANSLATED, WITH AN
INTRODUCTION AND COMMENTARY,
BY ROGER T. AMES

SUN PIN: THE ART OF WARFARE
A RECENTLY REDISCOVERED CLASSIC
TRANSLATED, WITH AN
INTRODUCTION AND COMMENTARY,
BY D. C. LAU AND ROGER T. AMES

I CHING: THE CLASSIC OF CHANGES
THE FIRST ENGLISH TRANSLATION
OF THE NEWLY DISCOVERED
SECOND-CENTURY B.C. MAWANGDUI TEXTS.
TRANSLATED, WITH AN
INTRODUCTION AND COMMENTARY,
BY EDWARD L. SHAUGHNESSY

FIVE LOST CLASSICS: TAO, HUANGLAO, AND YIN-YANG IN HAN CHINA

TRANSLATED,
WITH AN INTRODUCTION AND
COMMENTARY, BY
ROBIN D. S. YATES

BALLANTINE BOOKS · NEW YORK

http://www.randomhouse.com

Library of Congress Cataloging-in-Publication Data
Five lost classics : Tao, Huang-Lao, and Yin-yang in Han China /
translated by Robin D.S. Yates
p. cm.—(Classics of ancient China)
1. Taoism—Sacred books. 2. Yin-yang. 3. Philosophy,
Chinese—221 B.C.–960 A.D. 4. Manuscripts, Chinese—China—Ma-wang-
tui Site. I. Yates, Robin D. S., 1948– . II. Series.
BL1900.A1F58 1997
181'.114—dc21 97–2880
CIP

Text design by Holly Johnson

Manufactured in the United States of America

First Edition: July 1997

10 9 8 7 6 5 4 3 2 1

For Grace

CONTENTS

ACKNOWLEDGMENTS

This book has long been in gestation and, as a consequence, I have many scholars and friends to thank for their assistance, support, and advice, not all of whom can be acknowledged: for my omissions, I beg indulgence.

I first began work on the texts that are translated in this book in the early 1980s while I was teaching at Harvard University. These texts formed the basis of the curriculum for my third-year Classical (literary) Chinese course and I was privileged to have in that class many fine scholars who helped my understanding of these difficult yet exciting texts. Several of them, including Karen Turner and Susan Weld, have gone on to publish their own important studies of early Chinese thought and history. To their enthusiasm and insights I am much indebted.

While I was at Dartmouth College, Robert Henricks, the general editor of this series, solicited my contribution, and I am most grateful to him for his encouragement, advice, and the intellectual stimulation he gave me through conversation and correspondence. I must also thank him and Owen Lock, senior editor of the series, for their patience in awaiting this volume. Owen lent enthusiastic support for the project. In the course of preparing the volume, I also benefited greatly from conversations with Roger T. Ames of the University of Hawaii, who wrote two of the previous volumes of the series, the translation of Sun-tzu's *Art of War*, and Sun Pin's *Art of War*, the latter with D. C. Lau. Roger has done great service to the field with his publications on the history of Chinese thought and through his superb editorship of *Philosophy East and West*.

In the course of preparing this volume, I greatly benefited from the opportunity for presenting my preliminary conclusions about the nature of these texts at the New England Symposia on Chinese Thought, ably organized by Kidder Smith of Bowdoin College and Harold Roth of Brown University. I also had the opportunity to present a paper at the International Symposium of Mawangdui Studies in Changsha, Hunan, in 1992, organized by Fu Juyou and Chen Songchang to celebrate the twentieth anniversary of the discovery of Mawangdui. I would like to express my gratitude to those scholars and the many others who participated in the discussions, from whose wisdom, knowledge, and insights given me both in conversation and in their written work I have learned enormously. They include my former teacher Benjamin I. Schwartz, Tu Wei-ming, Peter Bol, Sarah Queen, John Major, Carine Defoort, who graciously sent me a copy of her excellent doctoral dissertation on the *Heguanzi*, Li Xueqin, Qiu Xigui, Li Ling, Yu Mingguang, Chen Guuying, Wu Jiulong, and Wei Qipeng. I would also like to express my appreciation to R. P. Peerenboom and Leo S. Chang, who generously shared their work on these texts before their publication, and whose expertise I found exceptionally helpful. The staff of the Harvard–Yenching, Dartmouth College, and McLennan–Redpath, McGill University, libraries provided me over the years with much-needed assistance to track down essential materials, and I thank them for their patience and understanding in responding to my pressing requests. In Beijing, Wang Yongjiang welcomed me to Yanbeiyuan most warmly and I would not have been able to revise the translations without his generous hospitality. Finally, I must offer a special word of thanks to Grace S. Fong, without whose support, encouragement, and constructive suggestions this book would not have been finished.

Yanbeiyuan, Beijing
June 25, 1994

PART ONE:
INTRODUCTION

The texts translated in this book were found in late 1973 in the richly furnished tomb no. 3, Mawangdui, Changsha, Hunan province, in a cache of manuscripts written on silk. They appear to have been part of the private library of a member of the Western Han dynasty aristocracy, the son of Li Cang, chief minister of the southern kingdom of Changsha, who died in approximately 168 B.C.E. Their retrieval was of immense, worldwide significance, comparable to the discovery of the Dead Sea Scrolls in the West. For the library contained, in addition to the two earliest manuscripts of the famous Daoist philosophical work *Laozi*, which have been already published in this series (Henricks 1989), esoteric medical, sexological, astrological, and philosophical texts, maps and charts from various schools and traditions that scholars knew had originally existed because they were recorded in the Han imperial library catalog, but which had been lost in antiquity.

Most importantly, copied in front of the second manuscript of *Laozi*, dubbed the B version by scholars assigned to the difficult task of transcribing these ancient works into modern Chinese characters, were texts that apparently reflected the philosophical tradition of HuangLao Daoism. This tradition is referred to in many ancient histories, philosophical treatises, and literary anecdotes as being extremely popular at the end of the Warring States period and beginning of the Han dynasty (206 B.C.E.). Indeed, it is recorded as being almost the state ideology of the early Han until it was displaced by Confucianism under the powerful emperor Wu in about 140 B.C.E. Unfortunately, the treatises in the silk manuscripts, which seem to be quite syncretic, are anonymous, and this fact has led to enormously varied interpretations as to their date of composition: some place the manuscripts at the very beginning of the tradition, others at the very end; the complex problems involved are discussed in the two appendices to this book. In addition, quite frequently there are gaps in the text because the silk decomposed where it was folded: the resulting lacunae make the translation and interpretation of these passages impossible.

HuangLao, meaning the philosophy of the Yellow Emperor and Laozi, was one of the three traditions of ancient Daoism, the others being those of the *Laozi* text itself and the famous mystic Zhuangzi (Chuang-tzu), that developed in the period of intense philosophical debate known as the Hundred Schools after the death of Confucius in 479 B.C.E. and prior to the unification of China under the First Emperor of Qin in 221 B.C.E. It was known to have been popular at the famous Jixia Academy in the eastern state of Qi patronized by the ruling house of Tian that had previously usurped the throne there. In the Warring States period, it had influenced a diverse range of intellectuals, including the political "Dao-legalist" theorists Shen Dao, Shen Buhai, Hanfeizi, and Heguanzi, and the Daoist Jixia academicians Tian Pian and Jiezi. In addition, it was the philosophy or technique of greatest interest to the early Han emperors Wen (reigned 179–157 B.C.E.) and Jing (reigned 156–141 B.C.E.), the powerful Empress Dowager Dou, Liu An (ca. 180–122 B.C.E.), the Han prince who sponsored the syncretic Daoist book *Huainanzi*, and a wide range of leading Han politicians, including the prime minister. Early Han economic and social policies apparently were based to a large extent on HuangLao principles. Sima Tan argued that the Daoists *(Daojia)* adopted the best elements of all the philosophical traditions handed down to his time; this view was incorporated by his son Sima Qian, the grand astrologer of Emperor Wu, in his *Shiji (Historical Records)*, the first of China's twenty-four dynastic histories.

In short, prior to the adoption of the Confucianism of Dong Zhongshu under Emperor Wu (reigned 140–87 B.C.E.), the HuangLao Daoist tradition was the most important philosophy among the Han elite. After the imperial sponsorship of Confucianism, however, it gradually became more and more associated with what eventually was to be recognized as religious Daoism and by the third and fourth centuries C.E., it was virtually forgotten and the tradition was interrupted, nevermore to influence intellectuals and the political, social, and economic policies of Chinese governments. The books and treatises were thrown away or abandoned and the texts eventually completely lost.

As a consequence, later scholars had no way to determine with any precision exactly what constituted the main elements or features of HuangLao Daoist philosophical speculation until the discovery of the Mawangdui hoard, nor was there any way to determine what was HuangLao in the philosophical works of those schools that had survived the vicissitudes of history and had been passed down through the centuries. The analysis of the East Asian philosophical tradition was deeply flawed and inadequate. Thus there is no complete counterpart to these silk manuscripts in any of the books that have been handed down and commented on over the centuries; these manuscripts have not been read by anyone, Chinese or Western, for close to two thousand years. They are truly Lost Classics.

As a result, their discovery and publication caused a sensation in China and offered the opportunity to rewrite the history of the development of Chinese philosophy. They were even perceived to be a miracle by the followers of one of Taiwan's new cults, the religion of the Yellow Emperor, and the texts have been adopted as their official scriptures, and are venerated as containing holy writ (Jochim 1990). We will not, however, pursue this aspect of these new texts; rather we will concern ourselves with their role in the emergence of the Chinese philosophic tradition.

Although many Chinese, Japanese, and Western scholars have offered their preliminary assessments of these works, much more analysis needs to be done. R. P. Peerenboom's (1993) excellent study is the first book in the English-speaking world to devote itself entirely to these treatises (though without complete translations) and Yu Mingguang (1993[a]) has provided the first translation into modern Chinese in China, which includes Leo Chang's preliminary rendition into English. In Taiwan, Hu Xintian has published two tomes devoted to the translation into modern Chinese and analysis of the works (1984, 1992), and Jacques Decaux (1989) has published a French translation there, too. In Japan, it is probably Asano Yuichi's (1992) volume that has explored the complex problems concerning the nature and development of HuangLao in the most substantial way. Thus this book offers Western readers for the first time a complete, easily accessible, English translation of these remarkable texts.

5

2. THE HISTORICAL BACKGROUND TO THE SILK MANUSCRIPTS

What were the problems confronting society in the late Eastern Zhou period, the last three hundred years or so between Confucius' lifetime and the unification of China by the First Emperor of Qin in 221 B.C.E.? And what changes were occurring in social, political, and economic spheres that made it imperative for philosophers and statesmen to devote their attention primarily to questions of social and political philosophy, rather than to more abstract questions such as those being addressed by their Western counterparts—Socrates, Plato and Aristotle—at roughly the same time?

First of all, on the political front, the power of Eastern Zhou rulers, who had at one time claimed title to and control over the entire East Asian subcontinent we know as China, was only a shadow of its former self. The Eastern Zhou court actually dominated only a very small area around what is now Luoyang, just south of the Yellow River in the north China plain. Certainly the Zhou ruling house was still recognized as possessing ritual authority, an authority which was considered so potent for many hundreds of years that it enabled them to claim to have direct access to the supramundane world: the Zhou king was Son of Heaven and only he could worship Heaven and maintain thereby the harmony between the world of men and the spirit world. But practically speaking, the territory of China was controlled by a number of different city-states organized into regional systems. The ruling houses of these city-states were related by marriage to the Zhou and to each other, yet they were fighting each other in increasingly bitter wars to gain control of the whole country. Traditionally, this period has been characterized as "feudal" and the rulers of the states are called "feudal lords." In the Eastern Zhou, the chief of the "feudal lords" was called the "hegemon" and he was responsible for keeping the other lords in line. Over time, the larger states attacked and absorbed the smaller until the era of the Warring States, in which seven great kingdoms were left to fight to the bitter conclusion. It was the state of Qin, located in the northwest, that finally defeated all its rivals—the Wei, Han, Zhao, Yan, Qi (the state that had destroyed Confucius' home state of Lu), and Chu in the south—and united China into an empire that was to endure until the present century.

This condition of political fragmentation was not generally acceptable to the intellectual elite, as far as we know, although the people as a whole seem to have identified with the states of which they were citizens. Certainly, the Chinese at the time believed that they were living in an age of degeneration and decline and they longed to return to a golden past, an age of "Great Peace" when the order and harmony of unity under a single, politically powerful, and legitimate central authority prevailed in the world. Each of the different philosophers and philosophical schools offered their rulers and patrons different remedies and policies and they located the golden age at different time periods in the past. For the writer(s) of the *Nine Rulers* text, the last essay translated in this book, it was Tang, the founder of the Shang dynasty, who was the epitome of the wise and perfect ruler; for the Yin-Yang specialists, it seems to have been the Yellow Emperor who filled this role.

Virtually all of the philosophers, of whatever persuasion, also offered their suggestions as to how best to prosecute the endemic wars of the period: Sunzi and Sun Bin were only the most famous of the military theoreticians. The essays on war in the second book of the silk manuscripts are typical of the kind of advice the rulers and kings were receiving. These rulers were all seeking the single cure for their woes: how to forestall the incursions of their neighbors, how to organize their bureaucracy and appoint the best officials to help them run their countries, how best to unify the disparate elements of their own population and encourage them to develop the state's economic and natural resources, and how best to cultivate their own moral and ethical behavior so that they could be "true kings" and win the allegiance of the whole world.

From an economic point of view, the foundation of wealth still remained agricultural production of grain and probably most people lived in the rural areas. Yet cities were growing rapidly and perhaps

7

were the largest in the world: the capital of the state of Qi, for example, may well have had a population of seven hundred thousand people. The rural population was able to support such concentrated urban agglomerations because of new farming techniques: cast iron agricultural tools were fast becoming popular at the expense of stone and bronze implements, and the states themselves controlled much of the iron production and marketing of pottery, lacquer, bone, stone, and other handicrafts. New systems of land tenure began to emerge, replacing what may have been a manorial-type. It became possible to buy and sell land, even though most immobile property probably still remained ultimately under the ownership of the state. But peasants, instead of being tied by heredity to the same plots over multiple generations, began to move around, either from one region to another within the same state, or to migrate into the cities, or from one state to another. Regional specialization in products was developing, as was long-distance trade. This trade and movement the states tried to control by the introduction of new systems of tallies and passports, which gave permission to private individuals to engage in cross-border activities. Trade was lubricated by the development of metal and cloth currency, and although many states possessed their own currency, gradually a system of exchange rates was formalized.

The development of the economy in turn led to the loosening of the rigid social status system. Members of the old aristocracy of earlier Zhou times seem to have eliminated each other in the innumerable wars and a new class of entrepreneurs and landowners seems to have risen to prominence. The states tried to fix the male population into a new hierarchy of graded social ranks which were not dependent on wealth, but on service that the individuals rendered to the states, especially service in warfare, where cutting off enemy heads in battle was rewarded with rank. Such success in battle was not a particularly attractive method of promotion, but at least it was an objective and rational criterion. As in the past, the family nested within a lineage remained the basic unit of society, the accepted ideology was patriarchy, and the accepted system of inheritance was patriliny, even though it is likely that some groups of non-Chinese tribespeople living in close proximity to or within the borders of the states practiced matriliny and matriarchy.

At the same time, the states were becoming more centralized, bureaucratized, and hierarchized, and the loyalty of the officials was to the person of the ruler alone, and not to the official's family or lineage. Many of the philosophers wrestled with the problems of how to choose and promote officials for the new centralized polities. The most effective in theorizing and advocating new policies were the legalists, such as Lord Shang in Qin, who recommended the imposition of a strict system of laws and the establishment of precise rewards and punishments to force the officials and the people to obey orders and carry out the dictates of the ruler.

The reader of the silk manuscripts should remember, therefore, that the essays were written to advise rulers of states in a rapidly changing political, social, and economic climate. It is for this reason that the recommendations they present are at times almost obsessively precise, and at other times seemingly unnecessarily vague and irrelevant. Nowadays, we just do not care very much about the personal techniques of self-cultivation on the part of our rulers. That a Ronald Reagan or a Boris Yeltsin has recourse to the advice of a personal astrologer seems vaguely whimsical or amusing, but certainly not something to be taken seriously, on a par with concrete issues and policies. But for the ancient Chinese, and especially the HuangLao Daoists and Yin–Yang specialists, the necessity for the ruler and his advisers to be attuned to the ever-changing forces of the cosmos was crucial. Without the esoteric knowledge that these essays reveal, survival and success in the savage world of the Warring States was simply not possible.

3. HUANGLAO DAOISM
AND YIN-YANG THOUGHT

How have scholars defined HuangLao? From the point of view of the term itself, all scholars agree that "Huang" means the "Yellow Emperor" and "Lao" is Laozi. When the term refers to written texts, it means the "Books of the Yellow Emperor" (*Huangdi shu* 黃帝書) and the *Laozi*.[1] Certainly, early references in the philosophical texts and the historical records also allude to a close association between "HuangLao" and the doctrine of *xingming* 刑名 "forms and names," which is often associated with the legalist tradition. As a consequence, many scholars, including Anne Cheng, following Tang Lan, have interpreted the resultant combination "HuangLao" as a Daoism strongly influenced by "legalism" or as *Laozi* reinterpreted by "legist thought," which has nevertheless a strong "quietist" streak to it.[2] Harold Roth argues that the earliest evidence for HuangLao is in the *Guanzi* chapters, such as the "Inner Training" (*Nei ye*) and "Techniques of the Heart-Mind A and B" *(Xin shu shang, xia)*, where the theory and practice of breath-control meditation—in other words psychophysiological techniques—are advocated for use by a ruler who can thereby achieve self-transcendence and such "clarity of mind and metaphysical vision" that he can govern the world by means of *wuwei* ("nonaction" or "nonpurposive action").[3] Thus for Roth, there are three basic orientations for HuangLao Daoism: "cosmology, psychology (or psychophysiology) and self-cultivation, and political thought." Of these three, cosmology is the foundation, for not only must government be based on, and be in harmony with, the constant patterns and regularities of Heaven and Earth, otherwise disaster will strike, but also the ruler must phenomenologically unify himself with the omnipresent Dao, and apply that mystical knowledge in his practice of government.

John Major, looking at it from the point of view of the early Han Daoist compendium *Huainanzi*, interprets the precepts of HuangLao as follows:

1. *Dao* is the highest and most primary expression of universal potentiality, order, and potency. "It is undifferentiated, indeterminate, and ineffable. Yet it is generative, autonomous, unchangeable, and complete."

2. Dao is expressed in cosmic order, which embraces both the world of nature and the human world; the human order is a subset of the natural order. "Huang-Lao privileges the cosmic natural order: the natural order has normative priority."

3. The human order presupposes the existence of royal government. But royal government must conform to natural order. For a king to act "contrary to nature" is both futile and wrong; the proper stance of the king is *wuwei*, "non-striving" or "taking no action contrary to nature."

4. "A defining characteristic of the true king is the acquisition of . . . penetrating insight." The king must learn all that can be learned about the natural order, so as to make his actions conform to it.

5. The government of the true king is neither sentimental nor vacillating, and neither arbitrary nor domineering. Being in all respects in conformity with the patterns of the Dao as expressed in the natural order, it is balanced, moderate, and irresistably strong.[4]

Hans van Ess takes HuangLao as a specific political faction at the court of the early Han emperors,[5] while some Japanese scholars emphasize HuangLao's religious dimensions, which become apparent especially as HuangLao evolved in the later Han dynasty, in the first three centuries of the common era. During those times, HuangLao became associated with the techniques aimed at achieving physical longevity and the sage Laozi himself became divinised, being worshipped as Taishang Laojun, Lord Lao of the Supreme Ultimate. Taishang Laojun is still worshipped to this day, the personification of the very Dao itself, who "became embodied through spontaneity, was born before the Supreme Void, arose from the Causeless, regulates the rhythm of Heaven and Earth; and whose ends and beginnings are innumerable," in the words of the third-century commentary by Ge Xuan on the text of *Laozi*.[6]

Mark Csikszentmihalyi, on the other hand, correctly observes that the strategy of trying to find a "correct" definition of what HuangLao was in Warring States and early Han times "operates on the basis of a fundamental misconception. It assumes the existence of a definite phenomenon called HuangLao during the period of the Mawangdui texts to which [each scholar] is unambiguously referring."[7] HuangLao was rather a *tradition* or *group of traditions*, he argues, which included many different aspects, including mythological, politico-philosophical, military, divinatory, and medical.[8] This latter opinion seems to me to be the most consistent with the evidence currently available.

Yet in all of the analyses of the development of HuangLao thought, it seems to me that there is an extremely important element missing: there is no discussion of the role Yin-Yang speculation played in its history. Sima Tan, in his summary of the six different traditions or schools (*jia*, literally "families") describes the Daoists in the following way:

> The Daoists enable man's Numinous Essence *(jingshen)* to be concentrated and unified, enable him to move in unison with the Formless *(wuxing)*, and to provide adequately for the myriad things. As for its methods, it follows the great compliance of the Yin-Yang specialists, picks out the best of the Confucians and Mohists, and adopts the essentials of the Terminologists and Legalists. It shifts with the times, changes in response to things, and in establishing customs and in practical applications it is nowhere unsuitable. The general drift of its teachings is simple and easy to hold onto; there is much achievement for little effort.[9]

This characterization Harold Roth interprets as actually referring to the tradition of HuangLao Daoism, not the Daoism of Laozi and Zhuangzi, as all previous scholars have thought. What has been generally agreed, however, is that both Sima Tan and his son Sima Qian were especially influenced by Daoist thinking, even though their lord and master, Emperor Wu, favored Confucianism. In analyzing this summary, virtually all scholars have failed to notice that Sima Tan places Yin-Yang first among the traditions that the Daoists drew from. Yin-Yang theory must, therefore, have played an unusually important role in Daoist speculation as it was evolving in early Han times. What Yin-Yang thinking was, however, and what role it played in the development of the HuangLao Daoist tradition in particular and in the evolution of Chinese philosophical thought as a whole remains unclear.

Sima Tan places the Yin-Yang specialists first of all the six schools:

> "I have examined the techniques of Yin-Yang; they value the auspicious and multiply restrictions and taboos; they cause people to be restrained by increasing in number what they (sc. the people) fear; but their giving precedence to general compliance with the four seasons cannot be neglected."

Then the summary runs:

> "Each of the Yin-Yang four seasons, eight positions (possibly the eight hexagrams), the twelve degrees (the twelve zodiacal stations), and the twenty-four solar nodes in the calendar have teachings and orders related to them. If you follow (are compliant with) them you grow glorious, if you oppose them, and do not die, then you are lost. That is not necessarily so. That's why I say "they cause people to be restrained by increasing in number what they (sc. the people) fear." Now in spring things are born; in summer they grow; in autumn they are harvested; in winter they are stored away. This is the great constant order of the Way of Heaven; if you do not follow it, then there would be no way to make rules and regulations for the world. Thus I say, "their giving precedence to general compliance with the four seasons cannot be neglected."[10]

It is quite evident that there were strong links between the Daoists described by Sima Tan and specialists in the Yin-Yang tradition, although he denigrates the latter by saying that they give too much weight to what some would call magic and superstition. Most particularly, in comparison to the Confucians and the Mohists, and some of the legalists, both Daoists and Yin-Yang masters emphasized that the dependence of man on the cosmos, and the necessity of man to harmonize with the movements of the cosmos in all his daily activities, was implicit in the very nature of things, the Dao and the Way of Heaven.

One could even say that there were two basic trends of philosophical speculation in early China. The one represented by the Confucians, Mohists, and some of the legalists, was essentially humanistic, in the sense that these philosophers argued that the solution to the often intractable problems facing contemporary society could be achieved through the (re)formation of interpersonal relationships. The other was represented by the Daoists and Yin-Yang specialists. They believed that to solve the existential and socio-political crises at that time, man—especially, of course, the ruler—had to orient himself to the hidden order of the cosmos and abide completely by its norms. This order was only revealed by their own secret observations and speculations.

While we are nowadays perhaps more sympathetic to the humanistic strain, especially since in China from the tenth century it became the dominant philosophy in Chinese civilization among the social and intellectual elite, in fact the early Chinese found the esoteric and cos-mologically oriented strain more comprehensible and more compatible with their own cultural values and personal aspirations. Thus for Con-fucianism to triumph as the state ideology under Emperor Wu of the Han, it had to absorb in large measure the cosmological speculation of its rival and to transform itself into accepting its theoretical basis.

Unfortunately, prior to the archaeological discoveries in the last twenty-five years, there were very few texts that could be assigned with certainty to the Yin-Yang tradition and so it was impossible to under-stand what Sima Tan meant when he said that the Yin-Yang masters "value the auspicious and multiply restrictions and taboos; they cause people to be restrained by increasing in number what they (sc. the people) fear." In 1972, another hoard of manuscripts was discovered at Yinqueshan (Wu Jiulong 1985), this time written on narrow slips of bamboo, among which were the military treatises, *The Art of War* by Sunzi, and that of his descendant, Sun Bin (Lau and Ames, 1996). A number of the Yinqueshan texts can be reconstructed and shown to be lost Yin-Yang works, where taboos and restrictions are enumerated and the dire consequences of acting in contradiction to the forces of nature are spelled out in detail (Yates 1994[a]). The following is an example, to which the modern Chinese scholars who worked on the transcription of the texts gave the name "The Responses of Not Being Timely." One assumes that it is the ruler who acts in the untimely fashion and so brings down various disasters on his state:

> In the three months of spring, one unseasonable act will result in the germinating seeds not maturing; two unseason-able acts will result in two types of seeds not maturing; three unseasonable acts will result in three types of seeds not maturing; four unseasonable acts will result in four types of seeds not

maturing; five unseasonable acts will result in five types of seeds not maturing; six unseasonable acts will result in three unproductive (?) harvests failing as though from a disease.

In the three months of summer, if one unseasonable act occurs, then the four-footed animals will be barren; if two unseasonable acts occur, then the four-footed animals will not enter the settlements; . . . ; if three unseasonable acts occur, then there will be funerals; if four unseasonable acts occur, then you will see bloody weapons; . . . ; if five unseasonable acts occur, then there will be rebellion; if six unseasonable acts occur, three unproductive (?) harvests will fail as though [from a disease].

In the three months of autumn, one unseasonable act will result in much talk of sorcery; two unseasonable (acts will result in much . . . (three graphs indecipherable); three un- . . . [seasonable] acts will result in many executions and deaths; four unseasonable acts will result in four-footed animals being barren; five unseasonable acts will result in epidemic diseases; six unseasonable acts will result in three unproductive (?) harvests failing as though from a disease.

In the three months of winter, if one unseasonable act occurs, then the state will know winds; if two unseasonable acts occur, [then] there will be many destructive caterpillars; if three unseasonable acts occur, [then] there will be a drought; if four unseasonable acts occur, then there will be floods; if five unseasonable acts occur, [then] first there will be a drought, later a flood; if six unseasonable acts occur, [then] three unproductive (?) harvests will fail as though from a disease.

Other Yin–Yang texts are lists of objects and persons in the natural world, defining them as either Yin or Yang, therefore implying what correlations and oppositions exist between them, and providing the reader and owner of the texts with valuable information about how he should treat or interact with them. Yet others provide information on the stars and constellations and the powerful astral deities that inhabit them or are their manifestations. What can be seen from the above is that Yin–Yang texts were specific about the dangers that could result from taking actions that were not in accord with what was appropriate to a particular season, so it is small wonder that Sima Tan was not impressed by them. But the external physical world, what we would

15

call the environment, was perceived by the ancient Chinese to be populated by ghosts and spirits that could harm man and beast and was full of dangers that could quickly bring death and destruction. The skin of man's body was not viewed as an impermeable boundary: these ghosts and spirits could invade it and cause internal violence and decay. Further, the Chinese applied the metaphor of the body with its conduits for the flow of blood and qi, the rarified, quintessential energy-matter out of which all things in the entire cosmos were believed to be made, to the state itself, seeing it as subject to the same dangerous, destructive forces.

The Yin-Yang masters provided secret knowledge that gave mastery over these unseen, often noxious, forces. It was not surprising, therefore, that their texts, which are translated in this book, and their charts were placed in the tombs of their owners, for not only did the written characters possess the power to ward off evil spirits that might attack the dead as they lay in their graves, but they also provided the dead with esoteric knowledge that might be useful to them as their souls tried to negotiate the difficult passage through various obstacles that confronted them on their way to paradise.

I will argue below in the section on "The Nature and Organization of the Silk Manuscripts" that the silk scrolls translated in this book are composed of two types of texts: some belong to what has been identified as the HuangLao Daoist tradition, others belong to this more esoteric, lesser known Yin-Yang tradition. But the reader should remember that these and *all* the texts that have been recovered by archaeologists in recent years and that are translated in this series were placed in *tombs:* when the ancient Chinese placed them in the tombs they conceived them to possess extraordinary spiritual power and efficacy and to contain insight into the inner workings of the cosmos. We must respect and appreciate this aspect of the beliefs and social practice of the ancient Chinese. For them, the power of language in written text lay in its ability to explain and interpret, transform and control, and harness for one's own benefit the forces of the natural order and ward off its dangers.

4. THE MYTH OF THE YELLOW EMPEROR AND THE ORIGINS OF HUANGLAO DAOISM

In the first century B.C.E., Sima Qian contributed to and reflected early Chinese mythological thinking by placing the Yellow Emperor at the very beginning of time, at the head of the list of Five Emperors in his 130-chapter history of the world, the *Historical Records*.[11] In his historico-mythological account, which reflects contemporary Chinese social practice, Sima Qian emphasizes family links and lineages, and assigns the Yellow Emperor the surname Gongsun, with a given name *(ming)* of Xuanyuan, and claims he was the son of Shao Dian. Under the Yellow Emperor's beneficent rule, the Chinese people learned how to cultivate silkworms to make silk and to construct boats and chariots. Writing was developed, as were various other esoteric arts, including how to calculate the calendar, musical notes, mathematics, and medicine. In the latter discipline, he appears not only as the fount and origin of the entire corpus of the traditional Chinese healing arts, whose primary text is *Huangdi neijing (The Yellow Emperor's Classic of Internal Medicine)*,[12] but also of its esoteric sexual techniques and practices, being instructed in these by the mysterious female divinity, the Plain Maiden (Sunü).[13] He was seen to be the veritable ancestral father of the Chinese people, who saved the world from catastrophe when the denizen Chi You, who came to be worshipped as the God of War later in Han times, invented weapons and started a rebellion, trying to seize the throne. Some of the stories relating the events of these times are found in the second book of the texts translated here, the *Canon*. This war has parallels with the battles recounted in the newly discovered Yinqueshan text associated with the *Sunzi, Huangdi fa Chidi (The Yellow Emperor Attacks the Red*

17

Emperor), translated by Roger T. Ames (1993) in this series.[14] Here it is implied, in accordance with Five Phase (*Wu Xing*) theorizing, that the Yellow Emperor is the emperor of the center and he attacks in turn the emperors of the four quarters, respectively Red (south), Green (east), Black (north), and White (west), thereby permitting the grains in the fields to flourish, in other words providing sustenance to the people of the world, and amnesty for criminals. The story mentions the latter act of grace because it was believed that if people committed crimes it was evidence that the cosmos was out of order and the emperor was responsible for remedying the dangerous situation and averting disaster. The whole text, therefore, is a kind of Chinese equivalent of the peace and harmony among all creatures found in the Garden of Eden at the Beginning of Creation and recounted in Genesis.

Charles Le Blanc (1985/1986) has examined the myth of the Yellow Emperor in many different sources and has determined that there were at least twenty different themes in stories associated with him, which can be subdivided into two main categories. The first of these he calls the Yellow Emperor as an "historicized (not *historical*) persona" and the second as a "deified persona." The Yellow Emperor as a deity, Le Blanc notes, appears in later texts and he is characterized as having become an immortal god, having given birth to the primal cosmic forces Yin-Yang, as being the God of the *axis mundi*, Mount Kunlun, often located geographically to the west of China, the God of the earth and the God of the center, because yellow was the color of earth and of the center in the Five Phase system, and as God of one of the five planets, Saturn, also according to Five Phase theorizing. The Yellow Emperor as ancestor, sage, and paradigmatic emperor and unifier of the world appears in earlier texts, but it is not possible at present to determine whether, in fact, historically speaking, these features of his characterization were prior: the stories about the Yellow Emperor as deity could have been transmitted orally, and only have been written down later, after his popularity as historicized figure had been accepted.[15]

As I discuss below, a number of the characteristic features of the Yellow Emperor as deity appear in essays in the *Canon* of the silk manuscripts. These I believe to emanate from the Yin-Yang school in late Warring States times. The earliest extant reference of the Yellow Emperor as an historicized figure, on the other hand, appears in a bronze inscription dedicated by King Wei of the eastern state of Qi (reigned 357–320), although Liu Weihua and Miao Runtian (1986) argue that the HuangLao Daoist tradition, partly composed of a strain associated with the name of the Yellow Emperor (Huangdi) and partly of a strain associated with that of Laozi, goes back to Spring and Autumn times, several centuries earlier, when, they say, references to the Yellow Emperor begin to appear in the texts. On the bronze, the king refers to the Yellow Emperor as his "high ancestor" (*gaozu*), as well as being the "Bright Beginning" of the imperial system (Le Blanc 1985/1986: 53).[16]

The first appearance of the name of the Yellow Emperor associated with the royal house of Tian of the northeastern state of Qi is significant, for it was in Qi, as remarked above, that many of the philosophers later associated with the HuangLao tradition, such as Tian Pian and Shen Dao, Song Xing and Yin Wen, gathered to debate their ideas among themselves and before the kings as members of the famous Jixia Academy.[17] The HuangLao tradition may, therefore, have originated in the state of Qi in Warring States times.

5. THE ORGANIZATION AND PHILOSOPHY OF THE SILK MANUSCRIPTS

Because the silk manuscripts are so new and yet so old, scholars have not yet had the time to pore over them, to determine by comparisons with other texts the meaning of obscure passages. Indeed, there are a number of issues surrounding these texts which are crucial for understanding their significance in the history of Chinese philosophical ideas. Are they a single original work? In my discussion and translation, I refer to the four main parts of the silk manuscripts as "books," and the smaller subsections within them as "essays," although "treatises" might also serve the purpose. Are they really products of the HuangLao Daoist tradition? If not, what school or tradition of philosophy do they belong to? What was the original date of composition? Once we have resolved these difficult problems, we will be in a better position to understand the overall philosophy and the particular issues raised in each of the essays in the manuscripts. Scholars in China, Japan, and the West who have worked on them since their discovery have come to sometimes startlingly different interpretations. In this introduction, I offer my own opinions based on my own understanding of the content of each book and each essay. The reader should be aware, however, that since the texts were lost for two thousand years, they have not been subjected to intense scrutiny by scholars over the generations: there is no commentarial tradition to rely on as there is for the interpretation and translation of the *Laozi*, the *Sunzi*, Confucius' *Analects*, and the other canonical texts of early Chinese philosophy.

The main group of texts translated here are divided into four books. They were written before the B version of the *Laozi* by the same copyist in such a way that the late Tang Lan, a leading modern scholar who worked on the preliminary transcription and analysis, presumed that there must have been, in the eyes of that copyist, an intimate connection between the *Laozi* and these new manuscripts.

The ancient copyist, or perhaps the original author(s), appended the titles and the (approximate) number of graphs at the end of each book: *Jing Fa (The Canon: Law)* (5,000 graphs), *Jing (The Canon)* (4,500 graphs), *Cheng (Designations)* (1,600+ graphs), and *Dao Yuan (Dao the Origin)* (464 graphs). Originally the title of the second book was transcribed as the *Shi Da Jing (Ten Great Canons)*, but later as the *Shiliujing (Sixteen Canons)*, which left the last essay in it without a title. I believe that Li Xueqin (1993b) is correct in arguing that the words "Ten Great (Propositions)" refers to the last short essay and the title of the entire second book is *Jing (The Canon)*.

I have also included a fifth text, *Jiu Zhu (The Nine Rulers)*, the second of four previously unknown essays appended to the 'A' version of the *Laozi*, which have regrettably been ignored in the West. It too appears to belong to the HuangLao political tradition and bears striking resemblances to the four books that are the focus of this present volume.[18] I now turn to discuss briefly the philosophical contents and form of each of the books and *The Nine Rulers*.

A. THE CANON: LAW

The first and second books are divided into separate essays. *The Canon: Law* contains nine such essays with a total of five thousand characters, the same number traditionally attributed to the *Laozi*, and is written in a style that is fairly consistent, in such a way that it is reasonable to conclude that it was written by a single author or group of authors at a particular point in time. In comparison with the *Laozi*, however, apart from the first essay, "Dao and the Law," which seeks to describe the Dao and its relations to the Law in poetic language and which provides the metaphysical basis for the entire book, the rest of the essays in *The Canon: Law* are, for the most part, tightly argued treatises that set out various aspects of socioeconomic and political policy and philosophy, although they are not as logically developed as those found in the third century B.C.E. Ruist (Confucian) philosopher Xunzi. "Dao and the Law" has excited the interest of several Western scholars, because it opens with a series of propositions:

The Dao produces law. Law is what draws the line between gain and loss, and makes clear the curved and the straight. He who grasps the Dao, therefore, produces law and does not venture to transgress it, establishes law and does not venture to oppose it. . . . is able to draw himself with the line, only then may he be not confused when he sees and knows the world.

R. P. Peerenboom (1993) writes that this passage contradicts Joseph Needham's (1956) assertion, now well-accepted in the West, that China produced no theory of natural law (law derived from the divine or the processes of nature) and that for the Chinese, law was always contingent upon the whims and fancies of human lawgivers, most particularly the Chinese emperors. He (1990, 1993), Karen Turner (1989, 1993), and Cheng Chung-ying (1983), among others, have been exploring the consequences of these new silk manuscripts of HuangLao Daoism for understanding the philosophical basis and evolution of the Chinese legal tradition. Most particularly, the treatises emphasize that the ruler himself must abide by the law that emanates out of the transcendent, nameless, formless Dao, which is the origin of all phenomenal things in the universe. According to Peerenboom's interpretation, the ruler is not above the law, which is the position of legalists like the philosopher Hanfeizi, but rather is constrained by the law and the Dao; the ruler must gain the support of the people, not force them to obey every arbitrary order issued by the center. Further, the ruler is a kind of conduit for the Dao in practice; by legislating, he accords with the natural, normative order. While Peerenboom's analysis is certainly illuminating for the silk manuscripts, his characterization of Hanfei's thought lays too much emphasis on the perceived arbitrariness of the ruler. There are, in fact, very close correspondences between Hanfei and the author(s) of the *Canon: Law* and the other silk manuscripts. This can be seen in the fifth of Hanfei's essays, "The Dao of the Ruler," one phrase of which ("all affairs will be settled of themselves") also appears in the sixth treatise of the *Canon: Law*, "Assessments":

Tao [Dao] is the beginning of the myriad things, the standard of right and wrong. That being so, the intelligent ruler, by holding to the beginning, knows the source of everything, and, by keeping to the standard, knows the origin of good and evil. Therefore, by virtue of resting empty and reposed, he waits for the course of nature to enforce itself so that all names will be defined of themselves and all affairs will be settled of themselves. Empty, he knows the essence of fullness: reposed, he becomes the corrector of motion. Who utters a word creates himself a name; who has an affair creates himself a form. Compare forms and names and see if they are identical. Then the ruler will find nothing to worry about as everything is reduced to its reality.[19]

Such an emphasis is to be found in the first essay of the *Canon:Law* on the ruler's careful application of the theory of "forms and names" *(xingming)* in establishing the correct responsibilities for all different levels of his administrative hierarchy and for ensuring that his own position is not challenged by anyone else, including his wife, close relatives, son(s), and high officials. This doctrine in early times was particularly associated with those considered to be specialists in HuangLao, such as the Han (not the same Han as the dynasty, but an earlier state) prime minister Shen Buhai, who died in 337 B.C.E. and, as is clear, the legalist philosopher Hanfeizi. Liu Xiang, in his now-lost *Bielu,* affirmed quite categorically, "The doctrine of Shenzi (Shen Buhai) is called *xingming.* *Xingming* is to demand actual performance *(shi)* on the basis of the title *(ming)* held, thus honoring the ruler and humbling the minister, exalting superiors and curbing inferiors."[20] Herrlee G. Creel, in several classic studies, argued that this doctrine of "forms and names" originated with Shen Buhai and was, in fact, strong evidence that the so-called *fajia* should be divided into two groups, one the real "legalists," like Wei Yang (Lord Shang of the state of Qin in mid–fourth-century B.C.E.), who emphasized the strict application of rewards and punishments in governing a state and that the state's policies should only be concerned with its own self-strengthening by the means of concentrating on agriculture and warfare, and the other "administrators," like Shen Buhai. It was the latter, according to Creel, who created the theory of bureaucratic administration which was instituted in late Warring States China, generally applied in the Chinese empire by the introduction of the examination system for the recruitment and promotion of officials, eventually taken over to the West through the Kingdom of Sicily in the Middle Ages, and now is the prevalent system throughout the world for controlling and governing the administrations of nation states.[21]

Creel argued that essentially *xingming* "denoted a system for the organization and control of the corps of officials" and that the term meant, literally, "performance and title," the performance of the duties associated with the specific name of the office held by a particular administrator.[22] Unfortunately, the silk manuscripts had not been discovered at the time Creel was analyzing the data, for it is clear that the doctrine of "forms and names" was rather based upon a metaphysical foundation. As the "Way and the Law" states:

> The Dao of seeing and knowing is merely vacuity and nonexistence. As for vacuity and nonexistence, an autumn hair brings them into existence, for it then necessarily has a form and a name. If form and name are established, then the distinction between black and white has been made. Therefore the way in which he who grasps the Dao looks at the world is to be without tenacity, to be without location, be without action, be without partiality.
>
> For this reason, no worldly affair does not make a form and name, reputation and claim for itself. If forms and names have been established, reputations and appellations set up, then there is nowhere to conceal one's tracks or hide one's true aims.

What this means is that everything in the phenomenal world (all *things*) emanate from the nameless, formless, and empty Dao. As soon as they emanate, even if as small as the smallest thing possible ("the tip of an autumn hair"), they possess a shape or form and a name, and therefore they can be categorized and controlled by the ruler who himself—actionless, unlocatable, and unbiased—rests in that same Dao.

The last essay, "Names and Principles" in the *Canon: Law* is essentially a further exposition of this doctrine of "forms and names," and is the foundation stone of the HuangLao tradition's philosophy of language.[23] The author(s) draw on the concepts found in the other three books, especially the ideas of the Yin-Yang specialists, but give them a somewhat different twist, integrating them into the overall philosophy:

> When there is some affair in the world, you must fully investigate its name. Names . . . accord with names, and inquire where principles are applicable. When they are right, there will inevitably be good fortune; when they are wrong, there will inevitably be disaster. Right and wrong have their apportioned lots: decide them according to the law. Carefully listen in vacuity and quiescence, and take law as the tally. To

fully investigate and examine the principles of names and the beginnings and ends of names, this is called "Inquiring into Principles." If you are only public-spirited and without private bias, see and know and are not deluded, then your knowledge will rise up energetically.

In short, the *Canon: Law* is directed at the ruler of a state engaged in competition with rivals for the domination of the world. The advice the text offers is that he must conform his actions to the principles of Heaven and Earth and must forever observe and be constantly attuned to the objective conditions of his own state and those of his rivals. He must be trustworthy, conform his laws and regulations to the ever-changing principles of the cosmos, and under no circumstances oppose them. In his own personal behavior, he must conform to the Dao, be quiescent, be unbiased, and when action is called for, he must act immediately, ruthlessly, but dispassionately, then he will achieve his aims and be a true king:

The Six Handles: the first is observation; the second is assessment; the third is movement; the fourth is revolution; the fifth is change; the sixth is transformation.

If you observe, you know which states are dead and which alive. If you assess, you will know where preservation and destruction, rise and decline, are situated. If you move, you are able to break the strong and raise the weak. If you revolve, you do not lose the . . . of right and wrong. If you change, you can attack the dying and nourish the living. If you transform, you can brighten your potency and expel the noxious. If the Six Handles are in readiness, you will be a true king.

B. THE CANON

In the *Canon*, the second book, there are nine essays in which the Yellow Emperor and his assistants appear:

1. "Establishing the Mandate"
2. "Observation"
3. "The Five Regulators" (or "Five Governings")

25

4. "Guo Tong"
5. "Correcting the Rebellious"
6. "The Fights of the Surnames"
7. "The Female and Male Tally"
9. "Complete Laws"
14. "Compliance with the Dao"

Whereas there is no reference in the six remaining essays:

8. "The Features of Warfare"
10. "The Three Prohibitions"
11. "The Fundamental Types of Attack"
12. "Putting the Dao First"
13. "Rules for Conduct"
15. "Ten Great Propositions"

Most of the essays in which the Yellow Emperor appears are cast in the form of stories and dialogues between the Emperor and his leading officials and recount events at the beginning of time when order in the world was challenged by the evil monster Chi You, who was reputedly the creator of weapons of war. The Yellow Emperor seeks the advice of his assistants as to how to purge the world of this dangerous denizen and his allies, and, after fierce battles, the Yellow Emperor is victorious and inflicts various unpleasant punishments on the vanquished Chi You. The latter was, in fact, worshipped as the god of war in Han times and appears in Han iconography.[24]

"Establishing the Mandate" seems to have been placed first in the *Canon* because it details events at the very beginning of the Yellow Emperor's rule, perhaps at the very beginning of time. As mentioned above, Sima Qian begins his history with the Yellow Emperor, following what seems to be a HuangLao interpretation of the origins of phenomenal existence after the initial distinctions of Heaven and Earth, Yin and Yang out of the primordial undifferentiated Dao. "Establishing the Mandate" begins:

Of old, the Yellow Ancestral Model (the Yellow Emperor), as part of his essential nature, began by loving trustworthiness; he made himself into an exemplary image and faced the four directions to supplement his single heart-mind. Reaching out from the center to all directions, he consulted what was in front of him, he consulted what was behind him, he consulted what was to his left, he consulted what was to his right. He acted on his position and carried out his consultations, and, for this reason, he was able to be the ancestral model for the world.

The second essay, "Observation," seems to be composed of two parts. The first consists of a conversation between the Yellow Emperor and his assistant Li Hei, otherwise known as Li Mu, in the course of which it is revealed that the Yellow Emperor was responsible for the differentiation of the Yin and Yang, it was not a natural, spontaneous process, as other previously known Daoist works, such as the *Laozi*, suggest. In the *Laozi*, for example, one of the most famous passages in Book Two of the *Dao De Jing*, chapter 42, opens with the words, "The way begets one; one begets two; two begets three; three begets the myriad creatures," where the "two" is traditionally interpreted as Yin and Yang.[25] "Observation," on the other hand, explains the origin of life on earth in the Yellow Emperor's words:

> "Now I will begin by distinguishing them (Yin and Yang) into two and separate them to make Yin and Yang; I will divide them to make the four seasons . . . thereby act as its constants; when they are bright, they act as models, but it is the minute (and thus dark) Dao that is to be carried out. Carry out the models and follow . . . male and female; when male and female seek each other, hard will join with the soft. When soft and hard complete each other, male and female will then be formed. Below, they meet with Earth; above, they meet with Heaven. When they obtain Heaven's minuteness, the seasons then . . . are waiting for the emission of the Earth's qi, then those that are to sprout will sprout, and those that are to breed will breed; Heaven relies on that fact to bring them to completion."

This provides new and exciting evidence for studying early Chinese mythology and cosmogony, for, if I am right that this is a Yin-Yang text, we now know how the Yin-Yang tradition explained the origins of the universe.

The second part of "Observation," probably written later, is a more general disquisition on how to rule the world using the pair of concepts *xing* and *de* ("punishment" and "virtue" or "recision" and "accretion" [Major 1987]), cosmic powers that move in concert with Yin and Yang through the four seasons. Determining the time when each of these powers was in the ascendancy and what action to take in response was a highly complex task that required esoteric knowledge of the Heavens. In fact, a chart of *Xing* and *De* was found with two explanatory texts in the Mawangdui hoard (Fu Juyou and Chen Songchang 1992), but to date only Rao Zongyi (1993[b]) and Chen Songchang (1993[b]) have made a preliminary study of these fascinating materials, which have much to do with determining when to go to war to punish recalcitrant enemies.

"Compliance with the Dao," the fourteenth essay in the second book, seems to stand halfway between the dialogue/story form and the rhymed treatise or verse form of other essays of the silk manuscripts. It consists of a short introductory conversation between the Yellow Emperor and Li Hei and a long exposition by Li Hei in verse about the origins of the world.

In these "Yellow Emperor" essays, sometimes the Yellow Emperor appears in charge; in others, he relies heavily on his assistants. In comparing these essays with other works that were excavated at Yinqueshan in 1972 and with the titles of works in the bibliographic chapter of the *Han Shu (History of the Han)*, it seems as though it was a common practice of Yin Yang specialists to make use of the name of the Yellow Emperor and his assistants when explaining their ideas. So it is quite possible that these essays of the *Canon* are, in fact, original works of the Yin-Yang, not of the HuangLao, school. However, given that Sima Tan states that HuangLao took the best from the various schools, including Yin-Yang (see above), it is probably best to interpret these essays as being examples of Yin-Yang works from which the writers of the *Canon: Law* drew their ideas. It would be a mistake, however, in my view, to title the entire silk manuscripts *The Yellow Emperor Books*, as Li Xueqin (1990) and Qiu Xigui (1993) suggest. The Yellow Emperor essays are only a small portion of the silk manuscripts.

Of those essays with no reference to the Yellow Emperor, "Features of Warfare" emphasizes the triad Heaven, Earth, and Man, as well as the sage *(shengren)*, and timeliness. The entire essay is, in fact, a definition of the "Dao of Heaven" with respect to how one should engage in warfare:

If warfare does not take its form from Heaven, warfare cannot be initiated. If it does not take Earth as its model, warfare cannot be managed. If its form and model do not rely on Man, warfare cannot be brought to a successful conclusion. If these . . . it, Heaven and Earth form it, the sage relies on it and brings it to completion. Timeliness is what the sage uses in his tasks. He relies on the right moment and grasps the . . . , and for this reason he inevitably achieves success. The sage does not relax the punishments; he does not use tallies and passports: he relies on Heaven's seasons and with their aid he decides all matters. If a matter should be decided, and he fails to decide it, he will in turn suffer disorder as a result.

Heaven assuredly takes away and gives, is auspicious and . . . , and does not receive it, but follows it in turn with calamity. If the three are not followed, warfare will not achieve success. If the three are not followed, yet warfare achieves [success], . . . , you will not enjoy its success but will suffer calamity from it in recompense. If a state is fortunate, those who face it will suffer calamity. If a state lacks good fortune, yet wishes to lengthen its life, and, rushing and gushing out, it relies on the strength of the people, opposes the limit of Heaven, and furthermore values success, the state will be endangered from these actions: the altars of soil and grain will be devastated as a result, affairs will have no success, and, moreover, the rewards will not match the task. This is the Dao of Heaven.

Warfare must accord with the movements of Heaven, as represented in the changes of the seasons. One should only go on the offensive and attack another state, therefore, when it is clear that your own state is flourishing and the enemy's is not, and you should only attack when Heaven is in its own "attacking" and destructive mode, in other words in autumn and winter, when all of nature is in decline. If you do otherwise, instead of being successful and victorious, you will oppose what the text calls "the limit of Heaven" and will yourself suffer retribution and disaster from your inopportune activities. "Heaven's limit" and "Heavenly Success" are explicated in detail in the second essay of the first book, "The Priorities of a State."

"The Three Prohibitions" also emphasizes the triad Heaven, Earth, and Man: the "three" in the title indeed refers to them. In this essay, the Dao of Heaven appears as does the term "true king or lord." The essential argument is that the people must model themselves on Heaven.

"The Fundamental Types of Attack" discusses the Dao of Warfare, and states that there are three Dao or "ways" current at the time of composition. There are those who act for profit, those who act out of righteousness, and those who act out of anger. The best of these three is acting out of righteousness. No harm comes of acting for profit, but in fact no great profit accrues and yet no great danger results either. This view is in direct contradiction to the beliefs held by the Mohists who, although they considered an evaluation of a policy's benefits to be essential, regarded offensive warfare as being ruinous to both sides. Acting out of anger is the worst course to follow because it flies directly against the Dao. This idea has a parallel in passage no. 37 of the third book, *Designations:*

> In the world of men, there are three types of deaths which are not fated: death from being angry and not measuring the strength of one's opponent; death from limitless indulgence in one's desires; death from being solitary and not avoiding the crowd.

In contrast, the military theoretician Sunzi argued that one's own troops could be motivated to kill if they were stirred up by anger, but it was unwise for the officers and the commander himself to have their own emotions so stirred, since usually what results would be disastrous:

> "If your ranking officers are angry and insubordinate and, on encountering the enemy, allow their rancor to spur them into unauthorized engagements so that their commander does not know the strength of his own forces, the result will be ruin."[26]
> "As for the urgent business of the commander: He is calm and remote, correct and disciplined. He is able to blinker the ears and eyes of his officers and men, and to keep people ignorant."[27]

On the other hand, one had to be very careful if an angry enemy were to threaten you without either moving forward to engage or withdrawing from the field of battle.[28]

The term "Dao of Warfare" appears in the work of Shen Dao, so it would seem that this passage could have been influenced by his thinking. However, it is dangerous, in my opinion, to conclude definitively that this is the case because so many of the less important philosophical works of Warring States times have been lost and the important texts cannot be dated precisely enough so that we can reconstruct the evolution of philosophical thought decade by decade. Although great progress has been achieved in this reconstruction in recent years, led in the West by A. C. Graham[29] and Benjamin I. Schwartz,[30] in many cases it is now hard to reconstruct the contemporary intellectual arguments for which the leading philosophers developed their ideas. We must be aware that it is possible that some important ideas and concepts were originated by lesser-known figures whose writings were lost in the course of time. As a consequence, in analyzing the lost texts from Mawangdui, we must be careful not to jump to conclusions about the origins or affiliation of the texts based upon the occurrence of one or two terms, for those terms may simply have been part of the philosophical vocabulary common to those who were disputing at any one time and were not the exclusive intellectual property of a single philosophical school or tradition.

It is, however, possible that "The Fundamental Types of Attack" may have been composed at about the same time as the treatises in the *Lüshi chunqiu (Spring and Autumn Annals of Lü Buwei)*, presented to the King of Qin in 239 B.C.E., which argue for the use of "righteous warfare" *(yibing)* (chapter 7, treatise 2).

The essay whose original title has been unfortunately lost, to which the modern Chinese editors have given the name "Putting the Dao First," equally values the triad Heaven, Earth, and Man, where Man is again represented by the sage. The sage harmonizes with Heaven and Earth, conforms to the patterns or principles of the people, and is favorable to the ghosts and spirits. He benefits the masses and so the ruler employs him. The text uses the Ruist term "gentleman" *(junzi)* who humbles himself to follow the Dao, yet does not at all despise profit or benefit. He applies the Dao to control the age and softens himself to wait for the proper season when action can be initiated. Another Ruist term appears here, as in "The Three Prohibitions": the True King. This True King knows Heaven's seasons, the benefits of Earth, human affairs, is good at understanding and coordinating with the Yin and Yang, and satisfactorily ordering names into their appropriate categories. Finally, the text holds that the Dao can be used by both the small man in his daily activities, and by small and large states. This essay evidently draws upon quite disparate philosophical traditions, Ruist (Confucian), Mohist, Yin-Yang, and Daoist.

In "Rules for Conduct," we again find the triad Heaven, Earth, and Man. It seems that all three actively punish the ruler who fails to abide by the triad's rules. The text, therefore, is directed at the ruler. Furthermore, it contains an adage that also appears in the "Mountain Tree" chapter of *Zhuangzi*, "A straight tree is cut down; a straight man is killed." This may indicate that the essay was composed roughly at the same time as this part of the *Zhuangzi*. Forms and names are stated to be essential together with Heaven and Earth, and the term "male tally" also features, a term which is discussed at length in the section "The Female and Male Tally." No indication is specified as to the real relation between forms and names and Heaven, Earth, and Man, and certainly no suggestion that forms and names derive from the Dao. Dao, in fact, is not mentioned in this section at all.

The last short section in the book, "The Ten Great Propositions," strongly emphasizes the importance of understanding forms and names and nonaction or nonpurposive action *(wuwei)*. There are apparent quotations from "Gengsang Chu," chapter 23 of *Zhuangzi,* and questions very similar to those found in the *Guanzi* "Xin Shu xia" (Techniques of the Heart B), where the reader, not the ruler, is questioned as to whether he can be one, in other words at one with the Dao. The text rejects the advisability of looking at the past as a guide for action or practice in the present, in direct contradiction to the ten sections discussing the Yellow Emperor and his ministers, and also to the last few verses of advice to the ruler in *Dao the Origin*. However, this short section is written in the obscure style of *Dao Yuan (Dao the Origin)* and the "Dao and the Law" of the *Canon: Law* and is quite distinct from the other essays in this second book.

Given the eclectic nature of this second book, *The Canon*, it seems unlikely that it was composed by a single author at a single point in time. Whether or not it existed as a separate work in the late Warring States, Qin, and early Han times, and was transmitted independently, or whether it was a selection chosen by the owner of the Mawangdui library, is impossible to say at this time.

C. DESIGNATIONS

Cheng (Designations) is the third of the four lost books preceding the B text of the *Laozi* in the silk manuscripts. The text is composed in the form of aphorisms, of which about fifty-four have survived: some passages have been lost as a result of the rotting of the silk on which it was originally written. Each passage is divided by a black dot of ink, a technique of punctuation found in the A version of the *Laozi* silk manuscript. Generally speaking, it would appear that many of the passages are quotations from other texts, quite a large number of them now lost, but some of which can be identified, such as the *Shenzi*, the work of Shen Dao.

Li Xueqin (1993a), however, argues that the text was composed early and should be compared to one of the essays preserved in the *Yi Zhou shu*, the *Zhou Zhu (The Prayer-maker of Zhou)*, an early to mid–Warring States treatise. He explains the appearance of identical or similar wording of passages in *Designations* and in other philosophical works by saying that the latter are quoting the *Designations*, and not that *Designations* is quoting from them. His arguments are, however, not entirely convincing, for he fails to explain why the text is so philosophically eclectic, which is unlike the *Prayer-maker of Zhou*, and he fails to follow up the ramifications of his arguments. For example, at the end of the text there are long passages belonging to the Yin-Yang tradition. If the text is an integral whole dating from a relatively early period, Li needs to provide a history of Yin-Yang thought compatible with other data on the origins and development of this tradition.

In fact, the text is much closer in style to an essay now preserved in the *Guanzi, Shu Yan (Cardinal Sayings)*, translated by W. Allyn Rickett, whose first aphorism is put into the mouth of the reputed author of the entire book, Guan Zhong:

> Guanzi said: "In Heaven the Way is [manifested by] the sun. In man it is [manifested by] the mind. Therefore it is said that when the vital force is present, things live; when not, they die. What lives does so by virtue of its vital force. When there is [proper] terminology, good order prevails; when there is not, disorder ensues. What is ordered is so by virtue of [proper] terminology."[31]

This aphorism is very close in philosophical outlook to the silk manuscripts, although the "vital force" *(qi)* plays a minimal role in the latter. Furthermore, another passage is very close to one found in the essay "Assessments" of the *Canon:Law*. This reads:

> "The Three Names: the first is when the correction of names is established, then stop. The second is when the models of names are perverted, then there is rebellion. The third is headstrong rulers are obliterated and leave no reputation behind. When the Three Names are examined, then affairs will have correspondences."

This opaque, aphoristic passage seems almost to be expanded, commented upon, or explained in *Cardinal Sayings* in the following way,

33

suggesting that the latter text might have been written later than "Assessments":

"Generally speaking, there are three [categories of] terms involved in [governing] men: those dealing with good order in government, a sense of [honor and] shame, and management of affairs. There are two terms involved in the management of affairs: rectification and investigation. With these five, one can institute good order throughout the realm. When these terms are correctly adhered to, there is good order; when they are distorted, disorder prevails. If there is no terminology at all, death ensues. Therefore the former kings valued terminology."

Cardinal Sayings mixes what we have come to associate with Confucian, Daoist, Yin–Yang, and Legalist views, just as we find in *Designations*. In addition, at least two of the *Cardinal Sayings* passages are rhymed, just like several of those in *Designations*. All of this suggests that the abstraction of passages from other earlier essays from different philosophical sources and writing them down without much attention to creating a coherent new text was a not uncommon practice in late Warring States and early Han times.

There is some disagreement about the meaning of the title "Cheng." One possibility is that it should be translated "Sayings" or "Aphorisms" (Li Xueqin 1993a; Leo Chang in Yu Mingguang 1993a), but I suspect that it is rather a special HuangLao Daoist term which is the answer to the riddle in the opening passage of this third book:

Dao has no beginning, yet has a response. When it has not yet come, consider it nonexistent; when it has come, be similar to it. When an object is about to come, its form precedes it. Establish it by means of its form; name it by means of its name. When speaking about it, how do we refer to it?

We find the term *cheng* in the beginning of the first section of the HuangLao work *Yinwenzi*, "The Great Dao, A" ("Da Dao, shang"), which reads:

The Great Dao has no form; what are designated *(cheng)* "vessels" possess names. Names are what correct forms. If the correction of names derive from forms, then names cannot be

34

off the mark. Therefore Confucius said, "It is essential to correct names. If names are not correct, then words will not follow."[32] The Great Dao is not designated. If everything that must bear a name is produced from what is not designated, then all the various forms gain themselves.

Every phenomenon, every "thing" *(wu)* that exists, each "vessel" must have a "form" or shape and a name that distinguishes it from every other thing in the world. Only the Dao, the origin of all things, the "mother," as the *Laozi* refers to it, lacks form and name, and so is not "designated." The riddle at the beginning of this third book is, therefore, establishing the essential difference between the nameless, formless, constant Dao and all epiphenomena, the "designated" thing or "vessel." One should note that the term *cheng* also appears in aphorism 53 toward the end of the work, in a passage, unfortunately badly damaged, which appears to be giving advice to a ruler about how to control his state and gain power in the world. He is to use the technique of determining things by studying their forms and names and then is to take action at the appropriate time for each situation:

> . . . to observe (?) the front . . . in order to know the reverse; therefore . . . observe the crooked and the straight at the present time, and carefully examine their names in order to designate and decide about them. One who accumulates and hoards, waits for the proper moment and then uses his stores. Observe (?) those whom he appoints as officials to know how he shares his rule; how he accumulates cash to know the seasons . . . correct, noble . . . and survival and destruction.

In *Designations*, there are a great number of other quotations, aphorisms, and insights into the human condition and into problems, both political and military, facing the contemporary society. Some of them are so bereft of context that their precise meaning and implications are far from transparent; I have tried to identify and explain as many as possible in the notes to the translation. Of special interest is the long passage at the end, which I have designated no. 54, that seems to have been lifted from a long lost Yin-Yang text that has no parallel in any other known work. It and the other passages should be read in the light of the more extended essays in the other books translated here, for it appears very likely that in a number of instances they were the original sources of the ideas that are developed more extensively and more explicitly in the other essays.

D. DAO THE ORIGIN

The fourth section *Dao Yuan (Dao the Origin)* shares its title with the first section of the Daoist work *Wenzi* and, in reverse order, with the opening chapter of the *Huainanzi* ("Yuan Dao Xun" ["The Original Dao," or "Tracing the Dao to its Origins"] instead of our "Dao Yuan"). Written entirely in rhymed verse like most of the *Laozi*, its principal concern is to explicate the origin of all earthly phenomena from the Dao (cf. Jan Yün-hua 1980). Philosophically profound, it appears to draw or quote from several different works, including the *Laozi*, but seems to have been influential itself on later Daoist texts, such as those just mentioned, the *Wenzi* and *Huainanzi*.

At the beginning of eternal nonexistence,
Totally the same as the Great Void;
Vacuous and the same, it was the One;
Being the One constantly, it was nothing more.
Misty and blurred,
It did not yet possess light and dark.
Daemonic and faint, yet it filled everywhere,
Quintessentially quiescent, it was not luminous.
Therefore it did not possess form;
Immensely penetrating despite being nameless.
Heaven was unable to cover it;
Earth was unable to hold it up.
So small, it could bring smallness to completion;
So large, it could bring largeness to completion.
It filled up all within the Four Seas,
And embraced what was outside them.
In Yin it was not rotted,
In Yang it was not scorched. . . .

All living things, from the least insect, bird, or beast to every human being is what it is because of the Dao, but none of them is aware of its

36

presence, of its necessity for their very existence and for their every action. "It is only the Sage who is able to examine the formless" Dao and to harmonize himself with it. The ruler of a state is therefore urged to employ such a sage, for thereby he is able to unify the world and make all submit to him: notice that the ruler is not reckoned to be the sage, the ruler must find himself a sage to help him govern the world. With such a sage carrying out the orders of the ruler, everyone in the world can be assigned to their proper position, status, and occupation, and all can live in harmony in an ideal, peaceful state. One can see that this philosophy is very close to the basic tenets of the *Laozi*, but the essay closes by urging the ruler to:

"First know highest antiquity,
Later . . . quintessentially bright.
Embrace the Dao and control the measures
And the world can be unified.
Observe highest antiquity,
And (discern) everywhere where it can be used.
Search into matters before they are nothing;
Control them when you have the means."

The *Laozi* does not appeal to knowledge of the past as a guide for the ruler to take action in the present, so there is some slight difference in emphasis, suggesting a more "action-oriented" approach consistent with what scholars have interpreted as HuangLao Daoism.

Most of the effort of scholars to date has been put into the first and fourth books, because they are philosophically the most interesting, or rather because they recall or echo so strongly ideas found in the *Laozi* and *Guanzi*, especially the chapters "Techniques of the Heart A," "Inner Training," and other passages which have been associated with the HuangLao tradition, whereas the second book has drawn attention because it is the only one in which the Yellow Emperor actually appears. It is my opinion, however, that full understanding of the nature of the manuscripts will only be achieved through reading all of these four books together and carefully comparing the language and philosophical outlook of each essay with that in every other in the corpus and with the other works found at Mawangdui, as well as with the texts that have been transmitted from Warring States times. Only then can the basic questions posed above be satisfactorily answered.

The last essay translated in this book is regrettably quite fragmented, the result of the decaying of the silk on which it was written. Originally studied by Li Xueqin in 1974 (1979), it has only recently received attention from two other scholars, Yu Mingguang (1993[b]) and Wei Qipeng (1993). Wei considers the essay to be early in date, since some of the language is comparable to that found on Western Zhou bronze inscriptions and in the *Zuo Zhuan* and *Guoyu* texts. Hence he argues that possibly it is the remains of one of the fifty-one sections *(pian)* of the book called *Yi Yin*, now no longer extant, which stands at the beginning of the Daoist section in the Han imperial library catalog. As a result, Wei argues that it may have been the origin of the entire HuangLao Daoist tradition. Yu, on the other hand, considers it to be later in date than the other silk manuscripts translated here, and thus assigns it to the mid-Warring States period.

The essay is framed in the form of a conversation between the sage ruler Tang, the founder of the Shang dynasty, and his most important minister Yi Yin, and is very close in conception to a treatise called "The Seven Ministers and Seven Rulers," now found in the *Guanzi*. Yi Yin explains to his master that there are eight types of ruler who cause trouble in the world and bring disaster down upon themselves and their states. The best form of ruler is the ninth (hence the title *The Nine Rulers*) who abides by the law. It seems that originally the text was written to explain a chart or diagram, but regrettably this has now been badly fragmented:

> Yi Yin received the mandate from Tang, then assessed the four countries within the four seas . . . chart . . . "one who knows survival and destruction and how to match the two parts of the tally together gains control of the eight types of ruler. The eight types of ruler will encounter evil.
>
> "One variety: a ruler who bestows his monopoly of power on another; [one variety: a ruler who] labors; one variety: a ruler who is only a [half-ruler]; one variety: a parasitic [ruler]; two varieties of ruler who destroy their states; two varieties of ruler who extinguish their altars of soil. In all, together with the ruler who abides by the law, there are Nine Rulers. From ancient times to the present, those who survived and those

who perished . . . there were these nine. For the Nine Rulers I have completed a chart. I request to present it to you."

Tang then invited him to be the *Sangong* (prime minister), and Yi Yin displayed the chart and laid out the strategies in order to explain clearly rulers who abide by the law and ministers who abide by the law.

By explaining in sometimes lurid detail the faults of the eight types of ruler, Yi Yin aims to turn his own lord into the perfect, legitimate Son of Heaven who controls the entire known world.

The general ideas outlined in the essay are that the ruler must model himself on Heaven and his ministers and subjects must model themselves on Earth. Thus the ruler must practice the way of nonaction, while the ministers must concern themselves with carrying out his orders: ruler and minister have different responsibilities and duties. In this respect, the text differs from the *Laozi*, which advocates that all should model themselves on the Dao. The ruler, in conformity with the general tendency of the HuangLao tradition, is to base himself on the law. He is to take hold of the fundamentals, and control the essentials, to purify, empty, and protect himself; by getting others to work for him, he can exhaust their capabilities and knowledge without exhausting his own. He must follow the name of his subordinates' official positions to hold them responsible for their tasks. The text concludes with Tang withdrawing from active involvement in governing his realm and hiding himself behind double doors: the moral is that by following the precepts of HuangLao from that time forth the distinction between ruler and minister was fixed and order was brought to the entire world.

6. CONCLUSIONS

If we compare these new silk manuscripts with the *Laozi*, we can observe some striking philosophical parallels, as well as some striking differences. Both ground their philosophy in the constant Dao, the formless, nameless origin of all things. The authors of the silk manuscripts, however, do not consider the Dao to be a "mother," nor do they privilege the feminine and weakness or softness, the Yin of things and of activities, or treat water as a major image or symbol of the movement of the Dao, as does the *Laozi*. For them, what is most important is to follow or accommodate to *(yin)* the Way of Heaven, which may have been a concept developed by specialists in cosmological matters at the courts of the early rulers who eventually emerged as experts in Yin and Yang: Confucius in the *Analects* was said not to have talked about the Way of Heaven, implying that he knew about such speculation, but refused to be drawn into discussion of anything other than human affairs, of ethical matters and their expression in the rites. In fact, the silk manuscripts emphasize the triad Heaven, Earth, and Man and assert that all action must conform to the ever-changing patterns and seasons of the cosmos:

> The Way of Man is both hard and soft. If it is too hard, it is not sufficient to be used. If too soft, it is not sufficient to be relied on. Those who are hard and strong and have the dispositions of tigers will be emptied. Those who are dissolute and sunk in debauchery and are addicted to wine are lost. ("The Three Prohibitions")

Thus the silk manuscripts encourage the use of both Yin and Yang, of both civil virtue *(wen)* and martial vigor *(wu)*, much like the later Confucians emphasized moderation or centrality *(zhong)* in action and adhering to the Middle Way:

> Heaven has seasons for life and death; states have policies for life and death. To rely on Heaven's season of life to nourish the living is called *Wen* (Patterning); to rely on Heaven's season of killing to attack the dying is called *Wu* (Martiality). When both [*Wen* patterning] and *Wu* martiality are carried out, then the world will follow and obey. ("A Lord's Government")

This emphasis on both *wen* and *wu* was unusual in traditional China, because *wu* was associated with death, Yin, and the world of the ghosts and spirits, and so was generally avoided in discussions of the correct behavior of the ruler, who was to be a model for his people to follow. Throughout later Chinese imperial history, the literate elite, who commanded social prestige and controlled the administration of the country through their position of dominance in the bureaucracy, were known as *wenren* ("men of culture"), and they despised and downplayed the importance of soldiers, the men of *wu*, or violence.

Again, like the *Laozi*, the essays are directed to the attention of a ruler of a state, but the silk manuscripts are much more precise in providing practical advice on particular policies. This means, of course, that the *Laozi* can be understood on a much more abstract and generalized level than the silk manuscripts. Both certainly emphasize that the ruler should be without personal desires and prejudices, but the silk manuscripts repeatedly affirm that a state cannot be ruled justly and correctly unless a rigid status hierarchy is established and enforced so that no one challenges the power and charisma of the one ruler at the center:

> If there are two rulers, then the ruler will lose his brightness, male and female will contend for authority, the state will have rebellious soldiers: this is called a "Destroyed State." If the eldest son acts as the father, it is termed the "Highest Defiance." If the assembled ministers abandon their purposes, and great ministers act as rulers, it is termed the "Blocking Obstruction." Such a situation in a strong state will lead to it being pared down; in a middle-sized state it will lead to it being broken; in

a small state it will lead to it being destroyed. ("Great Distinctions")

There is no interest on the part of the authors of the silk manuscripts for the world to return to the simple village life, where the people are not even aware of what happens in the next village over, even though they can hear the sound of cocks crowing there and can see the smoke rising from the hearths. The authors recognize the extraordinary dangers of the world in which they were living: states were attacking each other vigorously and without remorse for the misery such warfare caused, or for the loss of life and destruction of property that resulted. So while both they and the *Laozi* considered that inauspicious weapons were instruments of ill-omen, the former were far more attuned to the practical needs of fighting for a just cause. They were conscious of the need for the soldiers' morale to be high; thus they advocated training the soldiers, and organizing and leading them in accordance with the inevitable and inexorable changes in the cosmic order:

> In the first year he follows their (the people's) customs; in the second, he uses their worthy men; in the third year, the people keep what they have obtained; in the fourth, he promulgates commands and orders; [in the fifth, he corrects them with punishments; in the sixth,] the people are awed and respectful; in the seventh, they can make punitive attacks.
>
> If, in the first year, the ruler follows the people's customs, then he will know their standards. If, in the second year, he uses [their worthy men], the people will exert their strength. If, for three years, there are no taxes, then the people will keep what they have obtained. If, in the fourth, he promulgates orders and commands, the people will be awed and respectful. If, in the fifth, he corrects them with punishments, the people will not rely on luck. If, in the sixth year . . . If, [in the seventh] year, when they can make punitive attacks, then they will conquer strong enemies. ("A Lord's Government")

Finally, I believe that the essays contained in these translations were not necessarily the work of a single individual author or group of authors composing at a single point in time. For those interested in this argument, please refer to Appendix Two. Indeed, I strongly suspect that a number of the essays emanate from the tradition of Yin-Yang specialists, rather than from the HuangLao Daoists, as most other scholars working on these texts have claimed. This is a preliminary assertion which must be examined and tested in the years to come. The manuscripts have been lost for two thousand years. Now recovered from their ancient resting place in the soil of China, may they be studied, interpreted, and learned from by readers throughout the world for many more years to come.

PART TWO:
TRANSLATION
WITH
COMMENTS
AND NOTES

A NOTE ON THE TRANSLATION

In the following translation, I have indicated missing graphs by three periods (. . .). These graphs have been lost as the result of the fraying and dissolving of the silk. Readers wishing to determine how many graphs have been lost in any given example should consult the Chinese text, which marks the missing graphs with squares. However, they should be aware that it is not really possible to determine the number of missing graphs in lacunae longer than five graphs. Lost words that can be reconstructed are enclosed in square brackets [ ]. Words or sentences that probably should be excised from the text are marked by { }.

In addition, I would like to bring the attention of readers who are conversant in Chinese to Chen Guuying's new book *Huangdi sijing jinzhu jinyi—Mawangdui Hanmu chutu boshu*. Unfortunately, this fine volume was published too late for me to refer to here.

1.

THE CANON:

LAW

(JING FA)

經　法

道法

道生法。法者，引得失以繩，而明曲直者殹（也）。故執道者，生法而弗敢犯殹（也），法立而弗敢廢【也】。□能自引以繩，然后見知天下而不惑矣。虛无刑（形），其裻冥冥，萬物之所從生。生有害，曰欲，曰不知足。生必動，動有害，曰不時，曰時而□。動有事，事有害，曰逆，曰不稱，不知所爲用。事必有言，言有害，曰不信，曰不知畏人，曰自誣，曰虛夸，以不足爲有餘。故同出冥冥，或以死，或以生；或以敗，或以成。禍福同道，莫知其所從生。見知之道，唯虛无有。虛无有，秋稿（毫）成之，必有刑（形）名。刑（形）名立，則黑白之分已。故執道者之觀天下殹（也），无執殹（也），无處也，无爲殹（也），无私殹（也）。是故天下有事，无不自爲刑（形）名聲號矣。刑（形）名已立，聲號已建，則无所逃迹匿正矣。公者明，至明者有功。

1 . THE DAO AND THE LAW

The Dao produces law. Law is what draws the line between gain and loss, and makes clear the curved and the straight. He who grasps the Dao, therefore, produces law and does not venture to transgress it, establishes law and does not venture to oppose it.[1] . . . [If] he is able to align himself, then he will not be confused when he sees and knows the world.[2]

> Vacuity without form, with its central seam dark and
>   mysterious:
> It is from it that the myriad phenomena grow.[3]

In birth and growth there is harm: this refers to desire, and not knowing when enough is enough.[4] Birth and growth entail movement; in movement there is harm; this refers to not acting at the proper season, and, though acting at the proper season, to . . .[5] In movement there are human affairs. In affairs there is harm; this refers to opposition, to lack of balance, and to ignorance of what to use them for. Affairs entail speech. In speech there is harm; this refers to unreliability, to not knowing that one should fear men, to false self-promotion,[6] to empty bragging, and to considering what is insufficient as being a surplus. Therefore, though they emerge together from the darkness, some die by it, some live by it; some are defeated through it, some come to completion through it. Disaster and good fortune share the same Dao, but no one knows where they grow from.[7]

The Dao of seeing and knowing is merely vacuity and nonexistence. As for vacuity and nonexistence, an autumn hair brings an object into existence, for it then necessarily has a form and a name.[8] If form and name are established, then the distinction between black and white has been made.[9] Therefore the way in which he who grasps the Dao looks at the world is to be without tenacity, to be without location, be without action, be without partiality.

For this reason, no worldly affair does not make a form and name, reputation and claim for itself.[10] If forms and names have been established, reputations and appellations set up, then there is nowhere to conceal one's tracks or hide one's true aims.[11]

> He who is dedicated to the public interest is intelligent;
> He who is most intelligent gains most success;

至正者靜，至靜者耵（聖）。无私者知（智），至知（智）者爲天下稽。稱以權衡，參以天當，天下有事，必有巧驗。事如直木，多如倉粟。斗石已具，尺寸已陳，則无所逃其神。故曰：度量已具，則治而制之矣。絕而復屬，亡而復存，孰知其神。死而復生，以禍爲福，孰知其極。反索之无刑（形），故知禍福之所從生。應化之道，平衡而止。輕重不稱，是胃（謂）失道。天地有恒常，萬民有恒事，貴賤有恒立（位），畜臣有恒道，使民有恒度。天地之恒常，四時、晦明、生殺，輮（柔）剛。萬民之恒事，男農，女工。貴賤之恒立（位），賢不宵（肖）不相放（妨）。畜臣之恒道，任能毋過其所長。

He who is most correct is quiescent;
He who is most quiescent is a sage.
He who is without private bias is knowledgeable;
He who is the most knowledgeable is the model for the world.[12]

Measure them by the steelyard and align them with the correspondence to Heaven.[13] Material affairs must receive minute examination.

For affairs are like straight trees[14]
And are as numerous as grains in a granary.
When the *dou* and *shi* measures have been provided
And the *chi* foot and *cun* inch rules have been arranged,
Then no item will escape its true spirit.[15]

Therefore it is said, when rules and measures have been provided, supervise and control them. Cut off, then reattached, disappeared, then present again: who knows its spirituality? Dead, then back to life, taking good fortune as disaster: who knows its limit? Trace it back to the formless: therefore you will know from what calamity and good fortune are born. The Dao of responding to transformation is to level the steelyard and then stop. If the light and the heavy weights are not balanced, this is called "Losing the Dao."

Heaven and Earth have constant regularities;
The myriad people have constant affairs;
Noble and base have constant positions;
There is a constant Dao for caring for ministers;
There are constant rules for employing the people.

The constant regularities of Heaven and Earth are:
the four seasons, darkness and light, growth and decay,
the soft and the hard.

The constant affairs of the myriad people are:
males perform agricultural work and females weave.

The constant positions of the noble and base are:
the worthy and the worthless do not hinder each other.

The constant Dao for caring for ministers is:
to employ the capable such that they do not exceed their duties.

使民之恒度，去私而立公。變恒過度，以奇相御。正、奇有立(位)。而名□弗去。凡事無小大，物自爲舍。逆順死生，物自爲名。名刑（形）已定，物自爲正。故唯執【道】者能上明於天之反，而中達君臣之半，富密察於萬物之所終始，而弗爲主。故能至素精，悎（浩）彌无刑（形），然后可以爲天下正。《道法》

The constant rules for employing the people are:
to remove private bias and establish the public interest.

Change and constancy, excess and abiding by the rules, control each other by the unorthodox.[16] When the orthodox and the unorthodox have their correct positions, then names [and realities][17] will not leave them.

In general, in affairs there is no great and no small, for things make dwellings for themselves.[18] In opposition or compliant, dying or living, things make names for themselves. When names and forms have been determined, things correct themselves.

Therefore, only he who grasps [the Dao] is able to understand the turnings of Heaven above and in the middle to comprehend the separation[19] between ruler and minister; he minutely[20] examines where the myriad phenomena begin and end, and does not act as their master. When, therefore, he is able to be most plain, most quintessential, grandly filling up the formless, only then can he be the rectifier of the world.

國次

國失其次，則社稷大匡。奪而无予，國不遂亡。不盡天極，衰者復昌。誅禁不當，反受其央（殃）。禁伐當罪當亡，必虛（墟）其國。兼之而勿擅，是胃（謂）天功。天地无私，四時不息。天地立（位），耶（聖）人故載。過極失【當】，天將降央（殃）。人強朕（勝）天，慎辟（避）勿當。天反朕（勝）人，因與俱行。先屈後信（伸）必盡天極，而毋擅天功。兼人之國。脩其國郭，處其郎（廊）廟，聽其鐘鼓，利其齎（資）財，妻其子女，○是胃（謂）□逆以芒（荒），國危破亡。故唯耶（聖）人能盡天極，能用天當。天地之道，不過三功。功成而不止，身危又（有）央（殃）。

When a state loses its priorities, the altars of soil and grain will be wronged.[21]

Though Heaven may take away from it and not give to it, a state will not perish as a result,[22]

For if the aggressor does not reach Heaven's Limit,[23] the defender who is failing may be glorious once again.

If punishments and prohibitions do not correspond, you will suffer calamity as a consequence.[24]

If the prohibitions and attacks correspond with the crimes and omissions committed by the other state,

You will inevitably empty that state.[25]

To annex it[26] and not monopolize it,[27] this is what is meant by "Heavenly Success."

Heaven and Earth have no private bias, the four seasons do not cease. Heaven and Earth are positioned, and so the sage performs his tasks. Should he exceed the limit and fail to make [the correspondence between his actions and Heaven and Earth],[28] Heaven will send down calamity.

Should Man[29] conquer Heaven by force, take care to avoid and not face him. Should Heaven in turn conquer Man, follow and march with it.[30]

If you are bent in front and stretched behind,[31] you will inevitably reach the Heavenly Limit and not monopolize the Heavenly Success.[32]

In a state of annexers, they repair the outer walls of their cities, locate their long palaces,[33] obey their bells and drums,[34] profit their property and wealth, and marry off their sons and daughters. This is what is meant by . . . Opposition leading to desolation: the state will be endangered, broken, and ruined.

Only a sage, therefore, is able to reach the Heavenly Limit and is able to employ the Heavenly Correspondence.

The Dao of Heaven and Earth does not exceed three accomplishments.[35] If the accomplishments are achieved and you do not then stop, you yourself will be endangered and in turn will suffer a calamity.

Therefore, when the sage attacks the state of an annexer, he tears down the inner and outer walls of his towns,[36] burns his bells and drums, disperses his property and wealth, scatters his sons and daughters, breaks open[37] his lands and enfeoffs the worthy with them: this is what is called the "Heavenly Success."

故耴（聖）人之伐殴（也），兼人之國，隋（墮）其郭城，梦（焚）其鐘鼓，布其齎（資）財，散其子女，列（裂）其地土，以封賢者，是胃（謂）天功。功成不廢，後不奉（逢）央（殃）。毋陽竊，毋陰竊，毋土敝，毋故執，毋黨別。陽竊者天奪【其光，陰竊】者土地芒（荒），土敝者天加之以兵，人執者流之四方，黨別【者】□內相功（攻）。陽竊者疾，陰竊者几（飢），土敝者亡地，人執者失民，黨別者亂，此胃（謂）五逆。五逆皆成，□□□□□地之剛（綱），變故亂常，擅制更爽，心欲是行，身危有【殃，是】胃（謂）過極失當。《國次》

If you are not negligent after the success is achieved, later you will not encounter calamity.

Do not be too exposed to Yang;
Do not be too exposed to Yin;[38]
Do not cover over the soil;[39]
Do not take the ancients as your standard;[40]
Do not divide into factions.

Heaven will remove [its light] from those who are too exposed
   to Yang;
The territory [of those too exposed to Yin] will be desolated;
Heaven will bring warfare on those who cover over the soil;
Those who take others as their standard, Heaven will spread to
   the four quarters;
Those who have factions . . . inside the state
   they will attack each other.

Those who are too exposed to Yang will grow sick;
Those who are too exposed to Yin will starve;
Those who cover over the soil will lose their land;
Those who take others as their standard will lose the people;
Those who have factions will engender rebellions.

These are what are called the Five Oppositions.
If all five oppositions come to pass
. . .[41] the covering over (?) of territory,
If a ruler changes the old and disorders the constant,
Monopolizes control of the government and alters the bright
   laws,
And acts on what his heart desires,
He personally will endanger himself and meet with [calamity.
This] is what is called exceeding the Heavenly Limit and losing
   the Heavenly Correspondence.

君正

■　一年從其俗，二年用其德，三年而民有得，四年而發號令，【五年而以刑正，六年而】民畏敬，七年而可以正（征）。一年從其俗，則知民則。二年用【其德】，民則力。三年无賦斂，則民有得。四年發號令，則民畏敬。五年以刑正，則民不幸（倖）。六年□□□□□□□。【七】年而可以正（征），則朕（勝）強適（敵）。俗者順民心毆（也）。德者愛勉之【也。有】得者，發禁拕（弛）關市之正（征）毆（也）。號令者，連爲什伍，巽（選）練賢不宵（肖）有別毆（也）。以刑正者，罪殺不赦毆（也）。□□□□□□□□毆（也）。可以正（征）者，民死節毆（也）。若號令發，必廄而上九，壹道同心，【上】下不赾（斥），民无它志，然后可以守單（戰）矣。號令發必行，俗也。男女勸勉，愛也。動之靜之，民无不聽，時也。受賞无德，受罪无怨，當也。貴賤有別，賢不宵（肖）衰（差）也。衣備（服）不相綸（逾），貴賤等也。

60

3 . A LORD'S GOVERNMENT

In the first year he follows the people's customs; in the second, he uses their worthy men;[42] in the third year, he lets the people keep what they have obtained; in the fourth, he promulgates commands and orders; [in the fifth, he corrects them with punishments; in the sixth,] the people are awed and respectful; in the seventh, they can make punitive attacks.[43]

If, in the first year, the ruler follows the people's customs, then he will know their standards. If, in the second year, he uses [their worthy men], the people will exert their strength. If, for three years, there are no taxes,[44] then the people will keep what they have obtained. If, in the fourth, he promulgates orders and commands, the people will be awed and respectful. If, in the fifth, he corrects them with punishments, the people will not be lucky.[45] If, in the sixth year . . . If, [in the seventh] year, when they can make punitive attacks, then they will conquer strong enemies.

Customs follow the hearts of the people. The worthy love them and make them work hard.[46] [So that they may keep] what they have obtained, do away with[47] the prohibitions and relax the taxes at the barriers and in the markets. By orders and commands, link them into five- and ten-man groups[48] and select and train them according to their distinctions of competence. To correct them by punishments means that crimes that warrant death are not pardoned[49] . . . That they may be used for punitive attacks means that the people die out of a sense of duty.[50]

If orders and commands are promulgated, inevitably they will assemble[51] and follow their superiors (?),[52] be of one Dao and have the same heart; when [the superiors] and inferiors do not censure each other,[53] the people will lack evil intent and only after that can they defend and fight.

When orders and commands have been promulgated, that they will inevitably be obeyed is because of customs;[54] that men and women are urged to labor is because of love; that the ruler moves them or keeps them quiescent, and all the people obey is because of timeliness;[55] that, when they receive rewards, they have no special affection and, when they suffer punishment, they harbor no resentment, is because of appropriateness;[56] that there are distinctions between noble and base, is because of the gradations between the worthy and the worthless; that types of clothing do not transgress[57] each other's codes is because of the ranks of noble and base.

61

國无盜賊，詐僞不生，民无邪心，衣食足而刑伐（罰）必也。以有餘守，不可拔也。以不足功（攻），反自伐也。天有死生之時，國有死生之正（政）。因天之生也以養生，胃（謂）之文，因天之殺也以伐死，胃（謂）之武。【文】武並行，則天下從矣。人之本在地，地之本在宜，宜之生在時，時之用在民，民之用在力，力之用在節。知地宜，須時而樹，節民力以使，則財生。賦斂有度，則民富，民富則有佴（恥），有佴（恥）則號令成俗而刑伐（罰）不犯，號令成俗而刑伐（罰）不犯則守固單（戰）胈（勝）之道也。法度者，正之至也。而以法度治者，不可亂也。而生法度者，不可亂也。精公无私而賞罰信，所以治也。苟事，節賦斂，毋奪民時，治之安。无父之行，不得子之用。无母之德，不能盡民之力。父母之行備，則天地之德也。三者備則事得矣。能收天下豪桀（傑）票（驃）雄，則守御（禦）之備具矣。審於行文武之道，則天下賓矣。

62

When the state lacks robbers and murderers, slanders and lies do not arise, and the people do not possess depraved hearts, it is because food and clothing is sufficient and mutilating punishments and fines[58] are inevitable.

Those who defend to keep a surplus cannot be eradicated. Those who attack because of an insufficiency will themselves be attacked in turn.[59]

Heaven has seasons for life and death; states have policies for life and death. To rely on Heaven's season of life to nourish the living is called *Wen* (Patterning); to rely on Heaven's season of killing to attack the dying is called *Wu* (Martiality). When both [*Wen* patterning] and *Wu* martiality are carried out, then the world will follow and obey.

The basis of Man lies in Earth. The basis of Earth lies in appropriateness;[60] production through appropriateness lies in the seasons; the use of the seasons lies in the people; use of the people lies in strength; use of strength lies in regulation. When the appropriateness of the Earth is known, wait for the proper season and then plant. If regulation of the people's strength is used to employ them, then wealth will be produced. If taxes have rules,[61] then the people will be wealthy; if the people are wealthy, they will have a sense of shame. If they have a sense of shame, then commands and orders will complete customs and prohibitions against crimes deserving mutilating punishments and fines will not be transgressed. If orders and commands complete customs, and prohibitions against crimes and fines are not transgressed, then that is the Dao of defending stoutly and conquering in battle.

Laws and measures are the epitome of rectification. He who is able to govern by means of laws and measures cannot be disordered. He who is able to promulgate laws and measures cannot be disordered. To be quintessential, public-spirited, and without private bias, and to have rewards and punishments reliable is the way to govern. [To reduce][62] harsh impositions, regulate taxes, not take the proper seasons away from the people: he who governs so will be safe.

If you fail to behave as a father, you will not acquire the use of sons. If you lack the potency of a mother, you will be unable to make full use of the people's strength. When conduct befitting a father or a mother is performed, then that is the potency of Heaven and Earth. When the three[63] are performed, then affairs will be accomplished. If you are able to gather the local magnates and the bravoes of the world, then preparations for defense will be readied. If you inquire carefully into the Dao of *Wen* and *Wu*, then the world will submit.

號令闔（合）於民心，則民聽令。兼愛无私，則民親上。《君正》

When commands and orders are harmonized in the hearts of the people, then they will obey orders. When there is universal love[64] and no private bias, then the people will feel close affection for their superiors.

六分

■　觀國者觀主，觀家觀父，能爲國則能爲主，能爲家則能爲父。凡觀國，有六逆：其子父，其臣主，雖強大不王。其〇謀臣在外立（位）者，其國不安，其主不晉（悟）則社稷殘。其主失立（位）則國无本，臣不失處則下有根，【國】憂而存。主失立（位）則國芒（荒），臣失處則令不行，此之胃（謂）頹（頹）國。主兩則失其明，男女挣（爭）威，國有亂兵，此胃（謂）亡國。適（嫡）子父，命曰上曠，群臣离志：大臣主，命曰雍（壅）塞；在強國削，在中國破，在小國亡。謀臣【在】外立（位）者，命曰逆成，國將不寧：在強國危，在中國削，在小國破。主失立（位），臣不失處，命曰外根，將與禍閵（鄰）；在強國憂，在中國危，在小國削。主失立（位），臣失處，命曰无本，上下无根，國將大損；在強國破，在中國亡。在小國威（滅）。

4. THE GREAT DISTINCTIONS[65]

When observing a state, observe the ruler; when observing a family, observe the father.[66] If you are able to act on behalf of a state, then you are able to be a ruler; if you are able to act on behalf of a family, then you are able to be a father.[67]

In general, in observing a state, there are six oppositions: that between son and father, that between minister and ruler, [and that between female and male].[68] Even if the ruler is strong and great, he will not be a true king if these six oppositions exist in his state. If the planners of strategy are in positions on the outside,[69] his state will not be stable, and if the ruler is not fully aware of the entire political situation, then the altars of the soil and grain will be ruined. If the ruler loses his position, then the state will lack a foundation, and if the ministers do not lose their posts, then there will be roots below: though [the state] will be in distress, yet it will survive.[70] If the ruler loses his position, then the state will be devastated; if the ministers lose their posts, then orders will not be carried out: this is what is called an "Undisciplined State."[71]

If there are two rulers,[72] then the ruler will lose his brightness, male and female will contend for authority, the state will have rebellious soldiers: this is called a "Destroyed State."

If the eldest son acts as the father, it is termed the "Highest Defiance."[73] If the assembled ministers abandon their purposes, and great ministers act as rulers, it is termed the "Blocking Obstruction." Such a situation in a strong state will lead to it being pared down; in a middle-sized state it will lead to it being broken; in a small state it will lead to it being destroyed.

When planners of strategy are in positions on the outside, it is termed the "Completion of Opposition," and the state will not be at peace. Such a situation in a strong state will lead to danger; in a middle-sized state, to it being pared down; and in a small state, to it being broken.

If the ruler loses his position, but the ministers do not lose their posts, it is termed the "Root Outside": misfortune will be close at hand.[74] Such a situation in a strong state will lead to distress; in a middle-sized state to danger; and in a small state to it being pared down.

If the ruler loses his position, and the ministers lose their posts, it is termed "Being Without a Basis" and "Superiors and Inferiors Lacking Roots": the state will suffer great injury. Such a situation in a strong state will lead to its being broken; in a middle-sized state to its being destroyed; and in a small state to its being obliterated.

主暴臣亂，命曰大芒（荒），外戎內戎，天將降央（殃）；國无小大，又（有）者威（滅）亡。主兩，男女分威，命曰大麋（迷）。國中有師；在強國破，在中國亡，在小國威（滅）。凡觀國，有大〈六〉順：主不失其立（位）則國【有本。臣】失其處則下无根，國憂而存。主惠臣忠者，其國安。主主臣臣，上下不赿者，其國強，主執度，臣循理者，其國朝（霸）昌。主得【位】臣楅（輻）屬者，王。六順六逆□存亡【興壞】之分也。主上者執六分以生殺，以賞□。以必伐。天下大（太）平，正以明德，參之於天地，而兼復（覆）載而无私也，故王天，王天下者之道，有天焉，有人焉，又（有）地焉。參（三）者參用之，□□而有天下矣。爲人主，南面而立。臣肅敬，不敢敝（蔽）其主。下比順，不敢敝（蔽）其上。萬民和輯而樂爲其主上用，地廣人眾兵強，天下无適（敵）。文德廄（究）於輕細，武刃於□□，王之本也。然而不知王述（術），不王天下。知王【術】者，驅騁馳獵而

If the ruler is violent and subjects are rebellious, it is termed the "Great Devastation"; there will be warfare both inside and outside the state,[75] and Heaven will send down calamities. No matter whether the state is large or small, those states that suffer "Great Devastation" will be obliterated and destroyed.

When there are two rulers, and male and female share authority, it is termed the "Great Delusion," and inside the state there is armed conflict. Such a situation in a strong state will lead to it being broken; in a middle-sized state to it being destroyed; and in a small state to it being obliterated.

In general, in observing a state, there are six compliances. If the ruler does not lose his position, then the state [possesses a basis. If the ministers] lose their posts, then there will be no roots below: though the state is in distress, yet it will survive. When the ruler is benevolent and the ministers loyal, the state is stable. When the ruler acts as a ruler and the ministers act as ministers, and superiors and inferiors do not censure[76] each other, the state is strong. When the ruler grasps the measures,[77] and the ministers follow the principles, the state is glorious like that of a lord-protector. When the ruler acquires . . . and the ministers are attached to him like the spokes of a wheel to a hub,[78] he will be a true king.

The six compliances and six oppositions . . . are the distinctions between survival and destruction, [prosperity and ruin]. The ruler above[79] grasps the six distinctions to give life or to kill, to reward or to . . . ,[80] and to be inevitable in punitive attacks. The world is at "Grand Peace,"[81] he rules with bright potency,[82] he makes a triad with Heaven and Earth, and is able to cover over and uphold concurrently[83] and to be without private bias: thus is he able to rule the world as a true king.[84] The Dao of him who rules the world as a true king has Heaven in it, has Earth in it, and has Man in it. He partakes of those three and uses them together and [therefore he rules as a true king] and possesses the world.

He who is a ruler of men stands facing south; his ministers are grave and reverential, and do not venture to hide their ruler.[85] Inferiors are harmonious and compliant[86] and do not venture to hide their superiors. The myriad people are agreeable and friendly and are pleased to be used by their ruler above[87]; the territory is broad, the population numerous, the army strong, and in the world he has no enemies.[88]

Civil potency penetrating to the light and fine people,[89] and martiality and (?) being inflicted upon[90] . . . is the basis of true kingship. Although that is so, if you do not know the technique of being a true king, you will not rule the world as a true king. He who knows [the

不禽芒（荒），飲食喜樂而不面（湎）康，玩好嬛好而惑心，俱與天下用兵，費少而有功，□□□□□□□□□□則國富而民□□□□□□其□【不】知王述（術）者，驅騁馳獵則禽芒（荒），飲食喜樂則面（湎）康，玩好嬛好則或（惑）心；俱與天下用兵，費多而无功，單（戰）朕（勝）而令不□□□失□□□□□□□空□與天□□則國貧而民芒（荒）。□耴（聖）之人弗留，天下弗與。如此而有（又）不能重士而師有道，則國人之國已（矣）。王天下者有玄德，有□□獨知□□□□王天下而天下莫知其所以。王天下者，輕縣國而重士，故國重而身安；賤財而貴有知（智），故功得而財生；賤身而貴有道，故身貴而令行。□□天下□天下則之。鞘（霸）主積甲士而正（征）不備（服），誅禁當罪而不私其利，故令行天下而莫敢不聽，自此以下，兵單（戰）力掙（爭），危亡无日，而莫知其所從來。夫言鞘（霸）王，其□□□唯王者能兼復（覆）載天下，物曲成焉。《六分》

70

technique], though he may urge his horses to a gallop in the hunt, yet he will not go so far as the abandoned wastelands[91] and, though he may drink and eat and enjoy entertainment, yet he will not go so far as to be dissipated in drink and reckless in his pleasure; though he may amuse himself with expensive trinkets and seductive girls, his heart will not be deluded. If he engages in warfare with the world, his expenses will be few, but he will achieve success . . . then the state will be rich and the people . . . their/his . . .

He who does [not] know the technique of a true king, when he urges his horse to a gallop in the hunt, goes as far as the abandoned wastelands; when he drinks and eats and enjoys entertainment, then he becomes dissipated in drink and reckless in his pleasure; when he amuses himself with expensive trinkets and seductive girls, his heart is deluded. When he engages in warfare with the world, his expenses are numerous, but he achieves no success; though he may be victorious in battle, yet his orders are not . . . loses . . . empty . . . with Heaven . . . then the state will be poor and the people devastated. . . . the sages do not stay with him and the world does not share with him. Under such circumstances, if he is also unable to value officer-knights or to have teachers who possess the Dao, his state will belong to another.

He who rules the world as a true king possesses Dark Potency[92]; he has . . . alone knows . . . rules the world as a true king, but no one in the world knows how he does it. He who rules the world as a true king treats the counties and kingdoms[93] lightly, but values the officer-knights, and therefore his state is respected and his person is safe. He disrespects material goods, but esteems those with knowledge, and therefore his aims are achieved and his material goods grow. He disrespects himself, but esteems those in possession of the Dao, and therefore he himself is esteemed and his orders are carried out. Therefore he rules the world as a true king and the world takes him as its model.

The ruler who is a lord-protector accumulates armored soldiers and punitively attacks the unsubmissive; he punishes and prohibits those who deserve to be held guilty of crimes and does not consider the profit to be for his own private ends. For this reason, his orders are carried out in the world and no one ventures to disobey. Furthermore, his soldiers do battle and he fights from strength, and danger and destruction follow soon after (?), and no one knows where they originate.

Now in speaking about the lord-protector and the true king, their . . . only the true king is able to cover over and uphold the world concurrently,[94] and the phenomena of the natural world are helped by him to come to completion.[95]

四度

■　君臣易立（位）胃（謂）之逆，賢不宵（肖）並立胃（謂）之亂，動靜不時胃（謂）之逆，生殺不當胃（謂）之暴。逆則失本，亂則失職，逆則失天，【暴】則失人。失本則□，失職則侵，失天則几（飢），失人則疾。周毚（遷）動作，天爲之稽。天道不遠，入與處，出與反。君臣當立（位）胃（謂）之靜，賢不宵（肖）當立（位）胃（謂）之正，動靜參於天地胃（謂）之文。誅□時當胃（謂）之武。靜則安，正治，文則【明】，武則強。安得本，治則得人，明則得天，強則威行。參於天地，閡（合）於民心，文武並立，命之曰上同。審知四度，可以定天下，可安一國。順治其內，

5. THE FOUR MEASURES[96]

If lord and subject change positions, it is called "Opposition"; if the worthy and the worthless stand together, it is called chaos; if movement and quiescence are not timely, it is called opposition; if life and death do not correspond to the appropriate season and circumstances, it is called violence.

If there is opposition, the basis will be lost;
If there is chaos, official duties will be lost;
If there is opposition, Heaven will be lost;
[If there is violence], Man will be lost.
If the basis is lost, then . . . ;
If official duties are lost, there will be encroachment;
If Heaven is lost, there will be famine;
If Man is lost, there will be epidemics.

For revolving[97] all around, movement and creation: Heaven is the model for these activities. The Dao of Heaven is not far off: on entering, take up position with it; on exiting, return with it.[98]

When ministers and lords match their right positions, it is called "Quiescence"; when the worthy and the worthless match their right positions, it is called correctness. To move and be quiescent, forming a triad with Heaven and Earth,[99] is called *Wen* (Civil Patterning); to punish . . . in a timely fashion is called *Wu* (Martiality).

If you are quiescent, then you will be safe;
If you are correct, you will govern well;
If you are refined, you will be [bright];
If you are martial, you will be strong;
If you are safe, you will gain the basis;
If you govern well, you will gain the Human;
If you are bright, you will gain Heaven;
If you are strong, your majesty will be put into operation.

When you form a triad with Heaven and Earth and harmonize with the hearts of the people, and when *Wen* (Civil Patterning) and *Wu* (Martiality) stand together, it is termed "The Highest Unity."

If you fully investigate and know the four measures, you can settle the world and can pacify a single state. When compliance governs the

逆用於外，功成而傷。逆治其內，順用其外，功成而亡。內外皆逆，是胃（謂）重央（殃），身危爲僇（戮），國危破亡。外內皆順，命曰天當，功成而不廢，後不奉（逢）央（殃）。○聲華□□者用也。順者，動也。正者，事之根也。執道循理，必從本始，順爲經紀，禁伐當罪，必中天理。伓（倍）約則窘（窘），達刑則傷。伓（倍）逆合當，爲若又（有）事，雖○无成功，亦无天央（殃）。毋□□□□，毋御死以生，毋爲虛聲。聲洫（溢）於實，是胃（謂）威（滅）名。極陽以殺，極陰以生，是胃（謂）逆陰陽之命。極陽殺於外，極陰生於內。已逆陰陽，有（又）逆其立（位）。大則國亡，小則身受其央（殃）。□□□□□□□□建生。當者有□。極而反，盛而衰，天地之道也，人之李（理）也。逆順同道而異理，審知逆順，是胃（謂）道紀。

inside of a state, but opposition is used on the outside, when the task is accomplished, harm will have resulted. If opposition governs the inside and compliance is used on the outside, when the task is accomplished, destruction will have resulted. When opposition is applied both inside and outside, this is called "Valuing Calamity": the individual ruler will be in danger and executed and the state will be in danger, defeated, and destroyed. If compliance is applied to both inside and outside, it is called "Matching Heaven" (*Tiandang*). When the task is achieved, you will not have failed and later will not encounter calamity.

When a ruler's reputation is magnificent, but . . . ,[100] it is used (?).[101] Compliance is movement, correctness is the root of affairs. He who grasps the Dao and follows principles must begin from the basis, compliantly act according to the constant standards, prohibit and punish those who deserve being held guilty of crimes, and must be centered on the principles of Heaven.

If you renege on agreements, you will suffer; if you extend punishment,[102] you will be harmed. If you go against the appropriate times for opposition and harmony,[103] when you have some affair at hand, although you will fail to achieve success, yet you will also not suffer a Heavenly calamity.

Do not . . .
Do not meet death with life;
Do not act for an empty reputation.

If the reputation overflows the reality, this is called "Destroying the Name."

To reach the extremity of Yang by means of death and to reach the extremity of Yin by means of life, this is called "Opposing the Name of Yin and Yang."[104] If extreme Yang is used to kill on the outside, and extreme Yin is used to live on the inside,[105] that is already in opposition to Yin and Yang, and also opposes their positions.[106] If it is a large state that acts in such a way, then it will be lost; if a small one, then the person of the ruler will suffer a calamity as a consequence.

. . . establish life: those who match it will possess . . . To reach the extremity and then return, to flourish and then decay is the Dao of Heaven and Earth, and the principle of Man.

Opposition and compliance have the same Dao but different principles. To fully investigate and know opposition and compliance, this is called the "Standard of the Dao."

以強下弱，以何國不克。以貴下賤，何人不得。以賢下不宵（肖），
□□不□。規之內曰員（圓），柜（矩）之內曰【方】，【縣】之
下曰正，水之曰平。尺寸之度曰小大短長，權衡之稱曰輕重不爽，
斗石之量曰小（少）多有數。八度者，用之稽也。日月星辰之期，
四時之度，【動靜】之立（位），外內之處，天之稽也。高【下】
不敝（蔽）其刑（形），美亞（惡）不匿其請（情），地之稽也。君
臣不失其立（位），士不失其處，任能毋過其所長，去私而公，人
之稽也。美亞（惡）有名，逆順有刑（形），請（情）偽有實，王
公執□以爲天下正。因天時，伐天毀，胃（謂）之武。武刃而以文
隨其後，則有成功矣。用二文一武者王。其主道離人理，處狂惑
之立（位）處不吾（悟），身必有瘳（戮）。柔弱者无罪而幾，不及
而翟，是胃（謂）柔弱。剛正而□者□□而不廄。名功相抱（孚），
是故長久。名功不相抱（孚），名進實退，是胃（謂）失道，其卒
必□身咎。

76

Were it to use the strong to subordinate the weak, what state would not be victorious? Were he to use the noble to subordinate the mean, what man would not gain his ends? If he used the worthy to subordinate the worthless [what] . . . would not . . . ?

Inside the compass is called round; inside the set-square is called [square]; beneath the [plumb-line] is called straight; [on the top of][107] the water is called level. The measures of inch and foot-rule are called small and large, long and short, the weighing of the pivot and beam of the steelyard means that the light and the heavy will not be mistaken; the measuring of the peck and picul means that the less and the more will be counted. These eight measures[108] are the models for use.

The periodicities of the sun and moon, planets, and constellations, the regularities of the four seasons, the positions [of movement and quiescence], the locations of inside and outside, are the models of Heaven.

That height and [lowness] do not hide their forms, beauty and ugliness do not conceal their true conditions, are the models of Earth.

That lord and subject do not lose their positions, that the officer-knights do not lose their posts, that those discharging duties are not able to exceed their responsibilities, private bias is removed, and public spirit is established, these are the models of Man.

Beauty and ugliness have their names, opposition and compliance have their forms, truth and falsehood have their realities: the king or lord[109] takes hold of . . . in order to make the world correct.

To rely on the times of Heaven to attack and punish those who are being destroyed by Heaven[110] is called *Wu* (Martiality). If you inflict damage[111] with martiality and follow it up with *Wen* (Civil Patterning), then success will be achieved.

He who uses *Wen* (Patterning) twice to once for *Wu* (Martiality) will be a true king. If, without realizing it,[112] he loses[113] the Dao of the ruler, abandons the principles of Man, and takes up the position of madness or folly, he himself will inevitably be executed.

The soft and weak rulers are those who are in danger, though guilty of no crime, and are afraid even before they are reached: they are called "The Soft and Weak."[114] Those rulers who are hard and upright and . . . are . . . and do not rest. Their reputation and achievement correspond to each other, and for this reason they long endure. If reputation and achievement do not correspond, if reputation advances but reality retreats, this is called "Losing the Dao," and their soldiers will necessarily . . ., and they themselves will encounter disaster.

黃金珠玉臧（藏）積，怨之本也。女樂玩好燔材，亂之基也。守怨之本，養亂之基，雖有耵（聖）人，不能爲謀。《四度》

Stores and piles of yellow gold and pearls and jade are the roots of resentment; wasting wealth[115] on female musicians and amusing jesters is the foundation of chaos. If a state guards the roots of resentment and nourishes the foundation of chaos, although it may possess a sage for a ruler, yet it will not be able to plan for the outcome.[116]

■ 人主者，天地之□也，號令之所出也，□□之命也。不天天則失其神，不重地則失根。不順【四時之度】而民疾。不處外內之立（位），不應動靜之化，則事窘（窘）於內而舉窘（窘）於【外。八】正皆失，□□□□。【天天則得其神，重地】則得其根。順四【時之度】□□□而民不□疾。【處】外【內之位，應動靜之化，則事】得於內，而得舉得於外。八正不失，則與天地總矣。天執一，明【三，定】二，建八正，行七法，然后□□□□□□□之中无不□□矣。岐（蚑）行喙息，扇蜚（飛）耎（蠕）動，无□□□□□□□□□□不失其常者，天之一也。天執一以明三。日信出信入，南北有極，【度之稽也。月信生信】死，進退有常，數之稽也。列星有數，而不失其行，信之稽也。天明三以定二，則壹晦壹明，□□□□□□□□【天】定二以建八正，則四時有度，動靜有立（位），

6 . ASSESSMENTS

The ruler of men is the . . .[117] Heaven and Earth and from him commands and orders issue, and he is the . . . of mandates.

If he does not treat Heaven as Heaven, then he loses his
    spirituality;
If he does not value Earth, then he loses his roots.

When he does not follow [the measures of the four seasons], the people suffer. If he does not fix the positions of inside and outside, and does not respond to the transformations of movement and quiescence, then affairs will be in disarray on the inside and his initiatives will be in disarray [on the outside. When the Eight] Corrections are all lost . . .

[If he treats Heaven as Heaven, then he acquires his spirituality;
If he values Earth], then he gains his roots.

When he follows the [regularities of the] four [seasons] . . . , the people do not . . . suffer. If he [fixes the positions of the] outside [and inside, and responds to the transformations of movement and quiescence, then affairs] are achieved on the inside and initiatives are successful on the outside. If the Eight Regulators are not lost,[118] then he is united with Heaven and Earth.

Heaven holds the One, brightens [the Three and determines][119] the Two, establishes the Eight Regulators, puts into practice the Seven Models,[120] and afterwards . . . in the center of . . . nothing does not . . . Creeping and sucking caterpillars and insects, flapping and wriggling birds and beasts[121] none . . .

What does not lose its constancy is Heaven. Heaven holds the One and uses it to brighten the Three.[122] That the sun faithfully emerges and faithfully reenters[123] and that North and South have poles [are the epitomes of measures. That the moon faithfully grows and faithfully] dies,[124] that advance and retreat have constancy, are the epitomes of enumeration. That the serried stars have number, but do not lose their ranks, is the epitome of faithfulness.[125]

If Heaven brightens the Three in order to determine the Two,[126] then one will be dark and the other bright . . . If [Heaven] determines the Two in order to establish the Eight Regulators, then the four seasons have regularities, movement and quiescence have their positions, and

而外內有處。天建【八正以行七法】。明以正者，天之道也。適者，天度也。信者，天之期也。極而【反】者，天之生（性）也。必者天之命也。□□□□□□□□□者，天之所以爲物命也。此之胃（謂）七法。七法各當其名，胃（謂）之物。物各□□□□胃（謂）之理。理之所在，胃（謂）之□。物有不合於道者，胃（謂）之失理。失理之所在，胃（謂）之逆。逆順各自命也，則存亡興壞可知【也。強生威，威】生惠（慧），惠（慧）生正，【正】生靜。靜則平，平則寧，寧則素，素則精，精則神。至神之極，【見】知不惑。帝王者，執此道也。是以守天地之極，與天俱見，盡□于四極之中，執六枋（柄）以令天下，審三名以爲萬事□，察逆順以觀于朝（霸）王危亡之理，知虛實動靜之所爲，達於名實【相】應，盡知請（情）僞而不惑，然后帝王之道成。六枋（柄）：一曰觀，二曰論，三曰僮（動），四曰轉，五曰變，六曰化。

82

outside and inside have their locations. Heaven establishes [the Eight Regulators in order to put into practice the Seven Models].

To brighten in order to regulate is the Dao of Heaven. Appropriateness is the measure of Heaven. Faithfulness is the periodicity of Heaven.[127] To go to the limit and then [turn back] is the nature of Heaven. Necessity is the mandate of Heaven . . . is what Heaven uses to make mandates for things. These are called the Seven Models.[128]

When each of the Seven Models matches its name, it is called a "thing." When each thing [is fitted with the Dao(?)], it is called "Principle." Where Principle is situated, it is called [Compliance].[129] When some things do not fit with the Dao, it is called "Losing Principle." Where Losing Principle is situated, it is called "Opposition." If Opposition and Compliance each mandate themselves,[130] then preservation and destruction, rise and decline can be known.

[Strength produces authority;
Authority][131] produces kindness;
Kindness produces correctness;
[Correctness] produces quiescence.
If you are quiescent, you are calm;
If you are calm, you are tranquil;
If you are tranquil, you are plain;
If you are plain, you are quintessentially pure;
If you are quintessentially pure, you are spiritual.

The [limit] of utmost spirituality brings about seeing and knowing without being deluded.[132] A true emperor or king grasps this Dao.

For this reason, if you guard the limits of Heaven and Earth, see as Heaven sees, exhaustively . . . the middle of the four poles[133]; hold on to the Six Handles and use them to issue orders to the world; fully investigate the Three Names and use them to . . . for the myriad affairs; examine opposition and compliance and use them to observe the principles by which hegemons and kings came to be endangered and destroyed; know where vacuity and reality, movement and quiescence, are to be used; penetrate to the [mutual] correspondences of name and reality, and know the facts and falsehoods completely and not be confused: only then is the Dao of the emperors and kings brought to completion.

The Six Handles: the first is observation; the second is assessment; the third is movement; the fourth is revolution[134]; the fifth is change; the sixth is transformation.

觀則知死生之國，論則知存亡興壞之所在，動則能破強興弱，槫（轉）則不失諱（韙）非之□，變則伐死養生，化則能明德徐（除）害。六枋（柄）備則王矣。三名：一曰正名一曰立（位）而偃，二曰倚名法而亂，三曰強主威（滅）而无名。三名察則事有應矣。動靜不時，種樹失地之宜，【則天】地之道逆矣。臣不親其主，下不親其上，百族不親其事，則內理逆矣。逆之所在，胃（謂）之死國，伐之。反此之胃（謂）順之所在，胃（謂）之生國，生國養之。逆順有理，則請（情）偽密矣。實者視（示）【人】虛，不足者視（示）人有餘。以其有事起之則天下聽，以其无事安之則天下靜。名實不相應則定，名實不相應則靜（爭）。勿（物）自正也，名自命也，事自定也。三名察則盡知請（情）偽而【不】惑矣。

If you observe, you know which states are dead and which alive.[135] If you assess, you will know where preservation and destruction, rise and decline, are situated. If you move, you are able to break the strong and raise the weak. If you revolve, you do not lose the . . . of right and wrong. If you change, you [can] attack the dying and nourish the living. If you transform, you can brighten your potency and expel the noxious. If the Six Handles are in readiness, you will be a true king.

The Three Names: the first is when the correction of names is established, then stop.[136] The second is when the models of names are perverted,[137] then there is rebellion. The third is when headstrong rulers are obliterated and leave no reputation behind. When the Three Names are examined, then affairs will have correspondences.

If movement and quiescence are not timely, and sowing and planting miss the appropriate factors of Earth, [then] the Dao of [Heaven] and Earth is opposed. If ministers do not treat their lord affectionately, and inferiors do not treat their superiors affectionately, and if the hundred clans do not treat their affairs affectionately, then the principles internal to the state are opposed.

Where opposition is situated is called a "Dead State": attack it.[138] The reverse of this is called "compliance"; where [compliance] is situated is called a "Living State": nourish a living state.

> If opposition and compliance have principles, then facts and
>   falsehoods are meticulously (clarified?).
> Fullness reveals vacuity [to men];
>   insufficiency reveals excess to them.
> If you begin something only when there is business to do,
>   then the world will listen and obey.
> If you keep it quiet when there is nothing to do,
>   then the world will be quiescent.
> If names and realities do not correspond with each other,
>   then settle them.
> If names and realities do not correspond with each other,
>   then there will be fighting.[139]

> Things correct themselves;
> Names name themselves;
> Affairs settle themselves.[140]

If the Three Names are examined, then you will know the facts and falsehoods completely and [not] be deluded.

有國將昌，當罪先亡。《論》

He who possesses a state will be glorious;
Those who deserve being held guilty of crimes will be
   destroyed first.

亡論

■ 凡犯禁絕理，天誅必至。一國而服（備）六危者戚（滅），一國而服（備）三不辜者死，廢令者亡。一國之君而服（備）三壅者，亡地更君。一國而服（備）三凶者，禍反【自】及也。上洫（溢）者死，下洫（溢）者刑。德溥（薄）而功厚者隋（隳），名禁而不王者死。抹（昧）利，襦傳，達刑，爲亂首，爲怨媒，此五者，禍皆反自及也。守國而侍（恃）其地險者削，用國而侍（恃）其強者弱。興兵失理，所伐不當，天降二央（殃）。逆節不成，是胃（謂）得天。逆節果成，天將不盈其命而重其刑。贏極必靜，動舉必正。贏極而不靜，是胃（謂）失天。動舉而不正，【是】胃（謂）後命。大殺服民，僇（戮）降人，刑无罪，過（禍）皆反自及也。所伐當罪，其禍五之。所伐不當，其禍什之。國受兵而不知固守，下邪恒以地界爲私者□。救人而弗能存，反爲禍門，是胃（謂）危根。聲華實寡，危國亡土。夏起大土功，

88

In general, when prohibitions are transgressed and principles are eliminated,[141] Heaven's punishment will inevitably befall. A state that prepares the Six Dangers[142] will be obliterated. A state that prepares the Three Crimes against the Innocent[143] will die, and one that sets aside the orders will perish. He who is the ruler[144] of a state and prepares the Three Blockages[145] will lose territory and change rulers. Misfortune [will befall in turn] a state that prepares the Three Evils.[146] Superiors[147] who are excessive die; inferiors who are excessive are punished.[148] Those whose virtue is thin and whose accomplishments[149] are great are exterminated; he whose fame is hindered and does not act like a true king[150] dies.

Greed for profit, trusting to tallies and passports,[151] extending punishment,[152] starting chaos, transmitting resentment: misfortune will befall all of these five in turn.

He who defends his state by relying on the ruggedness of the terrain will be pared down; he who uses his state to fight by relying on his strength, will be weakened.[153] On him who raises soldiers against the principles and if those whom he attacks do not deserve [to be held guilty of a crime], Heaven sends down a double calamity. When criminal conduct[154] does not fully develop, this is called "Acquiring Heaven." When criminal conduct really does develop fully, Heaven will not complete his fate[155] but rather double his punishment.

When you reach the limit, you must be quiescent, and in moving and initiating affairs you must be correct. To reach the limit and not be quiescent, this is called "Losing Heaven." To move and initiate affairs and not be correct, [this] is called "Being Behind Fate." To massacre a submissive people, to execute surrendered prisoners, to punish the innocent, misfortune will befall all of these in turn. If those whom he attacks deserve to be held guilty of a crime, his good fortune[156] will be fivefold. If those whom he attacks do not deserve to be held guilty of a crime, his misfortune will be tenfold.

When a state keeps soldiers but does not know how to defend itself securely, those inferiors who pervert the constant regulations and turn the land boundaries into their personal possession are . . . To rescue people, but then be unable to preserve them and instead create a gateway to misfortune, this is called the "Root of Danger."

When a ruler's reputation is magnificent, but the reality is slight,[157] the state is in danger and territory is lost. To start great earthmoving

命曰絕理。犯禁絕理，天誅必至。六危：一曰適（嫡）子父。二曰大臣主。三曰謀臣【離】其志。四曰聽諸侯之所廢置。五曰左右比周以雍（壅）塞。六曰父兄黨以儥。危不朕（勝），禍及於身。【三】下辜：一曰妄殺殺賢。二曰殺服民。三曰刑无罪。此三不辜。三雍（壅）：內立（位）朕（勝）胃（謂）之塞，外立（位）朕（勝）胃（謂）之儥，外內皆朕（勝）則君孤直（特）。以此有國，守不固，單（戰）不克。此胃（謂）一雍（壅）。從中令外【謂之】惑，從外令中胃（謂）之□，

90

projects in the summer is termed "Eliminating Principles."[158] When prohibitions are transgressed and principles are eliminated, Heaven's punishment will inevitably befall.[159]

The Six Dangers:

The first is the eldest son acts as the father[160];
The second is great ministers act as rulers;
The third is planners of strategy (?) . . .[161] their purposes;
The fourth is agreeing with the appointments and dismissals
    made by the feudal lords[162];
The fifth is courtiers colluding[163] to block and obstruct the ruler;
The sixth is the ruler's uncles and elder brothers forming a
    faction to defy him.[164]

If the [Six] Dangers are not conquered, misfortune will befall the ruler's person.

The [Three] Crimes against the Innocent:

The first is recklessly to murder the worthy;
The second is to murder a submissive people;
The third is to punish the guiltless.

These are the Three Crimes against the Innocent.[165]

The Three Blockages:

When the inner court[166] is victorious, it is called "Obstruction";
When the outer court[167] is victorious, it is called "Defiance"[168];

If both inner and outer courts are victorious, then the lord is solitary and alone. If you possess a state with these blockages, your defense will not be secure, and in battle you will not conquer. This is called the "First Blockage."

To issue orders to the outside from the center [is
    called] "Delusion";
To issue orders from the outside to the center is called
    [treason][169];

外內逐靜（爭），則危都國。此胃（謂）二雍（壅）。一人主擅主，命曰蔽光。從中外周，此胃（謂）重雍（壅），外內為一，國乃更。此胃（謂）三雍（壅）。三凶：一曰好凶器。二曰行逆德。三曰縱心欲。此胃（謂）【三凶。眛】天【下之】利，受天下之患。抹（眛）一國之利者，受一國之禍。約而倍之，胃（謂）之襦傳。伐當罪，見利而反，胃（謂）之達刑。上殺父兄，下走子弟，胃（謂）之亂首。外約不信，胃（謂）之怨媒。有國將亡，當□□昌。《亡論》

If the inner and the outer are pursuing competition[170] for power,
the capital of the state is endangered.

This is called the "Second Blockage."

If another person[171] on his own authority[172] acts as the ruler,
it is termed "Concealing the Light"[173];
To surround the outer from the center, this is called the
"Double Blockage";
When the outer and inner are one, then the state will change
its ruler.[174]

This is called the "Third Blockage."

The Three Evils:

The first is liking ill-omened instruments[175];
The second is practicing "Oppositional Virtue"[176];
The third is following the heart's desires.
These are called [the Three Evils.

He who is greedy] for profit from the world will suffer calamity
from it. He who is greedy for the profit from one state will receive that
state's misfortune.

To make agreements and then to repudiate them is called "Untrustworthiness." To attack those who deserve to be held guilty of a crime,
to see profit and to bring it back home is called "Extending Punishment."[177] To murder fathers and uncles and elder brothers[178] on the one
hand, and, on the other, to exile sons and younger brothers is called the
"Start of Chaos." To make agreements with foreign governments that
are not reliable is called "Transmitting Resentment."

If you possess a state and engage in these five practices, you will be
destroyed; . . . deserves . . . glorious.

論約

■　始於文而卒於武，天地之道也。四時有度，天地之李（理）也。日月星晨（辰）有數，天地之紀也。三時成功，一時刑殺，天地之道也。四時時而定，不爽不代（忒），常有法式，□□□，一立一廢，一生一殺，四時代正，冬（終）而復始。【人】事之理也，逆順是守。功洫（溢）於天，故有死刑。功不及天，退而无名。功合於天，名乃大成。人事之理也。順則生，理則成，逆則死，失□□名。怀（倍）天之道，國乃无主。无主之國，逆順相功（攻）。伐本隋（墮）功。亂生國亡。爲若得天，亡地更君。不循天常，不節民力，周遷而无功。養死伐生，命曰逆成。不有人僇（戮），必有天刑。逆節始生，慎毋【先】正，皮（彼）且自氏（抵），其刑。故執道者之觀於天下也，必審觀事之所始起，審其刑（形）名。刑（形）名已定，逆順有立（位），死生有分，存亡興壞有處。然后參之於天地之恒道，

94

8. ASSESSING ESSENTIALS [179]

To begin in patterning (*Wen*) and to end in martiality (*Wu*) is the Dao of Heaven and Earth.[180] That the four seasons have regularities is the principle of Heaven and Earth. That the sun, moon, stars, and constellations have number is the main thread of Heaven and Earth. That three seasons are for coming to completion and achievement and one season is for punishment and killing is the Dao of Heaven and Earth.[181] The four seasons are timely and fixed,[182] they do not fail and do not err.[183] They constantly have their laws and models . . . As one is being established, one is giving way; as one is being born, another is dying: the four seasons govern in turn, they end and begin again. The principles of [human] affairs consist solely of opposition and compliance. If their achievement overflows into Heaven, as a result there will be death and punishment.[184] If their achievement does not reach Heaven, they withdraw without a reputation. If their achievement harmonizes with Heaven, then their reputation is fully realized. These are the principles of human affairs.

If they are compliant, they live; if they are principled, they are brought to completion. If they are in opposition, they die; if they lose . . . reputation. When they oppose the Dao of Heaven, the state will then be without a ruler. In a state without a ruler, opposing and compliant groups will assault each other.

When the foundation of the state is attacked and its achievements are destroyed, chaos grows and the state is lost. If a state acts as though it has obtained Heaven, it loses Earth and changes its ruler. Not to follow the Heavenly Constants, not to economize the people's strength,[185] to revolve all around without success, to nourish the dying and to attack the living, this is termed the "Completion of Opposition." If there is not execution at the hands of humans for this type of behavior, inevitably there will be Punishment from Heaven.

When criminal conduct begins to grow, take care not to correct it [first], for it will, moreover, bring about[186] its own punishment.

For this reason, the way he who grasps the Dao observes the world is that he necessarily fully investigates and observes where affairs begin to arise, and fully investigates their forms and names. When forms and names have been fixed, opposition and compliance have their positions, the dying and the living have their distinctions, and survival and destruction, rise and decline have their places. When after that he compares them with the Constant Dao of Heaven and Earth, then he determines

95

乃定禍福死生存亡興壞之所在。是故萬舉不失理，論天下而无遺
筴。故能立天子，置三公，而天下化之，之胃（謂）有道。《論
約》

where misfortune and good fortune, death and life, survival and destruction, rise and decline, are located.

For this reason, in initiating a myriad affairs, he does not lose the principles, and he assesses the world without any miscalculations.

Therefore, to be able to establish the Son of Heaven, to appoint the Sangong,[187] and have the world obey them,[188] is called "Possessing the Dao."

名理

■　道者，神明之原也。神明者，處於度之內而見於度之外者也。處於度之【內】者，不言而信。見於度之外者，言而不可易也。處於度之內者，靜而不可移也。見於度之外者，動而〇不可化也。動而靜而不移，動而不化，故曰神。神明者，見知之稽也。有物始□，建於地而洫（溢）於天，莫見其刑（形），大盈冬（終）天地之間而莫知其名。莫能見知，故有逆成，物乃下生，故有逆刑。禍及其身。養其所以死，伐其所以生。伐其本而離其親。伐其與而□□□，後必亂而卒无名。如燔如卒（淬），事之反也。如繇（由）如驕（矯），生之反也。凡萬物群財（材），銚（佻）長非恒者，其死必應之。三者皆動於度之外而欲成功者也，功必不成，禍必反□□□。以剛爲柔者栝（活），以柔爲剛者伐。重柔者吉，重剛者威（滅）。若（諾）者，言之符也。已者，言之絕也。已若（諾）不信，則知（智）大惑矣。已若（諾）必信，則處於度之內也。天下有事，必審

98

Dao is the source of Spirituality and Brightness.[189] Spirituality and Brightness are what are placed inside measurement,[190] but are visible outside measurement. That they are placed [inside] is because they are trustworthy even though they do not speak. That they are visible outside measurement is because they cannot be changed even though they speak. That they are placed inside measurement is because they cannot be shifted even though they are quiescent. That they are visible outside measurement is because they cannot be transformed even though they move.

It moves and then is quiescent, yet does not shift[191]; it moves but does not transform: for that reason it is called "Spirituality."[192] Spirituality and Brightness are the epitome of perception and knowledge.

Something with substance[193] begins and [ends]; although it is established on Earth and overflows into Heaven, no one sees its form; although it grandly fills up every point between Heaven and Earth, no one knows its name. As no one is able to see or know it, therefore there is the Completion of Opposition[194]; then things are born below, and so there is Punishment of Opposition, and misfortune falls on his own person.[195]

When an individual nourishes the causes of his own death and attacks the causes of his own life; attacks his foundation and abandons his relatives; attacks those with whom he shares and . . . , later on chaos will be inevitable and he will perish in namelessness.

{First heated, then quenched, so are human affairs reversed; first submissive, then conceited, such is the reversal of life.[196] In general, those of the myriad phenomena that multiply their resources,[197] are haughty,[198] and deny the constant, will inevitably die in response to their behavior.}[199]

Although all these three types of individuals might[200] move outside measurement, yet they desire to accomplish their tasks. Their tasks will inevitably not be accomplished; rather, misfortune will inevitably [befall them in turn].

He who makes the hard into the soft will live[201]; he who makes the soft into hard will be attacked. He who values the soft is fortunate; he who values the hard will be obliterated. "Yes" is the tally[202] of speech; "no" is the end of speech. If "no" and "yes" are not reliable, then knowledge will be much deluded. If "yes" and "no" are inevitably reliable, then they are placed inside measurement.

When there is some affair in the world, you must fully investigate

其名。名□□循名廄（究）理之所之，是必爲福，非必爲衬（災）。是非有分，以法斷之。虛靜謹聽，以法爲符。審察名理名冬（終）始，是胃（謂）廄（究）理。唯公无私，見知不惑，乃知奮起。故執道者之觀於天下，□見正道循理，能與（舉）曲直，能與（舉）冬（終）始。故能循名廄（究）理。刑名出聲，聲實調合，禍衬（災）廢立，如景（影）之隋（隨）刑（形），如向（響）之隋（隨）聲，如衡之不臧（藏）重與輕。故唯執道者能虛靜公正，乃見□□，乃得名理之誠。亂積於內而稱失於外者伐。亡刑（形）成於內而舉失於外者戚（滅）。逆則上洫（溢）而不知止者亡。國舉襲虛，其事若不成，是胃（謂）得天；其事若果成，身必无名。重逆□□，守道是行，國危有央（殃）。兩逆相功（攻），交相爲央（殃），國皆危亡。《名理》《經法》凡五千

100

its name. Names . . . accord with names, and inquire where principles are applicable. When they are right, there will inevitably be good fortune; when they are wrong, there will inevitably be disaster. Right and wrong have their apportioned lots: decide them according to the law. Carefully listen in vacuity and quiescence, and take law as the tally. To fully investigate and examine the principles of names and the beginnings and ends of names,[203] this is called "Inquiring into Principles." If you are only public-spirited and without private bias, see and know and are not deluded, then your knowledge will rise up energetically.

The way, therefore, in which he who grasps the Dao observes the world . . . sees the correct Dao and accords with the principles, is able to enumerate the curved and the straight, and is able to enumerate the ends and beginnings. He is therefore able to accord with names and inquire into principles.

Forms and names derive from reputations.[204] When the reputation and the reality blend and harmonize,[205] misfortune and disaster[206] abandon their positions, like a shadow[207] following the form, like the echo following the sound, like the beam of a steelyard not concealing the light and the heavy weights.

Only he who grasps the Dao, therefore, is able to be vacuous and quiescent, public-spirited and correct; then he sees . . . , then he obtains the truth about the principles of names.

A state in which disorder piles up on the inside and its estimations fail on the outside will be attacked. One in which the appearance of destruction[208] is complete on the inside and its initiatives fail on the outside will be obliterated. When criminal behavior[209] overflows above[210] and the perpetrators do not know when to stop, the state will be destroyed. If a state initiates an invasion of an empty state,[211] even if the affair is not completed, this is called "Acquiring Heaven"; but even though the affair really is completed, the ruler personally will inevitably not have a name[212] from this adventure.

If you value opposition . . . and it is the Way of Defense that you practice, your state will be in danger and suffer calamity.

If two states in opposition to the Dao attack each other, they will create mutual calamity for each other, and both states will be in danger and be destroyed.

The Canon: Law. Five thousand graphs in total.

2.

THE CANON

(JING)

十大經

立命

■■昔者黄宗質始好信，作自爲象（像），方四面，傳一心。四達自中，前參後參，左參右參，踐立（位）履參，是以能爲天下宗。吾受命於天，定立（位）於地，成名於人。唯佘一人□乃肥（配）天，乃立王、三公，立國，置君、三卿。數日，曆（歷）月，計歲，以當日月之行。允地廣裕，吾類大明。吾畏天愛地親【民】，□无命，執虛信。吾畏天愛【地】親民，立有命，執虛信。吾愛民而民不亡，吾愛地而地不兄（曠）。吾受民□□□□□□□□死。吾位不□。吾句（苟）能親親而興賢，吾不遺亦至矣。《立【命】》

1. ESTABLISHING
[THE MANDATE] [213]

Of old, the Yellow Ancestral Model,[214] as part of his essential nature,[215] began by loving trustworthiness[216]; he made[217] himself[218] into an exemplary image and faced the four directions[219] to supplement[220] his single heart-mind. Reaching out from the center to all directions, he consulted[221] what was in front of him, he consulted what was behind him, he consulted what was to his left, he consulted what was to his right. He acted on his position and carried out his consultations,[222] and, for this reason, he was able to be the ancestral model for the world.

The Yellow Emperor stated,[223] "I received the mandate from Heaven, established my position on Earth and gained my reputation from Man.[224] Only I, the one man . . . then match Heaven, then establish kings and the *Sangong*, establish states and set up their lords and their three noble ministers.[225]

I number the days, reckon the months, and compute the years in order to match the movements of the sun and moon.[226]

[I] follow (?)[227] the breadth and abundance of Earth; I am classified with the great brightness of Heaven.[228] I am in awe of Heaven, love[229] Earth, and am intimate with [the people].[230] . . . those who lack the mandate by grasping emptiness and good faith.[231] I am in awe of Heaven, love [Earth], and love[232] the people. I establish those in possession of the mandate[233] by grasping emptiness and good faith.

I love the people and the people are not lost. I love Earth, and the Earth is not neglected. I love the people . . . die. My position is not . . . If I were able to treat my intimates intimately and promote the worthy, my success would be complete."

105

觀

【■黃帝】令力黑浸行伏匿，周留（流）四國，以觀无恒善之法，則力黑視（示）象（像），見黑則黑，見白則白。地□□□□□□□□□則亞（惡）。人則視（示）亮（鏡），人靜則靜，人作則作。力黑已布制建極，□□□□□曰：天地已成，而民生，逆順无紀，德瘧（虐）无刑，靜作无時，先後無○名。今吾欲得逆順之【紀】，□□□□□□□以爲天下正，靜作之時，因而勒之，爲之若何？黃帝曰：群群□□□□□□爲一囷，无晦无明，未有陰陽。陰陽未定，吾未有以名。今始判爲兩，分爲陰陽。離爲○四【時】，□□□□□□□□□□□因以爲常，其明以爲法而微道是行。行法循□□□牝牡，牝牡相求，會剛與柔。柔剛相成，牝牡若刑（形）。下會於地，上會於天。得天之微，時若□□□□□□□□□□寺（待）地氣之發也，乃夢（萌）者夢（萌）而茲（孳）者茲（孳），天因而成之。弗因則不成，【弗】養則不生。夫民之生也，規規生食與繼。不會不繼，无與守地；不

106

2. OBSERVATION

PART ONE

[The Yellow Emperor] ordered Li Hei[234] to go out secretly[235] under cover and travel[236] all around to all the states in order to observe those laws and rules that were not constantly excellent.[237] Li Hei instructed the phenomena[238]: when he was blackened, then they were black; when he was whitened, then they were white.

As for Earth . . . then they were ugly.

As for Man, he mirrored them[239]: when man was quiescent, he was quiescent; when man was active, he was active.

When Li Hei had announced the restrictions and established the limits, . . . [Li Hei] said,

"Heaven and Earth are completed and the people are born. Opposition and compliance lack rules; virtue and tyranny lack patterns,[240] quiescence and action have no proper seasons, front and rear have no name. Now I wish to obtain [the rules] for opposition and compliance, [the patterns for virtue and tyranny, and the seasons for quiescence and action] in order to make the world correct, and rely on the seasons of quiescence and action in order to control it. How should I proceed?"

The Yellow Emperor replied, "Crowding together . . . make a single granary,[241] without darkness, without light, Yin and Yang are not yet existent. As Yin and Yang are not yet fixed, I don't yet have any way to name the myriad phenomena. Now I will begin by distinguishing them into two and separate them to make Yin and Yang; I will divide them to make the four seasons . . . thereby act as its constants; when they are bright, they act as models, but it is the minute Dao that is to be carried out.[242] Carry out the models and follow. . . male and female; when male and female seek each other, hard will join with the soft. When soft and hard complete each other, male and female will then be formed.[243] Below, they meet with Earth; above, they meet with Heaven. When they obtain Heaven's minuteness, the seasons then . . . are waiting for the emission of the Earth's qi, then those that are to sprout will sprout, and those that are to breed will breed; Heaven relies on that fact to bring them to completion. If Heaven did not rely on it, then it would not bring them to completion. If it did [not] nourish them, they would not live. Now as for the life of the people, from the very first beginnings of life[244] they eat and reproduce. If they did not copulate and reproduce, they would not participate in preserving Earth. If they

107

食不人，无與守天。是□□贏陰布德，□□□□民功者，所以食之也。宿陽脩刑，童（重）陰○長夜氣閉地繩（孕）者，【所】以繼之也。不靡不黑，而正之以刑與德。春夏爲德，秋冬爲刑。先德後刑以養生。姓生已定，而適（敵）者生爭，不諶不定。凡諶之極，在刑與德。刑德皇皇，日月相望，以明其當，而盈□无匡。夫是故使民毋人埶，舉事毋陽察，力地毋陰敝。陰敝者土芒（荒），陽察者奪光，人埶者搣兵。是故爲人主者，時挃三樂，毋亂民功，毋逆天時。然則五穀溜孰（熟），民【乃】

did not eat and did not act as humans (?),[245] they would not share in preserving Heaven.[246]

[For] this reason . . . when Yin is full, to spread virtue *(de)* about . . . the people's efforts is the way to feed them. When Yang is at its peak, to overhaul the punishments *(xing)* and to value Yin in the long nights when qi hides the Earth's pregnancy is the [way] to reproduce them.[247]

When they are not scattered and not darkened,[248] correct them with punishments and virtue.[249] Spring and summer are the seasons of virtue; autumn and winter are the seasons of punishment.[250]

Place virtue first and punishment behind in order to nourish life.[251] When the livelihood of the surnames[252] has been determined and enemies start to fight, if one does not conquer them, you will not stabilize."

PART TWO

In general, the epitome of conquest lies in punishment
    and virtue.
Punishment and virtue are august indeed,
The sun and moon watch each other
In order to make clear their mutual complementarity
And fill . . . lack deficiency.

Now for this reason when making the people work, do not take Man as your standard;

When initiating affairs,
Do not be too exposed to Yang;
When engaging in labor in the earth,
Do not be too hidden by Yin.

The territory of the person who is too hidden by Yin will be desolated; from the person who is too exposed to Yang the light will be removed; he who takes Man as his standard will be struck by weapons.[253]

For this reason, he who is a ruler of men at the appropriate time regulates the work of each of the three seasons,[254] does not disorder the people's work, and does not oppose Heaven's seasons.[255] Under these conditions, the five types of grain ripen quickly, and the people [then]

蕃茲（滋）。君臣上下，交得其志。天因而成之。夫並時以養民功，先德後刑，順於天。其時贏而事絀，陰節復次，地尤復收。正名脩刑，執（蟄）虫不出，雪霜復清，孟穀乃蕭（肅），此衬（災）□生，如此者舉事將不成。其時絀而事贏，陽節復次，地尤不收。正名施（弛）刑，執（蟄）虫發聲，草苴復榮。已陽而有（又）陽，重時而无光，如此者舉事將不行。天道已既，地物乃備。散流相成，耵（聖）人之事。耵（聖）人不巧，時反是守。優未愛民，與天同道。耵（聖）人正以侍（待）天，靜以須人。不達天刑，不襦不傳。當天時，與之皆斷。當斷不斷，反受其亂。《觀》

multiply and proliferate. Ruler and subject, superior and inferior in their mutual relationships achieve their ambitions,[256] and Heaven, relying on that, brings them to completion.

Now you should encourage the people's efforts according to the proper season, place virtue first and punishment behind, and follow Heaven. Should the season be full, but affairs diminishing,[257] the Yin principle will return again, the qi of Earth will again withdraw. If, when correcting names, you overhaul punishments,[258] the hibernating insects will not appear, snow and frost will again be cold, and the sprouting grains will then shrivel up. These disasters . . . grow. Affairs initiated under these circumstances will not succeed.

Should the season be diminishing, but affairs full, the Yang principle will return again, and the qi of Earth will not withdraw. If, when correcting names, you lessen punishments, the hibernating insects will make noise, the withered foliage will again grow luxuriant: though it has already been the season of Yang, it will be Yang again and though the season repeats, there will be no light. Affairs initiated under these circumstances will not succeed.

When the Way of Heaven has been carried out, Earthly things will then be prepared. Scattered and flowing and completing each other are the affairs of the sage. The sage is not crafty: it is the alternation of the season that he preserves.[259] To love the people with excellent kindness is to have the same Dao as Heaven. The sage corrects in order to await Heaven; he is quiescent in order to wait for Man. He does not increase Heaven's punishment, he is not faithless, he is not untrustworthy.[260] He matches Heaven's seasons and decides everything with them. If he were not to decide what ought to be decided, he would in turn suffer disorder as the result.

五正

■　黃帝問閹冉曰：吾欲布施五正，焉止焉始？對曰：始在於身。中有正度，后及外人。外內交緩（接），乃正於事之所成。黃帝曰：吾既正既靜，吾國家愈（愈）不定，若何？對曰：后中實而外正，何【患】不定。左執規，右執柜（矩），何患天下？男女畢週，何患於國？五正既布，以司五明。左右執規，以寺（待）逆兵。黃帝曰：吾身未自知，若何？對曰：后身未自知，乃深伏於淵，以求內刑（型）。內刑（型）已得，后□自知屈后身。黃帝曰：吾欲屈吾身，屈吾身若何？對曰：道同者其事同，道異者其事異。今天下大爭，時至矣，后能慎勿爭乎？黃帝曰：勿爭若何？對曰：怒者血氣也，爭者外脂膚也。怒若不發浸廩是為癰疽。后能去四者，枯骨何能爭矣。黃帝於是辭其國大夫，上於博望之山，談臥三年以自求也。單（戰）才（哉）。閹冉乃上起黃帝曰：可矣，夫作爭者凶，

The Yellow Emperor asked Yan Ran, "I wish to publish and apply the Five Regulators; where do I stop and where do I begin?"

He replied, "Begin with yourself. If you possess correct measurement within yourself, you should, my lord, then extend it to others outside. If communication between the outside and the inside is established, then you will be correct in the accomplishment of your affairs."

The Yellow Emperor said, "I am both correct and quiescent, but my state still is not settled. What should be done?"

He replied, "If you, my lord, are true within yourself and are outwardly correct, what [troubles] will not be settled? If in your left hand you grasp the compass and in the right grasp the set-square, what will trouble the world? If the men and women are of entirely the same mind, what troubles will come to the state? When the Five Regulators have been published, use them to supervise the Five Brightnesses.[262] Grasp the compass and set-square in your left and right hand and with them await the opposing soldiers."[263]

The Yellow Emperor said, "I do not yet know myself; what should be done?"

He replied, "If you, my lord, do not know yourself, then hide yourself deep in a retreat in order to seek your inner form.[264] When your inner form has been achieved, you, my lord, . . . will know yourself completely."

The Yellow Emperor said, "I wish to know myself completely. What should I do to achieve that?"

He replied, "When the Dao of things is the same, their actions are the same. When the Dao of things is different, their actions are different. Now the world is fighting heavily, the time has come. Can you, my lord, be so cautious as not to fight?"

The Yellow Emperor said, "What should I do not to fight?"

He replied, "Anger is blood and qi. The outer fat of those who fight is greasy. If the anger does not issue forth, gradually[265] it will form ulcerations. If you, my lord, are able to purge yourself of these four,[266] how will your bare bones be able to fight?"

The Yellow Emperor thereupon yielded the throne to his nobles of the state, ascended Mount Bowang[267] and calmly[268] rested for three years to find himself. The battle was [intense]![269] Yan Ran then ascended and raised up the Yellow Emperor and said, "It is permissible to take action.

不爭【者】亦无成功。何不可矣？黃帝於是出其鏘鉞，奪其戎兵，身提鼓鞄（枹）以禺（遇）之（蚩）尤，因而禽（擒）之。帝箸之明（盟），明（盟）曰：反義逆時，其刑視之（蚩）尤。反義怀（倍）宗，其法死亡以窮。《五正》

Now to fight is inauspicious, but not to fight will also not complete the task of bringing good order to the world. Anything is permissible."

The Yellow Emperor thereupon brought out his square-holed ax and his great ax and seized his weapons. He personally held the drumstick to meet Chi You and thereby captured him. The Emperor composed a covenant for the occasion which stated:

Those who disobey righteousness and oppose the proper season, for their punishment look at Chi You! Those who disobey righteousness and rebel against the ruling house, the law is death and destruction forever!

果童

■　黃帝【問四】輔曰：唯余一人，兼有天下。今余欲畜而正之，均而平之，爲之若何？果童對曰：不險則不可平，不諶則不可正。觀天於上，視地於下，而稽之男女。夫天有榦，地有恒常。合□□常，是以有晦有明，有陰有陽。夫地有山有澤，有黑有白，有美有亞（惡）。地俗德以靜，而天正名以作。靜作相養，德瘧（虐）相成。兩若有名，相與則成。陰陽備，物化變乃生。有□□□重，任百則輕。人有其中，物又（有）其刑（形），因之若成。黃帝曰：夫民卬（仰）天而生，侍（待）地而食。以天爲父，以地爲母。今余欲畜而正之，均而平之，誰敵（適）緐（由）始？對曰：險若得平，諶□□□，【貴】賤必諶貧富又（有）等。前世法之，後世既員，緐（由）果童始。果童於是衣褐而穿，負幷（缾）而襲。營行氣（乞）食。周流四國，以視（示）貧賤之極。《果童》

116

4. GUO TONG [270]

The Yellow Emperor [asked his Four] [271] Assistants, saying, "It is only I, the one man, who possess the world. Now I wish to educate and correct it, to balance and pacify it: how should I proceed?"

Guo Tong replied, "If you are not thrifty, [272] you cannot pacify it; if you are not trustworthy, you cannot correct it. Regard Heaven above and look at Earth below, and investigate men and women. [273] Now Heaven possesses a [permanent] core, and Earth possesses a permanent constancy. Combine . . . constancy and for this reason there is darkness and light and there is Yin and Yang.

"Now Earth possesses mountains and possesses marshes; it has black and white; it has beauty and ugliness. Earth makes abundant [274] its potency [275] and thereby is quiescent, and Heaven corrects names and thereby is active. Quiescence and activity nourish each other; virtue and tyranny complete each other. If they both possess a name and share each other, then they are complete. When Yin and Yang are ready, things transform, change, and then are born.

"If there is . . . heavy, but when a hundred people assume responsibility for something, then it is light. [276] Men have their talents, [277] things have their forms. Rely on them and you can complete them."

The Yellow Emperor said, "Now the people are born facing Heaven, and wait for Earth to produce food before they eat. They consider Heaven to be their father and Earth their mother. [278] Now I wish to educate and correct them, to balance and pacify them; with whom should I start?"

He replied, "If you are thrifty, you will be able to pacify; if you are trustworthy . . . [279] [noble] and base must be examined [280]; rich and poor are to have their ranks. The older generation should be treated as a model; the younger generation should be cut off (?). [281] Begin with Guo Tong."

Guo Tong thereupon put on coarse clothing and bent over carrying a bottle on his back. [282] He arranged to travel [283] about begging, going through all the states in order to demonstrate extreme poverty and meanness.

正亂

■　力黑問□□□□□□□□□□□驕□陰謀，陰謀□□□□□
□□□□□高陽，□之若何？太山之稽曰：子勿患也。夫天行正
信，日月不處，啓然不台（怠），以臨天下。民生有極以欲涅
〈淫〉泏（溢），涅〈淫〉泏（溢）□失，豐而【爲】□，□而爲
既，予之爲害，致而爲費，緩而爲□。憂桐（恫）而窘（窘）之，
收而爲之咎。纍而高之，部（踣）而弗救也。將令之死而不得悔，
子勿患也。力黑曰：單（戰）數盈六十而高陽未夫，涅〈淫〉泏
（溢）蚤□□曰天佑，天佑而弗戒，天官地一也。爲之若何？
【太】山之稽曰：子勿言佑，交爲之備，【吾】將因其事，盈其
寺，軒其力，而投之代，子勿言也。上人正一，下人靜之，正以侍
（待）天，靜以須人。天地立名，□□自生，以隋（隨）天刑。天
刑不搴，逆順有類。勿驚□戒，其逆事乃始。吾將遂是其逆而僇
（戮）其身，更置六直而合以信。事成勿發，

118

5. CORRECTING
THE REBELLIOUS

Li Hei asked," . . . proud . . . made secret plans. In making secret plans . . .
Gao Yang,[284] what should be [done] about it?"

The Peak of Tai Shan[285] said, "Do not, sir, be troubled. Now Heaven's
path is correct and trustworthy; the sun and moon do not stop; clearly
they are not remiss in supervising the world. There is a limit to the
people's life: it is polluted by desires. When it is polluted . . . lost. En-
riching (life?) causes . . . causes it to end. Giving to it causes it harm;
extending it causes it destruction; delaying it causes it . . . ; worrying
about it puts it in difficulty; accepting it causes it disaster. Tie it up and
elevate it, kill it and do not save it.[286]

If you are going to let someone[287] die, you should not regret it. Do
not, sir, be troubled."

Li Hei said, "The number of battles that have been fought is a full
sixty, yet Gao Yang is still not yet adult.[288] Pollution that is . . . early is
called 'Heaven Helping.' That Heaven helps and is not afraid of him
(Chi You?), is because Heaven and Earth are one (?).[289] What should be
done about it?"

The Peak of [Tai] Shan replied, "Do not, sir, speak about helping.
Together we will make preparations against him (Chi You?). [I] will
rely on the situation to satisfy his ambitions[290] and push[291] his strength
to the limit and throw him to Dai.[292] You, sir, should not speak about it.

> The superior man corrects and unifies,[293]
> the inferior man keeps things quiescent.
> The one corrects in order to await Heaven;
> the other is quiescent in order to wait for Man.
> Heaven and Earth establish names,
> [Wise preparations] are produced by themselves
> in order to follow Heaven's Punishments.[294]
> When Heaven's Punishments are not in disarray,[295]
> opposition and obedience stay in their proper categories.
> Do not be alarmed, [do not] be afraid,
> though Chi You's opposition is now beginning.

"I will pursue and correct[296] his opposition and execute him. Further, I will appoint the Six Ministers (?)[297] and make them harmonious
by means of good faith. When the matter is over, do not initiate action,

119

胥備自生。我將觀其往事之卒而朵焉，寺（待）其來【事】之遂刑（形）而私〈和〉焉。壹朵壹禾（和），此天地之奇也。以其民作而自戲也，吾或（又）使之自靡也。單（戰）盈才（哉）。大（太）山之稽曰：可矣。於是出其鏘鉞，奮其戎兵。黃帝身禺（遇）之（蚩）尤，因而禽（擒）之。勑（剝）其□革以爲干侯，使人射之，多中者賞。翦（翦）其髮而建之天，名曰之（蚩）尤之旂（旌）。充其胃以爲鞠（鞠），使人執之，多中者賞。腐其骨肉，投之苦醢（醢），使天下囋（嚄）之。上帝以禁。帝曰：毋乏吾禁，毋留（流）吾醢（醢），毋亂吾民，毋絕吾道。止〈乏〉禁，留（流）醢（醢），亂民，絕道，反義逆時，非而行之，過極失當，擅制更爽，心欲是行，其上帝未先而擅興兵，視之（蚩）尤共工。屈其脊，使甘其箭。不死不生，憝（憝）爲地桯。帝曰：謹守吾正名，毋失吾恒刑，以視（示）後人。《正亂》

for wise preparations will be produced of themselves.[298] I will look over the conclusions of past matters and will move (?)[299] because of them; I will wait for the future to gain shape and harmonize with it, sometimes moving, at others harmonizing, for this is the secret[300] of Heaven and Earth. When he rises up with his people and personally fights,[301] I will also[302] make him defeat himself. The battle will be intense!"

The Peak of Tai Shan said, "Fine!"

Thereupon they took out their square-holed axes and their great axes and seized their weapons of war. The Yellow Emperor personally met Chi You and as a result captured him. He flayed his . . . hide and made it into a target and made men shoot at it: those who hit it many times were rewarded. He shaved off his hair and placed it in the heavens and called it Chi You's Banner.[303] He filled his belly and made it into a football, and made men kick (?)[304] it: those who hit it many times were rewarded.

He minced his bones and flesh and tossed them into a hash pickled with bitter herbs and made the world taste it. Shangdi used this to issue a prohibition. He declared:

"Do not violate my prohibitions! Do not stop the circulation of[305] my pickled hash! Do not disorder my people! Do not cut off my Dao! Those who violate the prohibitions, stop the pickled hash, disorder the people, cut off my Dao, counter righteousness and oppose the proper seasons, do what is wrong, exceed the limit and miss what is appropriate, take control without proper authority, change the straightforward and follow their heart's desires: they would not be putting Shangdi first, but rather raising armies without proper authority. They should look at Chi You and Gong Gong![306] I will bend their spines[307] and fetter their backs.[308] Neither dead nor living,[309] they will simply be pillars of the earth (?)."[310]

The Emperor[311] stated, "Take care to preserve the names that I have corrected; do not fail to carry out my constant punishments; use them to show later generations."

姓爭

■　高陽問力黑曰：天地【已】成，黔首乃生。莫循天德，謀相復（覆）頃（傾）。吾甚患之，爲之若何？力黑對曰：勿憂勿患，天制固然。天地已定，規（蚑）僥（蟯）畢掙（爭）。作爭者凶，不爭亦毋（無）以成功。順天者昌，逆天者亡。毋逆天道，則不失所守。天地已成，黔首乃生。胜（姓）生已定，敵者○生爭，不諶不定。凡諶之極，在刑與德。刑德皇皇，日月相望，以明其當。望失其當，環視其央（殃）。天德皇皇，非刑不行。繆（穆）繆（穆）天刑，非德必頃（傾）。刑德相養，逆順若成。

6 . THE FIGHTS
OF THE SURNAMES

Gao Yang[312] asked Li Hei, saying, "Heaven and Earth [have been] completed and the black-haired folk are now born,[313] but no one follows Heaven's potency, they rather plot to overthrow and overturn it. I am very troubled by this. What should I do about it?"

Li Hei replied, saying,

"Do not be worried, do not be troubled!
Heaven's rules are certain.
When Heaven and Earth were stabilized,
the wriggling insects ended by fighting each other.
Those that initiated the fighting were inauspicious,
but not to fight also meant that there was no way to survive.
Those that followed Heaven flourished,
whereas those that opposed Heaven perished.
If they did not oppose Heaven's Dao,
then they did not lose what they should have protected.
When Heaven and Earth were completed,
then the black-haired folk were born.
After the birth of the surnames was settled,
enemies started fights,
and they were neither trustworthy nor settled.

"In general, the acme of trustworthiness
lies in punishment and virtue.
Punishment and virtue are august, august,
and the sun and moon gaze at each other
in order to clarify where they match.
If their gaze failed to match,
they would in turn manifest disaster.[314]

"Heaven's virtue is august, august;
if it were not for punishment, it could not move.
Solemn, solemn are Heaven's punishments;
if it were not for virtue, they would be overturned.
When punishment and virtue nourish each other,
opposition and compliance are then completed.

123

刑晦而德明，刑陰而德陽，刑微而德章。其明者以爲法，而微道是行。明明至微，時反以爲幾（機）。天道環（還）於人，反爲之客。爭（靜）作得時，天地與之。爭不衰，時靜不靜，國家不定。可作不作，天稽環周，人反爲之【客】。靜作得時，天地與之。靜作失時，天地奪之。夫天地之道，寒涅（熱）燥濕，下能並立：剛柔陰陽，固不兩行。兩相養，時相成。居則有法，動作循名，其事若易成。若夫人事則无常。過極失當，變故易常。德則无有，昔（措）刑不當。

Punishment is dark and virtue bright;
punishment is Yin and virtue is Yang;
punishment is obscure and virtue conspicuous.
It is the bright that is to be taken as a model,
but it is the obscure Dao that is to be carried out.
The brightest clarity becomes obscure,
the seasons revolve and act as the key.[315]
Heaven's Way returns to man,
but he in turn acts as its guest.[316]
When quiescence and action are performed by someone in the
    proper season
Heaven and Earth will give to that person.
But if he fights with a state that is not declining
and, in the season of quiescence, he is not quiescent,
his state will not be stable.
Not to take action when action can be taken
and Heaven's plan revolves around,
man in turn acts as its [guest];
when {quiescence and action are performed by someone in the
    proper season,
Heaven and Earth will give to that person and}[317]
quiescence and action are not performed in the proper season,
Heaven and Earth will take away from that person.[318]
Now according to the Way of Heaven and Earth,
cold and heat, dryness and moisture
cannot stand together;
hardness and softness, Yin and Yang
assuredly cannot both move at the same time.
They both nourish each other,
and the seasons complete each other.
If at rest a person possesses laws,
and in movement and action he follows the correct names,
his affairs will then be easy to complete.
But if a person's affairs lack constancy;
he exceeds the limit and fails to correspond with what is
    appropriate;
he alters the old and changes the constant regulations,
and, as for virtue, he possesses it not;
in managing punishments, he does not match them with the
    crimes;

居則无法，動作爽名。是以僇受其刑。《姓爭》

at rest he lacks laws,
and in movement and rest, he is not in harmony with the
correct names.
For this reason, he will be executed,[319] receiving punishment
for his actions.

雌雄節

■　皇后屯曆（歷）吉凶之常，以辯（辨）雌雄之節，乃分禍福之鄉（向）。憲敖（傲）驕居（倨），是胃（謂）雄節；□□共（恭）驗（儉），是胃（謂）雌節。夫雄節者，涅之徒也。雌節者，兼之徒也。夫雄節以得，乃不爲福，雌節以亡，必得將有賞。夫雄節而數得，是胃（謂）積英（殃）。凶憂重至，幾於死亡。雌節而數亡，是胃（謂）積德。愼戒毋法，大祿將極。凡彼禍難也，先者恒凶，後者恒吉。先而不凶者，是恒備雌節存也。後【而不吉者，是】恒備雄節存也。先亦不凶，後亦不凶，是恒備雌節存也。先亦不吉，後亦不吉，是恒備雄節存也。凡人好用雄節，是胃（謂）方（妨）生。大人則毀，小人則亡。以守不寧，以作事【不成，以求不得，以戰不】克。厥身不壽，子孫不殖。是胃（謂）凶節，是胃（謂）散德。凡人好用【雌節】，是胃（謂）承祿。富者則昌，貧者則穀。以守則寧，以作事則成，以求

128

7. THE FEMALE
AND MALE TALLY

The Emperor[320] assiduously enumerated[321] the constant rules of auspiciousness and inauspiciousness in order to differentiate the female and male tallies,[322] and then he divided the directions of disaster and good fortune. Brazen[323] pride and haughty arrogance: this is what is meant by the "male tally." . . . and reverent moderation: this is what is meant by the "female tally."

Now the male tally is the companion of fullness[324]; the female tally is the companion of moderation.[325] Now if the male tally is used to gain one's ends, then you will not be fortunate; if the female tally is used to destroy, you will inevitably[326] be rewarded. Now repeatedly to gain your ends using the male tally, this is what is meant by piling up calamities: inauspicious troubles will come again and again so that you will be almost dead and destroyed. Repeatedly to destroy using the female tally, this is what is meant by piling up potency. If you take extreme care not to be wasted,[327] great wealth will come to you.

In general, as for such disasters and difficulties, being forward is always inauspicious, holding back is always auspicious. Those that are forward and do not suffer inauspicious fortune, do so because they always take precautions for the survival of the female tally. Those that hold back [and do not receive auspicious fortune, do so] because they always take precautions for the survival of the male tally. To be not inauspicious either when being forward or when holding back is so because one always takes precautions for the survival of the female tally. Not to be auspicious either when being forward or holding back is so because one always takes precautions for the survival of the male tally.

In general, when men love to use the male tally, this is what is meant by "obstructing life." If a great man uses it, he will be destroyed; if a small man uses it, he will be lost. Holding on to it, you will not be at peace; using it to initiate affairs, [you will not succeed; using it to seek, you will not gain; fighting with it, you will not] conquer. You yourself will not live long, and your children and grandchildren will not multiply. This is what is meant by the "Inauspicious Tally." This is what is meant by "Scattering Potency."

In general, when men love to use the [female tally], this is what is meant by "inheriting wealth." If a rich man uses it, he will flourish; if a poor man uses it, he will have enough to eat. Holding on to it, you will be at peace; using it to initiate affairs, you will succeed; using it to seek,

則得，以單（戰）則克。厥身【則壽，子孫則殖，是謂吉】節，是
胃（謂）絝德。故德積者昌，【殃】積者亡。觀其所積，乃知【禍
福】之鄉（向）。《雌雄節》

you will gain; fighting with it, you will conquer. You yourself will [live long and your children and grandchildren will multiply. This is what is meant by the auspicious] tally. This is what is meant by "Gathering in Potency."[328]

Therefore, he who piles up potency flourishes; he who accumulates [calamities] perishes. Examine how they are accumulated and then you will know the directions [of disaster and good fortune].

兵容

■　兵不刑天，兵不可動，不法地，兵不可昔（措）。刑法不人，兵不可成。參○□□□□□□□□□之，天地刑（形）之，耵（聖）人因而成之。耵（聖）人之功，時為之庸，因時秉□，是必有成功。耵（聖）人不達刑，不襦傳。因天時，與之皆斷。當斷不斷，反受其亂。天固有奪有予，有祥□□□□□弗受，反隋（隨）以央（殃）。三遂絕從，兵无成功。三遂絕從，兵有成【功】，□不鄉（饗）其功，環（還）受其央（殃）。國家有幸，當者受央（殃）。國家无幸，有延其命。莆莆陽陽，因民之力，逆天之極，有（又）重有功，其國家以危，社稷以匡，事无成功，慶且不鄉（饗）其功。此天之道也。《兵容》

132

8. THE FEATURES OF WARFARE

If warfare does not take its form from[329] Heaven, warfare cannot be initiated. If it does not take Earth as its model, warfare cannot be managed. If its form and model do not rely on Man,[330] warfare cannot be brought to a successful conclusion. If these . . . it, Heaven and Earth form[331] it, the sage relies on it and brings it to completion. Timeliness is what the sage uses in his tasks. He relies on the right moment and grasps the . . . , and for this reason he inevitably achieves success. The sage does not relax the punishments[332]; he does not use tallies and passports: he relies on Heaven's seasons and with their aid he decides all matters. If a matter should be decided, and he fails to decide it, he will in turn suffer disorder as a result.

Heaven assuredly takes away and gives, is auspicious and . . . , and does not receive it, but follows it in turn with calamity.[333] If the three are not followed,[334] warfare will not achieve success. If the three are not followed, yet warfare achieves [success], . . . , you will not enjoy[335] its success but will suffer calamity from it in recompense.[336] If a state is fortunate, those who face it will suffer calamity. If a state lacks good fortune, yet wishes to lengthen its life, and, rushing and gushing out,[337] it relies on the strength of the people, opposes the limit of Heaven, and furthermore values success, the state will be endangered from these actions: the altars of soil and grain will be devastated as a result, affairs will have no success, and, moreover, the rewards will not match[338] the task. This is the Dao of Heaven.

成法

■　黃帝問力黑，唯余一人兼有天下，滑（猾）民將生，年（佞）辯用知（智），不可法組。吾恐或用之以亂天下。請問天下有成法可以正民者？力黑曰：然。昔天地既成，正若有名，合若有刑（形），□以守一名。上拴之天，下施之四海。吾聞天下成法，故曰不多，一言而止。循名復一，民无亂紀。黃帝曰：請問天下猷（猶）有一虖（乎）？力黑曰：然。昔者皇天使馮（鳳）下道一言而止。五帝用之，以扒（扒）天地，【以】楑（揆）四海，以壞（懷）下民，以正一世之士。夫是故毚（讒）民皆退，賢人減（咸）起，五邪乃逃，年（佞）辯乃止。循名復一，民无亂紀。黃帝曰：一者一而已乎？其亦有長乎？力黑曰：一者道其本也。胡爲而无長？□□所失，莫能守一。一之解，察於天地。一之理，施於四海。何以知紃之至，遠近之稽？夫唯一不失，一以騮（趨）化，少以知多。夫達望四海，困極上下，四鄉（向）相枹（抱），各以其道。

134

9 . COMPLETE LAWS

The Yellow Emperor asked Li Hei, "It is only I, the One Man, who controls the world, but cunning people are beginning to grow in numbers, and crafty debaters are employing wisdom, and they cannot be blocked by the laws (?).[339] I am afraid that someone will use them to disorder the world. Please may I ask whether the world has complete laws that can be used to correct the people?"

Li Hei said, "Yes. In ancient times, when the Heaven and Earth were completed, then the names were correct, the forms were harmonized . . . was used to preserve the name of the One. Above, it was linked with (?)[340] Heaven; below, it was applied to all within the Four Seas. I have heard about the complete laws of the world. Therefore it is said, 'Speak not about the many but about the One and then stop. Follow names and go back to the One, and the people will not disorder[341] the rules.'"

The Yellow Emperor said, "Please may I ask, can the world still possess the One?"

Li Hei said, "In ancient times, august Heaven caused the phoenix-wind[342] to descend and say one word and then stop. The Five Emperors used it to split apart[343] Heaven and Earth; [used it] to administer all within the Four Seas; used it to cherish the people below; and used it to correct the officers of their generation.

"Now, for this reason, slanderers all withdrew and worthy men rose up all together, the Five Evils[344] then fled, and the cunning debaters then stopped. They followed the names and went back to the One and the people did not disorder the rules."[345]

The Yellow Emperor said, "Is the One just one and that's all, or does it also grow?"

Li Hei answered, "The One is the root of the Dao; how could it be that it would not grow? . . . what it lost (?), no one could preserve the One. For the explanation of the One, examine into Heaven and Earth; for the principle of the One, apply it to all within the Four Seas.[346]

"How can one know the beginning of an endless piece of string[347] and the end point between far and near? Now it is only the One that is used to hasten[348] transformation, and, by means of a few, is used to know the many.

"Now if you look thoroughly at the Four Seas to the farthest limit of Up and Down, and to the Four Directions that embrace each other,[349] you will see that each uses its own Dao.

夫百言本，千言有要，萬【言】有蔥（總）。萬物之多，皆閱一空。夫非正人也，孰能治此？罷（彼）必正人也，乃能操正以正奇，握一以知多，除民之所害，而寺（持）民之所宜。綷〈總〉凡守一，與天地同極，乃可以知天地之禍福。《成法》

"Now a hundred words have a basis, a thousand words have their essentials, and ten thousand [words] have their generalities.[350] The multitude of the myriad phenomena all pass through a single hole.[351]

"Now if he were not a Corrected Person, who could control them?[352] He must be a Corrected Person! For then he is able to grasp hold of correction to correct the incorrect, to lay hold of the One and use it to know the many; to expel what is harmful to the people and support what is appropriate for them. In the total collectivity,[353] he preserves the One and possesses the same ends as Heaven and Earth: then he can know the calamities and good fortune of Heaven and Earth."

三禁

■　行非恒者，天禁之。爽事，地禁之。失令者，君禁之。三者既脩，國家幾矣。地之禁，不【墮】高，不曾（增）下，毋服川，毋逆土毋逆土功，毋壅民明。進不氏，立不讓，俓（徑）遂凌節，是胃（謂）大凶。人道剛柔，剛不足以，柔不足寺（恃）。剛強而虎質者丘，康沈而流面（湎）者亡。憲古章物不實者死，專利及削浴（谷）以大居者虛。天道壽壽番（播）于下土，施于九州。是故王公慎令，民知所緐（由）。天有恒日，民自則之，爽則損命，環（還）自服之，天之道也。《三禁》

138

10. THE THREE PROHIBITIONS[354]

Heaven prohibits those who perform the inconstant; Earth prohibits those who fail in their duties[355]; the ruler prohibits those who disobey orders. When these three prohibitions are put into practice, the state is near to perfection.

According to the prohibitions of Earth, one is not [to take away] from the high, nor add to the low. Do not block up[356] the rivers; do not oppose agricultural tasks[357]; do not oppose the people's bright intelligence. To advance but not stop, to stand but not yield, to initiate action rashly[358] and exceed[359] the regulations: this is called Great Inauspiciousness.

The Way of Man is both hard and soft. If it is too hard, it is not sufficient to be used. If too soft, it is not sufficient to be relied on. Those who are hard and strong and have the dispositions of tigers will be emptied.[360] Those who are dissolute and sunk in debauchery and are addicted to wine are lost. Those who imitate[361] antiquity and display things that are not real will die.[362] Those who monopolize profit and remove desires[363] in order to gain a great position, are false.[364]

The Dao of Heaven is distant,[365] yet it spreads to the land below and is applied to the Nine Regions. For this reason, the true king or lord is careful about orders and the people know what to follow. Heaven has the sun which is constant, and the people naturally model themselves on it. If they failed to model themselves on it, they would destroy their lives and instead would naturally suffer Heaven's Punishment. That is the Dao of Heaven.

本伐

■ 諸（儲）庫臧（藏）兵之國，皆有兵道。世兵道三，有爲利者，有爲義者，有行忿者。所胃（謂）爲利者，見□□□飢，國家不叚（暇），上下不當，舉兵而栽（誅）之，唯（雖）无大利，亦无大害焉。所胃（謂）爲爲義者，伐亂禁暴，起賢廢不宵（肖），所胃（謂）義也。【義】者，众之所死也。是故以國戉（攻）天下，萬乘【之】主□□希不自此始，鮮能多（終）之，非心之恒也，窮而反（返）矣。所胃（謂）行忿者，心唯（雖）忿，能徒怒，怒必有爲也。成功而无以求也，即兼始逆矣。非道也。道之行也，繇（由）不得已。繇（由）不得已，則无窮。故□者，赼者【也】；禁者，使者也。是以方行不留。《本伐》

11. THE FUNDAMENTAL
TYPES OF ATTACK

All[366] states that have armories and store weapons[367] in every case possess a Dao of warfare. The Dao of warfare of the present generation are three: there are those who act for profit; those who act out of righteousness; and those who act out of anger.

What is meant by acting for profit is: the ruler sees . . . famine, the state is not at leisure, superiors and inferiors do not match each other,[368] yet the ruler raises soldiers and causes them misery. Although there is no great profit, yet there is also no great harm from it.

What is meant by acting for righteousness is: the ruler attacks the disorderly and prohibits the rebellious, raises the wise, and gets rid of the worthless: that is what is meant by righteousness. [Righteousness] is what the masses die for. For that reason, when using a single state to attack the world, that the lord [of] ten thousand chariot state . . . ,[369] hoping not to start from this righteousness, rarely is able to end it[370] is not because he lacks constancy of heart, but because when things reach the limit, they return.

What is meant by acting out of anger is: although the ruler's heart is angry, it is not only that he is able to be angry, but his anger must have something to act on.[371] When he sets out to accomplish his ends, he lacks the means to achieve them, and also he begins to be in opposition to the Dao. That is not Dao.

The success of action in accordance with the Dao derives from its inevitability.[372] If it derives from inevitability, then it is limitless. Therefore to . . . is to expand (?)[373]; to prohibit is to force. For this reason one may carry out the Dao everywhere without cease.[374]

前道

■ 耺（聖）【人】舉事也，闔（合）於天地，順於民，羊（祥）於鬼神，使民同利，萬夫賴之，所胃（謂）義也。身載於前，主上用之，長利國家社稷，世利萬夫百生（姓）。天下名軒執□士於是虛。壹言而利之者，士也。壹言而利國者，國士也。是故君子卑身以從道，知（智）以辯之，強以行之，責道以並世，柔身以寺（待）之時。王公若知之，國家之幸也。國大人眾，強國也。□身載於後，□□□□□□□□□□□□□□□□□□□□□而不□□□□□□□幸也。故王者不以幸治國，治國固有前道，上知天時，下知地利，中知人事。善陰陽□□□□□□□□□□□□□□□□□□□□□□□□□□□【名】正者治，名奇者亂。正名不奇，奇名不立。正道不台（殆），可後可始。乃可小夫，乃可國家。小夫得之以成，國家得之以寧。小國得之以守其野，大國【得之以】并兼天下。道有原而无端，用者實，

12. [PUTTING THE DAO FIRST] [375]

When sages initiate an affair, they harmonize with Heaven and Earth, conform to the people, [376] and are favorable to the ghosts and spirits; they cause the people to share benefits with them and the myriad masses to depend on them: this is what is called righteousness. They place themselves at the forefront and the ruler above uses them, thus they always benefit the altars of the grain and soil of the state, and from generation to generation [377] benefit the masses and the hundred surnames.

Officers with high reputations in the world who hold . . . are thereupon empty (?). [378] One who benefits it [379] by a single word is an officer; one who benefits the state by a single word is an officer of the state. For this reason, the gentleman humbles himself in order to follow the Dao, is wise in order to defend it in argument, is strong in order to carry it out, applies the Dao strictly (?) in order to control the age, softens himself in order to wait for the proper season. If the king or a duke knows him, it is very fortunate for the state.

When *guo daren* (great men in the state?) are numerous, the state is strong . . . he holds himself back [380] . . . and not . . . fortunate.

Therefore one who is a true king does not govern the state by means of luck, he governs the state by steadfastly putting the Dao first. [381]

> Above, he knows Heaven's seasons;
> Below, he knows the benefits of Earth;
> In the middle, he knows human affairs. [382]
> He is good at Yin and Yang . . .
>
> . . .
>
> One whose [names] are correct is well-ordered;
> One whose names are biased is disordered;
> Correct names are not biased;
> Biased names do not survive.

The correct Dao is not endangered.

It can be at the rear; it can be at the front; it can be both used by the small man and it can be used by the state. If a small man acquires it, he is successful; if a state acquires it, it is at peace. If a small state acquires it, it preserves its outlying countryside; if a large state [acquires it, it] takes control of the world.

The Dao has an origin, but is endless. [383] He who uses it is the fruit;

弗用者蘿合之而涅於美，循之而有常。古之堅者，道是之行。知此道，地且天，鬼且人。以居軍□，以居國其國昌。古之賢者，道是之行。《【前道】》

he who uses it not is the flower.[384] He harmonizes with it and is transformed[385] into beauty; he follows it and possesses constancy.

Those of the ancients who were firm, it was Dao that they carried out.

Know this Dao, Earth and Heaven, ghosts and Man!

He who dwells with it in the army, is . . . He who dwells with it in the state, his state is prosperous.

Those of the ancients who were wise, it was Dao that they carried out.

行守

■　天有恒榦，地有恒常。與民共事，與神同□。驕泆（溢）好爭。陰謀不羊（祥），刑於雄節，危於死亡。奪之而无予，其國乃不遂亡。近則將之，遠則行之。逆節夢（萌）生，其誰骨當之。天亞（惡）高，地亞（惡）廣，人亞（惡）荷（苛）。高而不已，天闕土〈之〉。廣而不已，地將絕之。苛而不已，人將殺之。有人將來，唯目之瞻。言之壹，行之壹，得而勿失。【言】之采，行之阺（熙），得而勿以。是故言者心之符【也】，色者心之華也，氣者心之浮也。有一言，無一行，胃（謂）之誣。故言寺首，行志（識）卒。直木伐，直人殺。无刑（形）无名，先天地生，至今未成。《行守》

146

Heaven possesses a permanent core;
Earth possesses a permanent constancy;
Work together with the people;
Share . . . with the spirits.
The arrogant and excessive love to fight
And secretly plan inauspicious activity:
They will be punished with the male tally[386]
And be endangered to the point of death and destruction.
Take away from them and do not give to them:
Their state will then perish as a consequence.[387]
Those nearby will harm[388] them,
Those far away will leave them.
When the sprouts of the tally of opposition grow,[389]
Who can[390] match them?[391]

Heaven hates height; Earth hates breadth; Man hates harshness. He who grows high without stopping, Heaven [will] consider [him] defective. One who broadens his lands without cease, Earth will cut him off. One who is harsh without end, Men will kill him.

When a man comes,[392] just look at him with your eyes. If his speech is one and his actions are one,[393] get him and do not lose him. If his [speech] is flowery and his actions are playful,[394] get him, but do not use him. For this reason, words are the tally of the heart[395]; coloring is the embellishment[396] of the heart; qi is the outward manifestation of the heart.

To have a word but lack a corresponding action is called "self-promotion."[397] Therefore words support[398] the beginning and actions distinguish the end.

A straight tree is cut down;
A straight man is killed.[399]

Up to the present, no one has been successful who lacked forms and lacked names and lived without[400] Heaven and Earth.

順道

■　黃帝問力黑曰：大茞（庭）氏之有天下也，不辨陰陽，不數日月，不志（識）四時，而天開以時，地成以財。其爲之若何？力黑曰：大茞（庭）之有天下也，安徐正靜，柔節先定。兒濕共（恭）僉（儉），卑約生柔。常後而不失膲（體），正信以仁，茲（慈）惠以愛人，端正勇，弗敢以先人。中請（情）不刾執一毋求。刑於女節，所生乃柔。□□□正德，好德不爭。立於不敢，行於不能。單（戰）視（示）不敢，明執不能。守弱節而堅之，胥雄節之窮而因之。

14. COMPLIANCE
WITH THE DAO

The Yellow Emperor asked Li Hei, saying, "When Da Ting[401] possessed the world, he did not differentiate Yin and Yang, he did not count the days and months, he did not recognize[402] the four seasons, and yet Heaven began matters at the proper season, and Earth completed them according to its resources. How did it happen like that?"

Li Hei replied,

"When Da Ting possessed the world
He was calm, gentle, correct, and quiescent;
He determined that the tally of softness should be first.[403]
He was tactful[404] and modest,[405] reverent and frugal;
Humble and restrained, he advocated[406] the soft;
Always putting himself behind and not in front.[407]
He was correct and trustworthy and thereby benevolent;
Kind and generous and thereby loved others.
He was upright, correct, and brave[408]
And did not dare to put himself before others.[409]
He was equable, quiescent,[410] and not rash,[411]
He grasped hold of the One and sought nothing;
He modeled himself on the female tally,
And what he produced was therefore soft.

. . . correct potency,
He loved potency and was not contentious.
He took his stand on not being daring,
And practiced not being capable.[412]
In battle, he showed he was not daring;
In understanding, he held on to[413] incapability.
He preserved the soft tally and confirmed it[414];
He waited for the extremity of the male tally and relied on it
  before he proceeded.[415]

"Under such circumstances, though his people worked, they were not . . . though they were hungry, they were not indolent; when they died, they were not resentful.

若此者其民勞不□，几（飢）不飴（怠），死不宛（怨）。不廣（曠）其眾，不以兵邾，不爲亂首，不爲宛（怨）謀（媒），不陰謀，不擅斷疑，不謀削人之野，不謀劫人之宇。慎案其眾，以隋（隨）天地之從（蹤）。不擅作事，以寺（待）逆節所窮。見地奪力，天逆其時，因而飾（飭）之，事環（還）克之。若此者，單（戰）朕（勝）不報，取地不反。單（戰）朕（勝）於外，福生於內。用力甚少，名殷（聲）章明。順之至也。《順道》

"He did not waste his masses[416];
He did not consider warfare crucial;
And did not create the beginning of disorder.[417]
He did not act as a transmitter of resentment;
He did not make secret plans;
He did not arbitrarily decide doubtful matters;
He did not plot to whittle away other people's lands;
He did not plot to seize other people's houses.
He was careful to secure his masses
In order to follow the footsteps of Heaven and Earth.
He did not arbitrarily initiate action,
but waited for the furthest point of his enemy's tally of
    opposition.
When he saw that Earth was taking away his enemy's strength,
And Heaven was opposing his seasons,[418]
He relied on that to correct the enemy,
And in the course of events he subdued him.

"Under these circumstances, when he was victorious in battle, he did not receive retribution; when he took away his land, it was not taken back.[419] In battles, he was victorious outside his state, and inside it good fortune grew. He used very little might, but his reputation was brilliantly bright.[420] It was the supreme example of being in compliance with the Dao."

■　欲知得失請（情），必審名察刑（形）。刑（形）恒自定，是我俞（愈）靜。○事恒自㐌（施），是我无爲。靜翳不動，來自至，去自往。能一乎？能止乎？能毋有己，能自擇而尊理乎？紓也，毛也，其如莫存。萬物群至，我无不能應。我不臧（藏）故，不挾陳。鄉（向）者已去，至者乃新。新故不翏，我有所周。《十大經》凡四千六□□六

15. THE TEN
GREAT PROPOSITIONS[421]

If you desire to know the true facts[422] about gain and loss,
   it is essential to investigate names fully and to examine
   into forms.

Forms constantly determine themselves
   and for this reason I am more at rest.

Affairs constantly manage themselves:
   for this reason I do not act.

Be at rest, hidden, and do not move:
   what comes, arrives by itself; what goes, departs by
   itself.[423]

Can you be one? Can you stop?

Can you be without a self? Can you choose yourself and yet
   honor the principles?[424]

Swaddled like a baby, hoarding your energy,[425] be as
   though not existent.

When the myriad phenomena come flocking together, I
   cannot but respond.

I do not store the old; I do not clasp the stale.
   The past is already gone; what comes is new.

The new and the old are not to be intermingled[426]:
   I encompass every thing every where.[427]

The Canon.[428]   In all four thousand . . . and six (graphs).

3.

DESIGNATIONS
(CHENG)

稱

■■道无始而有應。其未來也，无之；其已來，如之。有物將來，其刑（形）先之。建以其刑（形），名以其名。其言胃（謂）何？・環□傷威。㣇（弛）欲傷法。无隋傷道。數舉參（三）者，有身弗能葆（保），何國能守？【・】奇從奇，正從正，奇與正，恒不不同廷。・凡變之道，非益而損，非進而退。首變者凶。・有義（儀）而義（儀）則不過，侍（恃）表而望則不惑，案法而治則不亂。・耴（聖）人不爲始，不剸（專）己，不豫謀，不爲得，不辭福，因天之則。・失其天者死，欺其主者死。翟其上者危。・心之所欲則志歸之，志之志之所欲則力歸之。故巢居者察風，穴處者知雨，憂存故也。

1. Dao has no beginning, yet has a response. When it has not yet come, consider it nonexistent; when it has come, be similar to it. When an object is about to come, its form precedes it. Establish it by means of its form; name it by means of its name.[429] When speaking about it, how do we refer to it?[430]

2. Promoting . . .[431] harms authority. Desire for leniency harms the law. Not following[432] harms the Dao. Doing these three repeatedly, a person would not be able to protect his body, and what state could he guard?

3. The irregular follows the irregular; the regular follows the regular. The irregular and the regular never share the same court.[433]

4. In general, the way of change is that when it is not increasing, then it is falling short; when it is not advancing, then it is retreating.[434] To change the beginning is inauspicious.

5. If you measure with a measuring device, you will not go too far; if you watch relying on a gnomon, you will not be deluded.[435] If you rule judging on the basis of the law, there will not be chaos.

6. The sage does not create the beginning and does not monopolize himself[436]; he does not make plans beforehand, nor act for gain, nor reject good fortune, but relies on the laws of Heaven.

7. He who loses Heaven dies; he who cheats his ruler dies; he who surpasses (?)[437] his superior is in danger.

8. What the heart desires, the will concentrates on; what the will desires, the strength concentrates on. Therefore, the reason why inhabitants of nests examine the wind and cave-dwellers know about rain is

157

憂之則□，安之則久。弗能令者弗得有。•帝者臣，名臣，其實師也。王者臣，名臣，其實友也。朝（霸）者臣，名臣也，其實【賓也。危者】臣，名臣也，其實庸也。亡者臣，名臣也，其實虜也。•自光（廣）者人絕之：□□人者其生危，其死辱翳（也）。居不犯凶，困不擇時。•不受祿者，天子弗臣也。祿泊（薄）者，弗與犯難。故以人之自爲，□□□□□□□□。【•】不士（仕）於盛盈之國，不嫁子於盛盈之家，不友□□□易之【人】。【•】□□不執偃兵，不執用兵。兵者不得已而行。•知天之所始，察地之理，耵（聖）人麋論天地之紀，廣乎蜀（獨）見，□□蜀（獨）□□□□□□蜀（獨）在。•天子之地方千里，諸侯百里，所以胅合之也。故立天子【者，不】使諸侯疑焉。立正敵（嫡）者，〇不使庶孽疑焉。立正妻者，不使婢（嬖）妾疑焉。疑則相傷，雜則相方。•時若可行，亟應勿言。【時】若未可，塗其門，毋見其端。•天制寒暑，地制高下，人制取予。取予當，立爲□王。取

because their distress or survival depends on these elements.[438] If they are distressed by them, then . . . If they are easy about them, they remain there for a long time. One who is unable to issue orders to something cannot possess it.

9. The famous subjects of an emperor are in fact his teachers; the famous subjects of a true king are in fact his friends; the famous subjects of a hegemon are in fact [his guests. The subjects of a ruler in danger] are in fact his hired laborers. The famous subjects of a lost ruler are in fact his slaves.[439]

10. Others will destroy the man who illuminates[440] himself, . . . others, his life will be in danger and his death shameful. If you live without transgressing the inauspicious, difficulties will not choose a time to afflict you.

11. He who does not receive a salary, the son of Heaven will not appoint as a minister. He whose salary is meager will not join others in committing transgressions and making difficulties for the ruler. Therefore to use others who act for themselves . . .[441]

12. . . . do not serve in a flourishing state, do not marry their children into a flourishing family, do not befriend . . . a changeable [person].[442]

13. . . . [The sage or true king] is not scornful of[443] ending a war,[444] nor does he disparage using war. War is waged whenever it cannot be helped.[445]

14. Knowing where Heaven begins, examining the principles of Heaven, the sage extensively[446] controls the main thread of Heaven and Earth. Broad is his solitary vision! . . . solitary . . . solitary existence!

15. The territory of the Son of Heaven is one thousand square *li*; that of the feudal lords is one hundred square *li*; that is the means whereby they are able to join and unify them.[447] Therefore, [he who] establishes the Son of Heaven [does not] let the feudal lords encroach[448] on him. He who establishes the legal [heir] does not let the concubine's son encroach on him. He who establishes the legal wife does not let the slave or concubine[449] encroach on her. If they encroach, they will injure each other; if they are confused,[450] then they will interfere with each other.

16. If the time is right for something to be done, immediately respond without saying a word. If [the time] is not yet right, block the gate and do not see its beginnings.

17. Heaven controls cold and hot; Earth controls high and low; Man controls taking away and giving. When taking away and giving match what is appropriate, he is established as a . . .[451] When taking

予不當，流之死亡。天有環（還）刑，反受其央（殃）。・世恒不可，擇（釋）法而用我。用我不可，是以生禍。・有國存，天下弗能亡也。有國將亡，天下弗能存也。・時極未至，而隱於德。既德其極，遠其德。○淺□以力，既成其功，環（還）復其從，人莫能代。・諸侯不報仇，不脩侀（恥），唯□所在。・隱忌妒妹賊妾如此者，下其等而遠其身。不下其德等，不遠其身，禍乃將起。內事不和，不得言外。細事不察，不得言【大】。・利不兼，賞不倍。戴角者无上齒。提正名以伐，得所欲而止。・實穀不華，至言不飾，至樂不笑。華之屬，必有覈（核），覈（核）中必有意。・天地之道，有左有右，有牝有牡。誥誥作事，毋從我冬（終）始。雷□爲車隆隆以爲馬。行而行，處而處。因地以爲齎（資），因民以爲師。弗因无犙也。・宮室過度，上帝所亞（惡），爲者弗居，唯（雖）居必路。・減衣衾，泊（薄）

away and giving do not match,[452] they banish him and he dies and is lost. Heaven inflicts punishment in retribution,[453] and he will in turn suffer disaster from it.[454]

18. If the constant way of the world is not possible, relax the laws and use yourself. If it is not possible to use yourself, from this disaster is born.[455]

19. The world cannot destroy a state that is to be preserved. The world cannot preserve a state that is to be destroyed.

20. When the crucial moment has not yet arrived, conceal your potency. When you reach the crucial moment, put your potency far away and lightly... use your strength. When you have accomplished the task, once again resume the track[456] and no other man will be able to replace you.[457]

21. A feudal lord does not avenge enmity and does not redress a humiliation he has suffered. It is only... where that exists (?).[458]

22. Those who harbor hatred, the jealous and the blind,[459] who abuse female slaves and other people such as these, reduce their ranks and keep them at a distance. If you do not lower their ranks, and do not keep them at a distance, disorder will then arise.

23. If you do not harmonize internal affairs, you should not speak about external matters.[460] If you have not examined the details, you should not speak about [generalities].

24. If the profit is not double, the reward is not twofold.[461] Beasts that bear horns lack upper teeth.[462]

25. Refer to the correct names in order to present rewards. When you gain what you desire, stop.

26. True grains do not bear flowers; the best words are not ornamented; the best music is not ridiculous.[463] Things that flower must have a pit; in the pit, there must be a bitter kernel.[464]

27. The Dao of Heaven and Earth has left and right, has female and male.[465] Purely and brightly[466] perform your tasks: do not follow my ends and beginnings. Thunderous [are] the chariot wheels; grand are the horses![467] Go, when you are going; stay still when you are staying still. Rely on the Earth for your matériel[468]; rely on the people to be your forces. If you do not rely on them, you will not achieve successful results (?).[469]

28. Palaces and buildings that exceed the rules are what Shangdi hates. He who creates them will not dwell in them. Though he may dwell in them, inevitably he will be exposed.[470]

29. To reduce the amount of clothing and coverlets, and diminish

棺椁，禁也。疾役可發澤，禁也。草莜可淺林，禁也。聚□□隋（墮）高增下，禁也，大水至而可也。‧毋先天成，毋非時而榮。先天成則毀，非時而榮則不果。‧日爲明，月爲晦。昏而休，明而起。毋失天極，廐（究）數而止。‧強則令，弱則聽，敵則循繩而爭。‧行曾（憎）而索愛，父弗得子。行母（侮）而索敬，君弗得臣。‧有宗將興，如伐於□。有宗將壞，如伐於山。貞良而亡，先人餘央（殃）。商（獝）闕（獗）而栝（活），先人之連（烈）。‧埤（卑）而正者增，高而倚者傰（崩）。‧山有木，其實屯屯。虎狼爲孟（猛）可揗，昆弟相居，不能相順。同則不肯，離則不能，傷國之神。□□□來，胡不來相教順弟兄茲，昆弟之親尙可易戈（哉）。‧‧天下有參（三）死：忿不量力死，

the widths of the outer and inner coffins is prohibited. To have rapid or harsh corvée labor projects that could destroy marshland[471] is prohibited. To pick foliage and pile up wood for coffins[472] that could inflict damage on forests is prohibited. To gather . . . to diminish heights and increase low ground is prohibited. When great floods occur, then these actions are permitted.

30. Do not precede Heaven's accomplishments[473]; do not flourish when it is not the right season. If you precede Heaven's accomplishments, you will be destroyed. If you flourish when it is not the right season, you will not obtain results.

31. The sun creates the light; the moon creates the dark. Rest when it is dark; arise when it is light. Do not miss Heaven's limits[474]: scrutinize the numbers and then stop.

32. If strong, issue orders; if weak, obey. If equally matched, follow the rules and then fight.

33. If they behaved hatefully but demanded love, fathers would not acquire sons. If they behaved insultingly but demanded reverence, rulers would not acquire subjects.[475]

34. When a lineage is going to flourish, it is like cutting (?)[476] in a . . . ; when a lineage is going to collapse, it is like cutting (?) on a mountain. When a true and good man perishes, it is more calamitous than when another ordinary man dies. When a savage and wild man lives, he is more fierce[477] than other men.[478]

35. What is low yet straight increases; what is high yet leaning to one side collapses.[479]

36.
Mountains have trees and their fruits are very abundant.
Tigers and wolves are fierce but they can be tamed.
As for elder and younger brothers who live together
And are unable to be obedient to each other:
When they are together, they are unwilling,
When separated, they are incapable.
This harms the spirits of the cemeteries.[480]
. . . come,
Why not come and instruct about love between elder and
   younger brothers?
The relations between elder and younger brothers can yet be
   changed!

37. In the world of men, there are three types of deaths which are not fated: death from being angry and not measuring the strength of

耆（嗜）欲无窮死，寡不辟（避）眾死。・毋籍（藉）賊兵，毋□盜量（糧）。籍（藉）賊兵，□盜量（糧），短者長，弱者強，羸絀變化，後將反苞（施）。・弗同而同，舉而爲同。弗異而異，舉而爲異。弗爲而自成，因而建事。・陽親而陰亞（惡），胃（謂）外其膚而內其勮。不有內亂，必有外客。膚既爲膚，勮既爲勮。內亂不至，外客乃却。・得焉者不受其賜。亡者不怨大□。【・】天有明而不憂民之晦也。【百】姓辟（闢）其戶牖而各取昭焉。天无事焉。地有【財】而不憂民之貧也。百姓斬木刑（刈）新（薪）而各取富焉。地亦无事焉。・諸侯有亂，正亂者失其理，亂國反行焉。其時未能也，至其子孫必行焉。故曰：制人而失其理，反制焉。・生人有居，【死】人有墓。令不得與死者從事。・惑而極（亟）反（返），□道不遠。・臣有兩位者，其國必危。國若不危，君與存也，失君必危。失君不危者，臣故駐（差）也。

one's opponent[481]; death from limitless indulgence in one's desires; death from being solitary and not avoiding the crowd.[482]

38. Do not loan murderers weapons; do not give (?)[483] robbers food. If you loan murderers weapons and give (?) robbers food, the short will become long and the weak strong; your own surplus and the enemy's shortage will change places and later on rebellion will occur.[484]

39. If things are not the same and yet you want them to be the same, initiate action and make them so. If things are not different and yet you want them to be different, initiate action and make them so. If things do not act yet work out by themselves, let them finish the matter.

40. To be close to Yang and hate Yin is called "putting the skin on the outside and the palate on the inside."[485] If you do not have internal disorders, inevitably there will be foreign aggression against your state. If you treat those close to you as close and those distant from you as distant, then internal disorders will not arise and foreign aggressors will withdraw.

41. Those who have attained it do not accept a reward for doing so; those who have lost it do not resent the great . . .[486]

42. Heaven possesses brightness and does not grieve that the people are in darkness. The [hundred] surnames open their doors and windows and each one takes light from it, yet Heaven has nothing to do with it. Earth has its [resources] and does not grieve that the people are poor. The hundred surnames cut down the trees and chop up[487] firewood and take their wealth from it, yet Earth also has nothing to do with it.[488]

43. When there is disorder among the feudal lords, if the one who corrects the disorder loses his principles, the disorderly state will take revenge on him in turn. If it is unable to take revenge on him at that time, when the sons or grandsons rule that state, it will inevitably take revenge on him. Therefore it is said, "If you lose your principles when controlling others, you will in turn be controlled by them."

44. The living have dwelling places; the [dead] have tombs. Do not let the living carry on business with the dead.

45. If you quickly return to your senses after you have been deluded, . . . the Dao is not far off.

46. If ministers have equal[489] positions, the state will inevitably be in danger. If the state is not in danger because the ruler still[490] survives, when it loses the ruler, it will inevitably be in danger. If it loses the ruler and is not in danger, it is because the ministers keep their former differences of rank.

子有兩位者，家必亂。家若不亂，親與存也，【失親必】危。失親不亂，子故毵（差）也。‧不用輔佐之助，不聽耴（聖）慧之慮，而侍（恃）其城郭之固，古（怙）其勇力之御。是胃（謂）身薄。身薄則貧（殆）。以守不固，以單（戰）不克。‧兩虎相爭，奴（駑）犬制其余。‧善爲國者，大（太）上无刑，其【次】□□【其】下鬭 果訟果，大（太）下不鬭 不訟有（又）不果。□大（太）上爭於□，其次爭於明，其下救（救）患禍。‧寒時而獨暑，暑時而獨寒，其生危，以其逆也。‧敬朕（勝）怠，敢朕（勝）疑。亡國之禍□□□不信其□而不信其可也，不可矣，而不信其□□□賈（觀）前□以知反，故□□賈（觀）今之曲直，審其名以稱斷之。積者積而居，胥時而用賈（觀），主樹以知與治合積化以知時，□□□正貴□存亡。‧凡論必以陰陽□大義。天陽地陰。春陽秋陰。夏陽冬陰。晝陽夜陰。大國陽，小國陰。重國陽，輕國陰。有事陽而无事陰。

If sons have equal positions, the family will inevitably be in disorder. If the family is not in disorder, it is because the relatives still survive to keep order. [If it loses the relatives, it will inevitably] be in danger. If it loses the relatives and is not in disorder, it is because the sons keep their former differences of rank.

47. Not to use the help of assistants and aides and not to listen to the thoughts of sages and intelligent men, but to rely on the solidity of inner and outer walls and depend on the service of the brave and strong, this is called "Slighting One's Self." If you slight yourself, you are in danger. If you defend in this way, you will not be firm; if you do battle, you will not conquer.

48. When two tigers fight, bad dogs control the leftovers.[491]

49. With regard to those who are expert at administering a state, the best have no punishments, the [next] . . . , [the] next are resolute in fights and resolute in disputes, and the worst do not fight, do not dispute, and furthermore are not resolute. . . . the best strive in the realm of . . . ; the next strive in the realm of intelligence; the next save the state from calamities and disasters.

50. To be the only one hot in the cold season; to be the only one cold in the hot season, his life is in danger because he is in opposition to the Heavenly seasons and everyone else.[492]

51. Be quick to conquer idleness. Be bold in conquering doubts. The misfortunes of a lost state[493] . . .

. . .

52. . . . do not believe its . . . , but not to believe that it is possible (?), is not acceptable; but not to believe its . . .

53. . . . to observe (?)[494] the front . . . in order to know the reverse; therefore . . . observe the crooked and the straight at the present time, and carefully examine their names in order to designate and decide about them. One who accumulates and hoards, waits for the proper moment and then uses his stores. Observe (?) those whom he appoints[495] as officials to know how he shares his rule; how he accumulates cash to know the seasons . . . correct, noble . . . and survival and destruction.[496]

54. In general, in making assessments, you must use the general meaning of the . . . of the Yin and Yang to decide whether a particular phenomenon is Yin or Yang.

Heaven is Yang and Earth Yin. Spring is Yang and autumn Yin; summer is Yang and winter Yin. The day is Yang and night is Yin. Large states are Yang; small states are Yin. Important states are Yang; unimportant states are Yin. To have affairs is Yang and to have no affairs is Yin.

信（伸）者陰者屈者陰。主陽臣陰。上陽下陰。男陽【女陰。父】陽【子】陰。兄陽弟陰。長陽少【陰】。貴【陽】賤陰。達陽窮陰取（娶）婦姓（生）子陽，有喪陰。制人者陽，制｛人者制｝於人者陰。客陽主人陰。師陽役陰。言陽黑（默）陰。予陽受陰。諸陽者法天，天貴正，過正曰詭□□□□祭乃反。諸陰者法地，地【之】德安徐正靜，柔節先定，善予不爭，此地之度而雌之節也。《稱》千六百

Those who stretch are Yang and those who bend are Yin. Masters are Yang, subordinates are Yin. Superiors are Yang, inferiors are Yin. Men are Yang, [women are Yin. Fathers] are Yang; [sons] are Yin. Elder brothers are Yang; younger brothers are Yin. Elders are Yang; juniors are [Yin]. The noble are [Yang]; the mean are Yin. The broad-minded are Yang; the narrow-minded are Yin. Marrying a wife and producing a son are Yang; having a death in the family is Yin. Controlling others is Yang; being controlled by others is Yin. Guests are Yang; hosts are Yin.[497] Military forces are Yang; corvée labor is Yin.[498] Speech is Yang; silence is Yin. Giving is Yang; receiving is Yin.

All that is Yang is modeled on Heaven. Heaven values the correct. To exceed the correct is called "Deceitful . . ." . . . sacrifices and then turns back (?).[499]

All that is Yin is modeled on Earth. The potency [of] Earth is to be peaceful, gentle, correct, and quiescent. It settles the tally of softness first and is good at giving and not contending. This is the rule of Earth and the tally of the female.[500]

Designations.   One thousand six hundred graphs.[501]

4.
DAO
THE ORIGIN
(DAO YUAN)

道原

■■恒无之初，迵同大虛。虛同爲一，恒一而止。濕濕夢夢，未有明晦。神微周盈，精靜不配（熙）。古（故）未有以，萬物莫以。古（故）无有刑（形），大迵无名。天弗能復（覆），地弗能載。小以成小，大以成大。盈四海之內，又包其外。在陰不腐，在陽不焦。一度不變，能適規（蚑）僥（蟯）。鳥得而蜚（飛），魚得而流（游），獸得而走，萬物得之以生，百事得之以成。

At the beginning of eternal nonexistence,[502]
Totally the same[503] as the Great Void;
Vacuous and the same, it was the One;
Being the One constantly, it was nothing more.[504]
Misty and blurred,[505]
It did not yet possess light and dark.
Daemonic and faint, yet it filled everywhere,
Quintessentially quiescent, it was not luminous.
Therefore it did not possess form;
Immensely penetrating despite being nameless.
Heaven was unable to cover it;
Earth was unable to hold it up.
So small, it could bring smallness to completion;
So large, it could bring largeness to completion.[506]
It filled up all within the Four Seas,
And embraced what was outside them.
In Yin it was not rotted,
In Yang it was not scorched.[507]
It took One as its measure and did not change[508]
And was able to be right for the crawling insects.
The birds flew by acquiring it;
The fish swam by acquiring it;
The wild animals ran by acquiring it.[509]
The myriad phenomena lived by acquiring it;
The numerous affairs were successfully completed by it[510];

173

人皆以之，莫知其名。人皆用之，莫見其刑（形）。一者其號也，虛其舍也，无爲其素也，和其用也。是故上道高而不可察也，深而不可則（測）也。顯明弗能爲名，廣大弗能爲刑（形），獨立不偶，萬物莫之能令。天地陰陽，【四】時日月，星辰雲氣，規（蚑）行僥（蟯）重（動），戴根之徒，皆取生，道弗爲益少；皆反焉，道弗爲益多。堅強而不摜，柔弱而不可化。精微之所不能至，稽極之所不能過。故唯耴（聖）人能察无刑（形），能聽无【聲】。知虛之實，后能大虛。乃通天地之精，通同而无間，周襲而不盈。服此道者，是胃（謂）能精。明者固能察極，知人之所不能知，

All men used it,
But no one knew its name.[511]
All men employed it,
But no one saw its form.
The One was its appellation[512];
The Void was its dwelling;
Nonaction was its original constitution[513];
Harmony was its use.
For this reason, the superior Dao is so high it cannot
    be scrutinized,
Is so deep it cannot be fathomed.[514]
It is clear and bright, but no one can name it;
It is broad and large, but no one can give it a form;
It stands alone and is not paired with anything else[515]
And none of the myriad phenomena is able to issue it orders.
Heaven and Earth, Yin and Yang,
The [four] seasons, the sun and moon,
The planets and constellations and cloudy vapors,
The wrigglers that walk and the crawlers that move,
And the plants that grow roots
All take their life from the Dao
But they do not decrease it.[516]
They all return to the Dao
But they do not increase it.[517]
It is hard and strong, yet it is not broken[518];
It is soft and weak, yet cannot be changed.
The subtlest of the fine cannot reach it;
The furthest of the distant cannot pass it.
Therefore it is only the Sage who is able to examine the
    formless,
Who is able to hear the [sound]less.[519]
When he knows the reality of the Void,
Later he is able to be supremely empty:
Then he penetrates to the quintessence of Heaven and Earth,
Penetrates to sameness and lacks differentiation,[520]
And harmonizes everywhere, yet is not full.[521]
One who practices this Dao
Is called "Capable of Being Quintessential."
He who is bright assuredly is able to examine into the distant,
He knows what other men cannot know,

人服人之所不能得。是胃（謂）察稽知〇極。耵（聖）王用此，天下服。无好无亞（惡），上用□□而民不褽（迷）惑。上虛下靜而道得其正。信能无欲，可爲民命。上信无事，則萬物周扁（遍）。分之以其分，而萬民不爭。授之以其名，而萬物自定。不爲治勸，不爲亂解（懈）。廣大，弗務及也。深微，弗索得也。夫爲一而不化。得道之本，握少以知多：得事之要，操正以政（正）畸（奇）。前知大古，后□精明。抱道執度，天下可一也。觀之大古，周其所以。索之未无，得之所以。《道原》四百六十四

He gains what others[522] cannot acquire:
This is called "Examining into the Far and Knowing the
Distant."
If the sage king uses such a one,
The world submits.
Without likes, without hates,
When the superiors use . . .
then the people are not deluded and confused.
When the superiors are empty and inferiors quiescent,
then the Dao gains its correct position.[523]
The trustworthy are able to be without desires,
And can issue commands to the people:
If you are extremely trustworthy and without affairs[524]
then the myriad phenomena are everywhere arranged.[525]
Divide them according to their natural divisions,
then the myriad people will not fight.
Bestow positions on them according to their names,
then the myriad phenomena will settle themselves.[526]
Do not labor on behalf of order,
Do not be idle because of disorder.
Broad and large, and troublesome tasks will not reach you;
Deep and subtle, and searching will not find you.
Now be One and not transform,
Gain the root of the Dao,
Grasp the few to know the many,
Gain the essentials of affairs,
Lay hold of the correct to correct the irregular.
First know highest antiquity,
Later . . . quintessentially bright.
Embrace the Dao and control the measures
And the world can be unified.
Observe highest antiquity,
And discern everywhere where it can be used.
Search into matters before they are nothing;
Control them when you have the means.[527]

Dao the Origin.[528]   Four hundred and sixty-four graphs.

Chart of the Nine Rulers

5.

THE NINE
RULERS
(YI YIN
JIU ZHU)

九主

・湯用伊尹，既放夏桀以君天，伊尹爲三公，天下大（太）平。湯乃自吾，吾至（政）伊尹，乃是其能，吾達伊尹。伊尹見之，□□於湯曰：『者（諸）侯時有儺罪，過不在主。干主之不明，膚下蔽（蔽）上□法亂常，以危主者，恒在臣。請明臣法，以繩適臣之罪。』湯曰：『非臣之罪也。主不失道□□□□□□□主法，以繩適主之罪。』乃許伊尹。伊尹受令（命）於湯，乃論洧（海）內四邦□□□□□□□□□圖，□智（知）存亡若會符者，得八主。八主適惡。剸（專）授之君一，勞□□□君一，寄一，破邦之主二，威（滅）社之主二，凡與法君

180

Tang[529] employed Yi Yin. When he resisted Jie of the Xia dynasty,[530] he ruled the world as lord; Yi Yin was to be *Sangong* minister and the world was at Grand Peace.[531]

Tang then thought to himself and five times caused Yi Yin to come before him: then he realized his ability and five times probed Yi Yin.[532] Yi Yin had an audience with him . . . said to Tang,

"At times, the feudal lords commit hateful[533] crimes: it is not the ruler's fault. To shield the ruler so that he is not bright, to control inferiors and keep superiors in the dark[534] . . . the laws and disorder the constants, in order to endanger the ruler, that always is the aim of ministers. I request to clarify the laws for ministers in order to control the crimes of these offensive[535] ministers."

Tang said, "It is not the crime of my subjects; it is I, the ruler, who has lost the Dao; . . . in charge of the law in order to control the crimes of these offensive ministers." He then gave permission to Yi Yin.

Yi Yin received the mandate from Tang, then assessed the four countries[536] within the four seas . . . chart . . . "one who knows survival and destruction and how to match the two parts of the tally together gains control of the eight types of ruler. The eight types of ruler will encounter evil.

"One variety: a ruler who bestows his monopoly of power on another[537]; [one variety: a ruler who] labors[538]; one variety: a ruler who is only a [half-ruler][539]; one variety: a parasitic [ruler][540]; two varieties of ruler who destroy their states; two varieties of ruler who extinguish their altars of soil. In all, together with the ruler who abides by the law,

181

爲九主。從古以來，存者亡者，□此九已。九主成圖，請效之湯。湯乃延三公，伊尹布圖陳筴（策），以明法君法臣。法君者，法天地之則者。志曰天，曰□曰四時，復（覆）生萬物，神聖是則，以肥（配）天地。禮數四則，曰天綸，唯天不失乏（範），四綸□則。古今四綸，道數不代（忒），聖王是法，法則明分。后曰：『天乏（範）何也？』伊尹對曰：『天乏（範）无□，復（覆）生萬物，生物不物，莫不以名，不可爲二名。此天乏（範）也。』后曰：『大矣才（哉）！大矣才（哉）！不失乏（範）。法則明分，何也？』伊尹對曰：『主法天，佐法地，輔臣法四時，民法萬物，此胃（謂）法則。天復（覆）地載，生長收臧（藏），分四時。故曰：事分在職臣。是故受職□□【臣】分□□□□□臣分也。有民，主分。以无職幷恥（聽）有職，主分也。恥（聽）□□敬□□誘□分□□之胃（謂）明分。分名暨（既）定，法君之佐佐主无聲。胃（謂）天之命四則，四則當□，天綸乃得。

182

there are Nine Rulers. From ancient times to the present, those who survived and those who perished . . . there were these nine. For the Nine Rulers I have completed a chart.[541] I request to present it to you."

Tang then invited him to be the *Sangong*, and Yi Yin displayed the chart and laid out the strategies in order to explain clearly rulers who abide by the law and ministers who abide by the law.

"The ruler who abides by the law is one who models himself on the rules of Heaven and Earth.

"The *Records*[542] refer to Heaven; they refer to [the Earth]; they refer to the four seasons. They cover over and give birth to the myriad phenomena: they are what the spiritual sages pattern themselves on in order to match Heaven and Earth. To enumerate in a ritually correct manner the four types of rule[543] is called the Heavenly Order. Only Heaven does not lose its form, the four types of order . . . rules. In the past and in the present, there were, and are, the four types of order, and the numbers of the Dao do not change or err.[544] It is what the sages and true kings model themselves on, and the laws and rules are clearly distinguished."

The Emperor stated, "What is Heaven's form?"

Yi Yin replied, "Heaven's form has no . . . it covers over and gives birth to the myriad phenomena; it gives birth to things but it is not itself a thing.[545] Everything is named by it, but it cannot make two names for something. This is the form of Heaven."

The Emperor said, "How Great! How great that it does not lose its model! What about the saying 'laws and rules are clearly distinguished'?"

Yi Yin replied, "The ruler models himself on Heaven; his helpers model themselves on Earth; his assistant ministers model themselves on the four seasons; the people model themselves on the myriad phenomena. This is what is meant by laws and rules. Heaven covers over; Earth supports; birth, growth, harvest, and storage are allotted to the four seasons.[546]

"Therefore it is said, 'Affairs are allotted among ministers with appropriately designated duties.' For this reason, give duties . . . [ministers] divide . . . is the allotted share of ministers. To possess the people is the allotted share of the ruler. To have no duties but at the same time to listen to those with duties is the allotted share of the ruler. To listen . . . respectful . . . seduce . . . allotted share . . . is called 'clarifying allotments.' When the names of the allotted shares are fixed, the helpers of the ruler who abides by the law assist the ruler without a sound. That is what is meant by Heaven commanding the Four Rules. When the Four Rules correspond with . . . , the Heavenly Order is then obtained.

得道之君，邦出乎一道，制命在主，下不別黨，邦无私門，諍（爭）李（理）皆塞。』【后】曰：『佐主无聲，何也？』伊君（尹）對曰：『故法君爲官求人，弗自求也。爲官者不以忘（妄）予人，故知臣者不敢誣能，□主不忘（妄）予，以分恥（聽）名。臣不以忘（妄）進，曰彊以受也。自彊者先名，先名者自責。夫先名者自彊之命已。名命者符節也，法君之所以彊也。法君執符以恥（聽），故自彊之臣莫【敢】僞會以當其君。佐者无扁（偏）職，有分守也，謂伞之命，佐主之明，并列百官之職者也。是故法君執符以職，則僞會不可□主。僞會不可□主矣，則賤不事貴，袁（遠）不事近，皆反其職，信□在忌（己）心。是故□□□□□□不出其身，晝夕不離其職。故法君之邦若无人。非无人也，皆居其職也。賤不事【貴】，袁（遠）不事，則法君之佐何道別主之臣以爲其黨，空主之廷朝之其門。所胃（謂）法君之佐佐主无聲者，此之胃（謂）也。』

184

"As for a ruler who has acquired the Dao, his state comes forth from a single Dao; orders and mandates rest with the ruler; subordinates do not divide into factions; the state has no access for private influence to insinuate itself, and the principles of contest are blocked up."

[The Emperor] said, "What about the clause 'assist the ruler without a sound'?"[547]

Yi Yin replied, "A ruler who abides by the law, when establishing his administration, seeks others, he does not seek himself for it. One who establishes an administration does not rashly give to others and therefore wise ministers do not dare to make false claims about their abilities,[548] and . . . ruler does not rashly bestow gifts in order to separate the names of those to whom he will listen and those whom he will not. When ministers do not rashly advance, it is called 'Promoting[549] in order to Receive.' Those who promote themselves have no name; those who lack names bring censure upon themselves. Now as for those who lack names, the commissions into which they have promoted themselves are terminated. As for those who possess names, on the other hand, their commissions bear tallies and passports and those are the means by which the ruler who abides by the law promotes them. The ruler who abides by the law holds their tally when he listens to them, and thus no minister who promotes himself [dares] falsely to have an audience in order to face his ruler. Those helpers who do not have deviant[550] posts guard their allotted shares, and this refers to commissions of . . . ,[551] the intelligence of those helping the ruler as well as the posts of all the ranked officials.

"For this reason, if the ruler who abides by the law holds the tallies in order to make appointments, then false audiences cannot . . . the ruler. If false audiences are not able to . . . the ruler, then the mean will not serve the noble, and the distant will not serve the near,[552] and all will reject their posts and trust will . . . be in their hearts.

"For this reason . . . do not make a show of themselves, and day and night they do not leave their posts.

"Therefore, if a state that has a ruler who abides by the law appears to have no one as an official, it is not that it actually has no one, but rather that they are all staying at their posts. If the mean do not serve [the noble] and the distant do not serve [the near], then how could the helpers of the ruler who abides by the law separate the ministers of the ruler and turn them into factions, or empty the ruler's court and go to their own gates?[553] This is what is meant by the saying, 'the helpers of the ruler who abides by the law assist the ruler without a sound.'"

后曰：『至矣才（哉）！至矣才（哉）！法君法臣。木直，繩弗能罪也。木其能侵繩乎？』伊尹或（又）請陳筴（策）以明八【適】變過之所道生。志曰：『唯天无勝，凡物有勝。』后曰：『天无勝，何也？』伊尹對曰：『勝者，物□□所以備也，所以得也。天不見端，故不可得原，是无勝。』后曰：『極卜不見？』伊尹對曰：『□故聖王□天。故曰主不法則，乃反爲物。崇見必得，得有巨才（哉）！得主之才（哉）！□□能用主，邦有二道，二道之邦，長諍（爭）之李（理），辨黨長爭，□□□无，爭道得主者蕘（萌）起，大干天綸，四則相侵，主輕臣重，邦多私門，挾主與□□□□□□□□□□□□失。膚詢可智，以命破威（滅）。』伊尹暨（既）明八裔之所道生。請命八裔□。【法】君明分，訨（法）臣分定，以繩八裔，八裔畢名。過在主者四，罪在臣者三，臣主同罪者二。【后曰】：『四主之罪，何也？』伊尹對曰：『劕（專）授

186

The Emperor said, "Superb! Superb! The ruler who abides by the law and the ministers who abide by the law! As for a straight tree, the marking line of a carpenter cannot find fault with it. But can a tree encroach upon the marking-line?"

Yi Yin again requested to lay out the chart in order to clarify what the misfortunate errors of the eight offenses are derived from. "The *Records* states, 'Only Heaven lacks external manifestations. In general, things leave external manifestations.'"

The Emperor said, "What about (the saying) 'Heaven lacks external manifestations'?"

Yi Yin replied, "External manifestations are the way in which things . . . make preparations against other things and the means by which they gain success. The end of Heaven, on the other hand, cannot be reached, and therefore its origin cannot be attained. For this reason, it lacks external manifestations."[554]

The Emperor said, "If you divined about it to the greatest extent possible,[555] would it not be apparent?"

Yi Yin replied, ". . . therefore the sage king [models himself on] Heaven. Thus it is said, 'If the ruler were not to model himself on the rules of Heaven, he would in turn be a thing.'[556] If the end is visible, inevitably it will be attained; the one who attains it will be the one to possess great ability and will obtain the ruler's ability[557] . . . is able to use the ruler, the state will have two Daos. A state with two Daos will generate principles of conflict, separate factions will struggle for a long time, . . . and then the Dao of struggle will sprout up,[558] and will greatly interfere with Heaven's rules, the four rules[559] will encroach upon one another, the ruler will be light and ministers heavy,[560] the state will have many access points for private influence, ministers will usurp the ruler's power and . . . lost. Worry and grief can be understood and thereby one may identify destruction and extermination."

When Yi Yin had clarified what the eight types of offenses derived from, he requested to name the . . . of the eight offenses.

"The ruler [who abides by the law] makes clear the allotted shares, and the allotted shares of ministers who abide by the law are settled, and thereby he controls the eight types of offenses. The complete names of the eight types of offense are (as follows): four of them are the ruler's fault, three of them are crimes of ministers, and for one, both ruler and minister share the blame."

[The Emperor said], "What are the four crimes of the ruler?"

Yi Yin replied, "The lord who bestows his monopoly of power on

失道之君也，故得乎人，非得人者也。作人邦，非用者也，用乎人者也。是□□得擅主之前，用主之邦，故制主之臣。是故觌（專）授失正之君也，過在主。雖然，酉（猶）【君也】主吾（悟）則酉（猶）制其臣者也。』后曰：『於（嗚）乎（呼）危才（哉）！得主之才（哉）！』『勞君者觌（專）授之能吾（悟）者也。□吾（悟）於觌（專）授主者也。能吾（悟）不能反道，自爲其邦者，主勞臣失（佚）。爲人君任臣之□□因主□□知，倚事於君，逆道也。兇歸於主不君，臣主□□侵君也，未免於□□。過在主。唯（雖）然，酉（猶）君也，自制其臣者也，非作人者。威（滅）【社之主】□□□□□能用威法其臣，其臣爲一，以恥（聽）其君，恐懼而不敢盡□□，是□□□昔撟□□施□伐□叴（仇）慇（讐），民知之无所告朔（愬）。是故同刑（形），共共謀爲一，民自□此王君所明號令，□无道，處安其民。故兵不而邦□舉。兩主異過同罪，威（滅）社之主也。過在上矣。』后曰：『差（嗟）！夏桀氏已夫。三臣之罪何？』伊尹對曰：『觌（專）授之臣擅主之前，【膚】下

another is one who has lost the Dao. As a result, he is acquired by others, it is not that he is the one who acquires others. He is a 'state servant,'[561] it is not that he is the one who makes use of others, but he is used by others. For this [reason, the minister] is able to arrogate authority ahead of the ruler, and uses the ruler's country, and thus is a minister who controls his ruler. It is for this reason the fault lies with the ruler for the case in which the lord bestows his monopoly of power on another and loses control of the government. Although this may be the case, he is still [a lord], so if the ruler realizes the situation, he still is one who may control his minister."

The Emperor said, "Alas! How dangerous that he obtains the ruler's abilities!"

"The lord who labors is one who is able to realize that he has bestowed the monopoly of power on another . . . he is a ruler who realizes that he has bestowed his monopoly on another; he can realize it, but not be able to change his ways. He himself works for his state, and the ruler labors while the ministers are idle and profligate. The lord of men takes responsibility for the minister's . . . and [the minister] relies on the ruler's . . . knowledge, and he transfers matters to the lord: that is in opposition to the Dao, for bad things redound to the ruler, and he is not a lord. The subject rules . . . and the . . . encroaches upon the lord. He does not avoid . . . The fault lies with the ruler. Although this may be the case, he is still the ruler, and he is one who controls his ministers himself; it is not that he is acting as another's servant.

"[A ruler who] destroys [the altars of soil] . . . is able to use awesome laws on his ministers, his ministers do the same when they listen to their ruler,[562] they are frightened and afraid and do not dare to completely . . . this . . . Formerly modest . . . apply . . . attack . . . enemies and rivals, and the people do not know where to lodge their complaints. For this reason, they bear the same appearance, and they conspire together for the same ends,[563] the people from . . . this. What you, my lord majesty, clarified as commands and orders . . . lack the proper Dao to settle and calm your people. Therefore when the army is of no use, the state . . . successful. Both rulers[564] have different faults, but the same crime. This is the ruler who extinguishes his altars of grain and soil. The fault lies with the superior."

The Emperor said, "Alas! Jie of Yin is finished![565] What about the crimes of ministers?"

Yi Yin replied, "The minister who is bestowed monopoly of power arrogates authority ahead of the ruler, [he controls his subordinates]

蔽（蔽）上。乘主之不吾（悟），以侵其君。是故擅主之臣罪亦大矣。半君者劖（專）授而【不悟】者也，【是】故擅主之臣，見主之不吾（悟），故用其主嚴殺僇，□臣恐懼，然后□□□利□主之臣，成黨於下，與主分權。是故□獲邦之【半】，主亦獲其半，則□□□□則□危，臣主橫危，危之至。是故半君之臣罪无□。』
【后】曰：『於（鳴）乎（呼），危才（哉）半君！』『寄主者半君之不吾（悟）者。□□□□臣見主之【不】能□□□□□□□□□□□□□則主寄矣。是故或聞道而能吾（悟），吾（悟）正其橫臣者□。□□□未聞寄主之能吾（悟）者也。』后曰：『哀才（哉）寄主！臣主同罪何也？』伊尹對曰：『破邦之主，劖（專）授之不吾（悟）者也。臣主同術爲一以筴（策）於民，百姓絕望於上，分倚父兄大臣，此王君之所因以破邦也。兩主異過同罪，破邦之李（理）也，故曰臣主同罪。』法君明分，法臣分定，八蕑畢名。后曰：『□□九主之圖，所胃（謂）守備搗具、外內无寇者，此之胃（謂）也。』后環擇吾見素，乃□三公，以爲葆守，藏之重屋。臣主始不相吾（忤）也。

190

and keeps his superiors in the dark.[566] He avails himself of the opportunity that the ruler is not aware and thereby encroaches on his lord. For this reason, the crime of the minister who arrogates the authority of the ruler is indeed great. He is a half-ruler who [unawares] bestows his monopoly of power on another. [For this] reason, the minister arrogates the ruler's authority and sees that the ruler is unaware, and so he uses his ruler's sternness to murder and execute, . . . the other ministers are frightened and afraid, and later on . . . benefits . . . the ministers of the ruler, and create factions below and share authority with the ruler. For this reason, if [the minister] captures [half] the state, and the ruler also holds his half, then . . . then . . . in danger. For the subject and the ruler to be equally endangered is the height of danger.[567] For this reason, no crime is [greater] than that of the minister of a half-ruler."

The [Emperor] said, "Alas! How dangerous to be a half-ruler!"

"A parasitic ruler is a half-ruler who is unaware . . . the minister sees that the ruler is [un]able . . . then the ruler is a parasite. For this reason, some (rulers) can become aware when they hear about the Dao. When they become aware, they correct their wayward ministers . . . but I have never yet heard of parasitic rulers being able to become aware."

The Emperor said, "Alas for parasitic rulers! What about ministers and rulers who commit the same crime?"

Yi Yin replied, "They are rulers who destroy their state and bestow their monopoly of power on others but are unaware. Ministers and the ruler share the same techniques and do the same things when making strategies for the people. The hundred surnames curtail looking at their superior, the ruler, and divide their dependence between their fathers, elder brothers, and the great ministers. This is what you, my lord majesty, would rely on to destroy the state. Each of the two rulers[568] has a different fault, but it is the same crime. These are the principles for destroying a state. Hence the saying, 'the minister and ruler share the same crime.'

"{The ruler who abides by the law clarifies the allotted shares and the shares of the ministers who abide by the law are settled. These are the complete names of the eight types of offense."}[569]

The Emperor said, ". . . the chart of the nine rulers. This is what is meant by guarding and readying the tools for attack so that neither inside nor outside the state will there be bandits."

The Emperor turned his behavior round and chose to appear plain[570]; and then he [appointed him] in order to make him a protector and guardian and hid him in a room with double doors.[571] From that time ministers and rulers started not to oppose each other.

In an influential essay that set the general framework for subsequent discussion of the silk manuscripts, Tang Lan (1974) argued that the four books were the long lost *Huangdi sijing (Four Classics of the Yellow Emperor)* mentioned in the bibliographic treatise of the Han dynastic history, the *Han Shu*. This latter work was composed by Ban Gu and completed by his sister Ban Zhao in the first century C.E., and relied in this part on the work of the scholar Liu Xiang who was responsible for the catalog of the imperial library and himself edited, and thus reorganized, many early texts. This interpretation has received wide, but not universal, acceptance, and can be seen especially in the work of Yu Mingguang (1989, 1993[a]), Chen Guuying, and Wang Bo. Without a doubt, it has strongly affected the interpretation of the philosophical content of the silk manuscripts and therefore has prejudiced the way scholars have perceived the influence of the manuscripts on Warring States, Qin, and Han intellectual discourse. Most recently, Qiu Xigui (1993) and the present author (Yates 1994[b]) have vigorously rejected the hypothesis that the silk manuscripts are the *Four Classics of the Yellow Emperor*: it remains to be seen whether this interpretation becomes generally accepted.

Without following the complexities of Tang's argument in too much detail, he bases his conclusions on the fact that the silk manuscripts are four in number and, in the middle of the Han dynasty, only the *Four Classics* are said to have consisted of four sections *(pian)*. Other works attributed to the Yellow Emperor were *Huangdi ming (The Yellow Emperor's Inscriptions)* (six sections), *Huangdi junchen (The Yellow Emperor: Lord and Subjects)* (ten sections), and the *Za Huangdi (Miscellaneous [Works of] the Yellow Emperor)* (fifty-eight sections). Further, two of the silk manuscripts bear the title *jing* (Canon or Classic), one of which contains the purported words of the Yellow Emperor himself, and the whole was copied in the early Han dynasty when HuangLao doctrines were popular at the very highest levels of government. Giving a work that claimed to represent the sayings of the ancient sage-ruler the name "Canon" would be in keeping with the social and intellectual proclivities of the early Han age. Tang also finds it significant that the silk manuscripts precede one version of the Daoist classic *Laozi*, for it is obvious to him that the copyist considered that the philosophical content of the silk manuscripts was intimately connected to that famous book. Hence his conclusion that they must be HuangLao works; they must be the *Four Classics of the Yellow Emperor*.

One year later, Gao Heng and Dong Zhian (1975) proposed to identify the second book of the silk manuscripts with another volume recorded in the Han bibliography, *The Yellow Emperor: Lord and Subjects*, but as Peerenboom (1993: 8) points out, the problem with this interpretation is that the number of essays in the second book does not match the number reported in the Han bibliography, and not all of the essays are framed as conversations between the Yellow Emperor and his ministers. So, despite the possibility that the copyist of the silk manuscripts might have divided the original ten sections into fourteen or sixteen essays, their conclusions also probably should not be accepted. In fact, Gao Zheng (1993) has argued that this second book should be called *Shisi jing* (*The Fourteen Classics*), but this is not as reasonable as Li Xueqin's (1993[b]) suggestion mentioned above that the original title was *Jing* (*The Canon*) (cf. Yates 1994 [b]).

APPENDIX TWO:
DATE OF THE COMPOSITION OF THE SILK MANUSCRIPTS

The date of composition of the texts has been disputed since their discovery. Cheng Chung-ying (1983) believes that they were written between 179 and 169 B.C.E. immediately prior to their deposition in the Mawangdui tomb. Tang Lan (1974), on the other hand, argues that the texts reflect the struggle between the Legalist and Confucian lines in the early Han, although he traces the origin of HuangLao thought back to about 400 B.C.E. A. C. Graham (1989[b]) suggests that the texts were written after the *Heguanzi*, which was composed in stages in the years of the Qin dynasty, the interregnum between the fall of the Qin and the rise of the Han, and the early Han. So he too implies that the texts were produced only a decade or so before they were consigned to the darkness of the tomb.

Various arguments have been used in support of one hypothesis or another. Wu Guang (1985) points out that myths surrounding the mythical sage Huangdi (the Yellow Emperor) began to circulate in the period of great social transformation between the Spring and Autumn and Warring States times (approximately the fifth century B.C.E.) down to the middle of the Warring States (fourth century B.C.E.). He argues that books ascribed to the authorship of the Yellow Emperor, or in which the Emperor figures as a hero, are primarily associated with the Daoist and Yin-Yang schools and can only have started after the myths were comparatively well-circulated and accepted by rulers, intellectuals, and people in general. In "Establishing the Mandate" of the *Canon*, it is stated that the Yellow Emperor had four faces. This story is also

195

found in the *Shizi*. Shizi was a student of Lord Shang in the mid-fourth century, but the present text includes much Ruist (Confucian) material. Although the currently extant book is probably not entirely original to Shizi, it does contain much early material. The *Canon* also contains much on the battles between the Yellow Emperor and Chi You, the ancient God of War. Stories about these terrifying encounters in ancient times are also found in pre-Qin texts, such as the Daoist *Zhuangzi* and the *Yi Zhou shu*, although, of course, the works included in the latter books were discovered only in the third century C.E., having been buried in the tomb of a prince of the state of Wei in late Warring States times.

With regard to passages in the manuscripts which are similar or the same in wording to that found in extant sources, the silk manuscripts quote extensively from the *Laozi*, though without ascribing the source, and so it is argued that they must have been written after the latter was put down in writing.

The manuscripts also quote from, or are similar in wording to, many other early texts. There are twenty-seven quotes from the *Guanzi* or proto-*Guanzi*; eighteen from the *Guoyu* "Yue Yu xia" (Discourses of the State of Yue, B) and *Heguanzi*; ten from the *Laozi*; and other references are to the military text *Weiliaozi*, parts of which were themselves found in the slightly later Han tomb at Yinqueshan, Shandong, in 1972; the *Shenzi* of the Han state politician Shen Buhai; Shen Dao's book; *Zhuangzi*; the Confucian *Xunzi, Li Ji (Records of Rites)*, and the commentary on the *Yi (Book of Changes)*. Of these, the manuscripts quote most extensively from Daoist works, followed by the so-called Legalists *(fajia)* and the Confucians *(Rujia)*. There is even one mention of the Mohists' famous concept of "universal love" ("inclusive love" or "loving everyone") *(jianai)*.

Some scholars argue that these references or quotations prove that the manuscripts were composed early and that they exerted strong influence on competing philosophies in late Warring States times. Wu Guang disputes this, saying that, for example, the *Guoyu* "Yue Yu xia" (Discourses of the State of Yue, B) was itself a late Warring States text, and if the manuscripts were genuinely early, composed in late Spring and Autumn times, they would have been treated like other texts of a comparable date, such as the *Shi (Book of Songs or Odes)* and the *Shu (Book of Documents)*, both of which were later incorporated into the Confucian canon. On the other hand, however, this is disputed by Wei Qipeng (1980), Li Xueqin (1990), Asano Yuichi, and Wang Bo (1993) who argue that, although the *Guoyu* "Yue Yu xia" is probably late, it may include passages of the long lost *Fan Li bingfa (Fan Li's Art of War)*, and that HuangLao Daoist thought might, in fact, originate with this early southeastern military theorist, sometime in the fifth century B.C.E.[1]

A careful analysis of the entire contents of the silk manuscripts reveal that the organization of the book is comparatively loose. One can see that they were composed not at a single point in time, nor are they from a single author's brush. The authors seem to have made selections from Daoist works, and additionally chosen passages from Ruist and Legalist texts, with the aim of developing their own theoretical system. This selection process can be seen most clearly in *Designations*. Here the passages are definitely taken from other works, and the whole chapter is divided into small paragraphs or even single sentences. The beginning of each new paragraph or passage is marked by a round black dot of ink. Further research needs to be done on the organization and structure of this section, but what can be determined is that the text opens with an aphorism that defines the relation of the multitudinous things of the cosmos to the Dao and closes with a Yin-Yang text that categorizes and enumerates archetypes of those things as being either Yin or Yang, thus providing essential knowledge for the ruler.

At the end of each essay in the manuscripts, there is a title. This is not the practice of early and middle Warring States texts, for example the *Analects* of Confucius and the *Laozi*. In the *Analects*, the chapter titles usually consist of the beginning words of the chapter. Chapter titles describing the actual contents only start to appear in the third century B.C.E., with the *Xunzi* and the *Hanfeizi*. The silk manuscripts not only give the essay heading, but chapter or book names too, at least in the *Canon: Law*. Furthermore, the titles are two graphs long: this is similar to Qin and Han practice. For example, the *Lüshi chunqiu (Spring and Autumn Annals of Lü Buwei)*, which was presented to the Qin throne in 239–238 B.C.E., contains subsection or essay titles, but not chapter titles and the books found at Yinqueshan show the same practice. In the latter texts, there are numerous examples of the number of graphs being provided at the end of the book or essay, although because the slips have been so badly fragmented in many cases it is not possible to determine which numbers originally referred to which texts. Nevertheless, this writing of the number of graphs in a given text was a convention of late pre-imperial times, though found associated with texts as early as *Sun Bin bingfa (Sun Bin's Art of War)*. It may have been a copyist's convention, rather than an authorial one. In the silk manuscripts,

197

the titles are all given at the end of the essay and book, whereas in the bamboo slip texts of Yinqueshan, some titles are given at the beginning and some at the end.

Many scholars have pointed out that the term *qianshou* ("blackhaired ones") appears. This first occurs in the *Spring and Autumn Annals of Lü Buwei* and in the *Hanfeizi*, the *Zhanguoce (Intrigues of the Warring States)*, and in Li Si's memorial objecting to the expulsion of aliens, a policy recommended to the Qin throne in 237 B.C.E. After the unification of China by the Qin, the First Emperor promoted this name "blackhaired ones" for the people. In "Fights of the Surnames" in *The Canon*, the term likewise appears, so it would seem that this essay must be of comparable date, in other words of late Warring States.

Furthermore, after the fall of Qin, Qin was subjected to intense criticism by philosophers and statesmen, not least because the First Emperor had ordered the burning of books at variance with legalist ideas at the suggestion of Li Si in 213 B.C.E. and refused to permit any discourse critical of the government's and the emperor's activities. In the early Han, a chorus of voices were raised against the Qin, which, of course, were partially aimed at justifying the Han's seizure of the Qin throne. Since there is no mention at all of criticism of the Qin in the silk manuscripts, it hardly seems likely that they could have been written as late as Cheng Chung-ying (1983) and Graham suggest, in the few years or decades immediately before they were placed in the tomb.

From a more general consideration of their contents, the silk manuscripts include much which can be described as concrete political and economic policies which the authors proposed to save the Chinese world from the chaos it was experiencing.

The text strongly advocates unification of the world by force and that there should be a single ruler. These ideas are present particularly in the Yellow Emperor essays of the second book. This suggests that, when these passages were written, the world had *not yet* been unified and certainly the consequences and ramifications and problems resulting from such a unification were not discussed at all. Indeed, both *The Canon: Law* and *The Canon* imply that China was still in a stage of competing "feudal" lords or "Warring States." For example, "Great Distinctions" explains the internal conditions of three types of states, the strong, the middle-sized, and the small. In "Assessing Destruction," the text warns that "[i]f you possess a state with these (blockages, previously defined), your defense will not be secure . . . ," and "Names and Principles" baldly states:

"A state in which chaos piles up on the inside and its estimations fail on the outside will be attacked. One in which the appearance of destruction is complete on the inside and its initiatives fail on the outside will be obliterated. When oppositional rules overflow above and the perpetrators do not know when to stop, the state will be destroyed. If a state initiates an invasion of an empty state, even if the affair is not completed, this is called "Acquiring Heaven"; but even though the affair really is completed, the ruler personally will inevitably not have a name from this adventure."

None of these passages indicate anything other than that the world *should* be unified, not that it is, and that the world is a dangerous place where destruction is inevitable unless the ruler follows the prescriptions advocated by the text. Graham (1989[b]) has also argued cogently that one of the three utopias in the *Heguanzi* was written during the struggles accompanying the fall of the Qin dynasty and before the rise of the Han. There is nothing in these silk manuscripts comparable to the despair he sees in that text, and this provides further evidence that they must have been written prior to the Qin unification.

In addition, "Fundamental Types of Attack" states that the best type of warfare is "righteous warfare." This position is in accord with chapter 7 of the *Spring and Autumn Annals of Lü Buwei*, composed in the late 240s B.C.E., where "righteous warfare" is also given pride of place.

Turning to the *form* of the texts, apart from what I have said above, some of the texts are composed in plain prose, some in a mixture of prose and rhymed four-line poetry, and some have the bulk of text written in verse, for example *Dao the Origin*. This type of mixture is seen as late as the *Huainanzi (The Art of Rulership*, chapter 9, Ames 1983) in the second century B.C.E. in the Han and as early as the "Inner Training" chapter of the *Guanzi* and, obviously, the *Laozi*. This seems to be a peculiarity of texts influenced by, or within the tradition of, "Daoism."

The rhyming pattern of these poetic passages may also provide some help in pinning down the date and affiliation of the texts. Long Hui (1975) pointed out the similarity of the rhyme schemes in the *Laozi*, the silk manuscripts, and the *Huainanzi*. This scholar also observes that some word usages seem to reflect peculiarly southern or Chu state practices: in "Three Prohibitions" the word *qiu* "hill" means *kong* "empty." Further work on this linguistic aspect of the manuscripts needs to be accomplished.

In addition, especially in the *Canon: Law*, many concepts are enumerated, a stylistic feature that is also to be seen in the *Hanfeizi*. For example, in "Priorities of a State" the "Five Oppositions" appear; there are "Six Compliances" in the section "Great Distinctions"; and "The Four Measures" is another section title. In "Assessments" the author analyzes the "Eight Corrections" and "Seven Models," "Six Handles" and "Three Names." In the late Warring States and Qin legalist text *Hanfeizi* are to be found "The Eight Villainies" and so on. This kind of enumeration becomes very popular in military texts by the fourth century B.C.E., in such texts as the *Art of War* of Sun Bin (Yates 1988).

With regard to actual concrete economic and political policies present in the silk manuscripts, "A Lord's Government" proclaims that:

> Customs follow the hearts of the people. The worthy love them and make them work hard. [So that they may keep] what they have obtained, do away with the prohibitions and relax the taxes at the barriers and in the markets. By orders and commands, link them into five- and ten-man groups and select and train them according to their distinctions of competence. To correct them by punishments means that crimes that warrant death are not remitted . . . That they may be used for punitive attacks is that the people die out of a sense of duty.

Division of the society into five- and ten-man groups follows the policy recommendations of Lord Shang, but his ideas do not seem to have actually been implemented in the state of Qin (Yates 1987: 223). Doing away with prohibitions and relaxing the taxes at the barriers and marketplaces seems to follow Mencius' or Xunzi's vision of ideal economic order, whereas not remitting or amnestying crimes seems to be "legalist" in inspiration. So this particular passage appears to have been influenced by both "legalist" and Confucian thinking. Certainly the text's emphasis on "love" is not "legalist," but rather follows Laozi, or to a lesser extent the Mohists, although the latter never extended "universal love" ("inclusive love") to the economic sphere. On the other hand, in the "Way and the Law" of *The Canon: Law*, the two lines "[n]oble and base have constant positions" and "[t]he constant affairs of the myriad people are: males perform agricultural work and females weave" recall similar ideas present in the inscriptions carved on the stelae that the First Emperor of Qin erected in the course of his travels through the country after the unification.

In many places, the texts urge the ruler to take action at the proper time, in accordance with the waxing and waning of Yin and Yang. Jan Yün-hua (1983) has noticed this feature as being particularly prominent in the *Canon* (he calls the section the *Shiliujing [Sixteen Canons].* An especially clear example is in "The Three Prohibitions:"

Heaven prohibits those who perform the inconstant; Earth prohibits those who fail in their duties; the ruler prohibits those who disobey orders. When these three prohibitions are put into practice, the state is near to perfection.

According to the prohibitions of Earth, one is not [to take away] from the high, nor add to the low. Do not block up the rivers; do not oppose agricultural tasks; do not oppose the people's bright intelligence. To advance but not stop, to stand but not yield, to initiate action rashly and exceed the regulations: this is called Great Inauspiciousness.

Although Yin and Yang are not specifically mentioned here, the ruler is strongly advised to follow the seasons of Heaven and in accordance with the "prohibitions of Earth" not to take away the people from their agricultural tasks at inappropriate times.

Indeed, Yin and Yang do not appear prominently in the texts *as a whole,* but do appear in sections and passages which may, perhaps, actually be Yin-Yang treatises, or quotations from them. For example, in a long quotation from an otherwise lost text incorporated at the end of *Designations,* many pairs of complementary opposites are designated Yin or Yang, presumably on the basis of some characteristic seen to be essential to their constitution. What is not to be found in the texts is influence from the "Five Phase" theorists. This implies that the texts originate from a time when "Five Phase" theorizing had not been united with the schemes of the Yin-Yang specialists. The "Five Phases" do appear on a few of the Qin almanac slips from Shuihudi and in one of the texts found at Yinqueshan categorized as "Yin-Yang" by Wu Jiulong (1985), but, generally speaking, the "Five Phases" are not important overall in newly discovered materials.

Finally, there is a remarkable lack of mention in the silk manuscripts of two terms most frequently associated with "legalist" thinkers, *shi* "positional advantage" and *shu* "techniques." This is strong evidence in favor of Tu Wei-ming's (1979–1980) rejection of Tang Lan and other scholars' interpretation that the texts are primarily legalist in orientation.

In the light of all the various pieces of evidence assembled above, therefore, I believe that the silk manuscripts were written in the third century prior to the unification of China by the First Emperor. They definitely cannot have been products of either the Qin or the early Han, as other scholars have maintained.

GRAPHIC ABBREVIATIONS AND TEXTUAL VARIANTS

In the silk manuscripts, quite a few words are consistently written in abbreviated form or in different ways than is usual. In the following list, I only provide the first occasion when these forms or ways appear.

DAO AND FA

殹 is an alternate form for 也.
Xing 刑 is an alternate form for *xing* 形.
Gao 槁 is a loan for *hao* 毫.
耶 is an abbreviation of *sheng* 聖 "sage."
Zhi 知 "know" is an abbreviation of *zhi* 智 "wise/wisdom."
Wei 胃 is an abbreviation of *wei* 謂 "call/mean/say."
Rou 糅 is an alternate form for *rou* 柔 "soft."
Li 立 "stand" is an abbreviation of *wei* 位 "position."
Xiao 宵 "night" is an alternate form for *xiao* 肖 "good."
The 1976 editors interpret *fang* 放 as *bing* 并 "level"; Guo Yuanxing (1979) suggests reading it as a loan for *fang* 妨 "hinder": this interpretation is accepted by the 1980 editors.
悎 is an alternate form for *hao* 浩 "grand."

PRIORITIES OF A STATE

Yang 央 "central" is an abbreviation of *yang* 殃 "calamity/disaster."

Xu 虛 "empty" is an abbreviation of *xu* 墟 "empty."

Zhen 朕 "I" is a loan for *sheng* 勝 "conquer."

Bi/pi 辟 "ruler/remote" is an abbreviation of *bi* 避 "avoid."

Xin 信 "reliable" is a loan for *shen* 伸 "stretch."

Lang 郎 "gentleman" is an abbreviation of *lang* 廊 "palace with exterior corridors."

Zi 齎 "type of vessel" is a loan for *zi* 資 "property."

Mang 芒 "beard" is an abbreviation of *huang* 荒 "desolate."

You 又 "more/again" is a loan for *you* 有 "have."

Sui 隋 is either an abbreviation of *duo* 墮 "fall/cause to fall," according to the *WW* editors, or of *hui* 隳 "destroy/exterminate," according to the 1976 editors.

Fen 棼 "beam/confused" is a loan for *fen* 焚 "burn."

Lie 列 "arrange" is an abbreviation of *lie* 裂 "split apart."

Feng 奉 "receive" may perhaps be a loan for *feng* 逢 "meet/encounter."

Gong 功 "task/success" is an alternate form for *gong* 攻 "attack."

Ji 几 "almost" is a loan for *ji* 饑 "hunger/starve."

The 1976 and 1980 editors take *gang* 剛 "hard" as a loan for *gang* 綱 "principle/law/bond/headrope of a fishing net." This is possible, but not certain given the lacuna. It may be an alternative form for *wang* 網 "net/cover over with a net."

A LORD'S GOVERNMENT

Zheng 正 "correct" is an abbreviation of *zheng* 政 "government."

Possibly *cong* 從 "follow" is an abbreviation of *zong* 縱 "indulge."

Zheng 正 "correct" is an abbreviation of *zheng* 征 "punitive attack/taxes."

Shi 適 "appropriate" is an alternate form for *di* 敵 "enemy."

Sun 巽 "mild" is an abbreviation of *xuan* 選 "select/choose."

Xiao 宵 "night" is an alternate form for *xiao* 肖 "good."

Possibly *lian* 練 "train" is a loan for *jian* 揀 "choose," as the 1976 editors claim.

Jiu 廄 "stable" is a loan for *jiu* 勼 "assemble, unite."

Dan 單 "single, solitary" is an abbreviation of *zhan* 戰 "fight."

Shuai 衰 "decline" is a loan for *cha* 差 "graduation."

Bei 備 "prepare" is a loan for *fu* 服 "clothing/submit."

Ru/xu/yao 繻 "tear silk" is an alternate form for *yu* 逾 "overstep/transgress/exceed."

Fa 伐 "punitive attack, punish" is a loan for *fa* 罰 "punish/fine."

Er 佴 "assistant" is a loan for *chi* 恥 "sense of shame."

Jie 桀 "a name" is an abbreviation of 傑 "hero/bravo."

Yu 御 "drive" is an abbreviation of *yu* 禦 "resist."

He 闔 "close" is a loan for *he* 合 "harmonize/join."

GREAT DISTINCTIONS

晉 is an alternate form for *wu* 悟.

Zheng 掙 is an alternate form for *zheng* 爭 "fight/contend."

Shi/di 適 "appropriate" is an alternate form for *di* 嫡 "principal wife."

威 is an abbreviation of *mie* 滅 "destroy."

Mi 麋 "deer" is a loan for *mi* 迷 "delude."

朝 is an abbreviation of *ba* 霸 "lord protector/hegemon."

Da 大 "great" is an abbreviation of *tai* 太 "grand."

Fu 復 "again" is an abbreviation of *fu* 覆 "cover over."

Bi 敝 "worn-out/shabby" is an abbreviation of *bi* 蔽 "cover."

Jiu 廄 "stable" is a loan for *jiu* 究 "penetrate/inquire into."

Shu 述 "record" is an alternative form for *shu* 術 "technique."

Mian 面 "face" is an abbreviation of *mian* 湎 "be polluted or dissipated by drink."

Huo 或 "or/some" is an abbreviation of *huo* 惑 "delude."

Yi 已 "stop/also" is an alternative form for *yi* 矣 "a final particle."

THE FOUR MEASURES

甅 is an abbreviation of *qian* 遷 "move/change."

Lu 僇 "despise" is an alternate form for *lu* 戮 "execute."

Bei/pei 伓 "name of a mountain" is a loan for *bei* 倍 "turn one's back on, renege."

Chun 窘 "massed" is an abbreviation of *jiong* 窘 "distressed."

Xu 洫 "ditch, overflow" is a loan for, or an abbreviation of *yi* 溢 "over-flow."

You 有 "have" is a loan for *you* 又 "also."

Li 李 "plum" is a loan for *li* 理 "principle."

Yuan 員 "personnel" is an abbreviation of *yuan* 圓 "round."

Ju 柜 "willow tree" is an alternate form for *ju* 矩 "carpenter's set-square."

Xiao 小 "small" is an abbreviation of *shao* 少 "less" according to the 1976 editors. The *WW* editors read the graph as *xiao*.

205

Ya 亞 "inferior" is an abbreviation of *e* 惡 "ugly/evil."

Qing 請 "please" is an alternate form for *qing* 情 "real facts/circumstances."

Wu 吾 "I" is an abbreviation of *wu* 悟 "realize."

Chou 瘳 "heal, injury" is an alternative form for *lu* 戮 "execute/kill."

Di 翟 "pheasant" is an abbreviation of *ti* 趯 "be afraid."

Bao 抱 "embrace" is a loan for *fu* 孚 "match accord with."

Zang 臧 "good" is an abbreviation of *zang* 藏 "store."

ASSESSMENTS

The *WW* editors understand *qi* 岐 "precipitous path" as *qi* 跂 "creep"; the 1976 editors take it as a loan for *qi* 蚑, which also means "creep."

Fei 蜚 is an alternative form for *fei* 飛 "fly."

Ruan 奭 is an abbreviation of *ruan* 蝡 "wriggle."

Sheng 生 "life/be born" is an abbreviation of *xing* 性 "nature."

Fang/bing 枋 is an alternate form of *bing* 柄 "handle" (of power and authority).

Tong 童 "boy" is a loan for *dong* 動 "movement."

Tuan 槫 "round" is an alternate form for *zhuan* 轉 "revolution."

Hui 諱 "taboo" is a loan for *wei* 韙 "right."

Xu 徐 "dignified" is an alternative form of *chu* 除 "expel/exorcise."

Shi 視 "see" is a loan for *shi* 示 "show/instruct."

Wu 勿 "do not" is an abbreviation of *wu* 物 "things."

ASSESSING DESTRUCTION

Fu 服 "submit" is a loan for *bei* 備 "prepare."

Pu 溥 "vast" is an abbreviation of *bo* 薄 "thin."

Mo 抹 "obliterate" is an alternate form for *mei* 眛 "avaricious."

Shi 侍 "serve" is an alternate form for *shi* 恃 "rely on."

Ying 贏 "abundance, excess" should be understood as *ying* 盈 "full," i.e., "(reach) the limit completely or fully."

Guo 過 "fault" is an alternate form for *huo* 禍 "calamity/disaster."

Yong 雍 "harmonious/obstruct" is an abbreviation of *yong* 壅 "block/obstruct."

Zhi 直 "straight" is a loan for *te* 特 "special/alone."

Chen 晨 "daybreak" is an alternate form for *chen* 辰 "constellations."
Dai 代 "replace" is a loan for *te* 忒 "err by excess, by going too far."
Dong 冬 "winter" is an abbreviation for *zhong* 終 "end."
Pi 皮 "leather" is an abbreviation of *bi* 彼 "that."

NAMES AND PRINCIPLES

Ruo 若 "like" is an abbreviation of *nuo* 諾 "assent."
Cai 衬 is a loan for *zai* 災 "disaster, calamity."
Yu 與 "share/with/and" is an abbreviation of *ju* 舉 "initiate/enumerate."
Jing 景 "bright/view" is an abbreviation of *ying* 影 "shadow."
Sui 隋 is an abbreviation of *sui* 隨 "follow."
Xiang 向 "towards" is an abbreviation of *xiang* 響 "echo."

ESTABLISHING THE MANDATE

Xiang 象 "resemble" is an abbreviation of *xiang* 像 "model/image."
Fei 肥 "fat" is a loan for *pei* 配 "match."
Mo 磨 is an alternate form for *li* 歷 "reckon" (the calendar).
Xiong 兄 "elder brother" is a loan for *kuang* 曠 "abandon, neglect."
Ju 句 "sentence" is an abbreviation of *gou* 苟 "if."

OBSERVATION

Nüe 瘧 "malaria" is an alternate form of *nüe* 虐 "tyrant," according to all the editors.
Si 寺 is an abbreviation of *dai* 待 "await."
Meng 夢 "dream" is a loan for *meng* 萌 "sprout."
Zi 茲 "this/now" is an abbreviation of *zi* 孳 "give birth/breed."
Tong 童 "youth" is a mistake for *zhong* 重 "heavy/value."
Sheng 繩 "rope" is a loan for *yun* 孕 "pregnant/pregnancy."
Chen 諶 "true" is a loan for *kan* 戡 "subdue/conquer."
Shu 孰 "who/what" is an abbreviation for *shu* 熟 "ripen."

Zi 茲 "this" is an abbreviation for *zi* 滋 "proliferate."

Zhi 執 "hold" is an abbreviation of *zhi* 蟄 "hibernate."

Qing 淸 "pure" is an alternate form for *jing* 淸 "cold."

Xiao 蕭 "desolate" is an alternate form for *su* 肅 "shrivel."

Shi 施 "apply" is an alternate form for *chi* 弛 "lessen/relax."

Wei 未 "not yet" is a loan for *hui* 惠 "kindness/benevolence."

Shi 侍 "serve" is an alternate form for *dai* 待 "await."

FIVE REGULATORS

Jie 綏 is an alternative form of *jie* 接 "join."

兪 is an alternate form of *yu* 愈 "still/even more."

Tong 迵 is an alternate form for *tong* 同 "same."

Pao 鞄 "vessel made of soft leather" is a loan for *fu* 枹 "drumstick."

禺 is an abbreviation of *yu* 遇 "meet."

Zhi 之 "it" is a loan for *Chi* 蚩 .

Qin 禽 "bird" is an abbreviation of *qin* 擒 "capture."

Ming 明 "bright" is an abbreviation of *meng* 盟 "covenant."

GUO TONG

卬 is an abbreviation of *yang* 仰 "face up."

Di 敵 "enemy" is an alternate form for *shi* 適 "appropriate."

You/yao 繇 "corvée labor" is an alternate form for *you* 由 "follow."

Bing 幷 is an abbreviation of *ping* 缾 "bottle."

Qi 氣 "qi" is a loan for *qi* 乞 "beg."

CORRECTING THE REBELLIOUS

Tai 台 "eminent" is an abbreviation for *dai* 怠 "lazy/remiss."

Tong 桐 "pawlonia" is an alternate form for *dong* 恫 "fear."

Bu 部 "section" is an alternate form for *bo* 踣 "kill."

He 禾 "grain" is an abbreviation of *he* 和 "harmonize."

勎 is an alternate form for *bo* 剝 "strip."

劗 is a loan for *jian* 翦 "shave/cut off."

The unknown graph 菁 is a loan for *jing* 旌 "banner/streamer."

Ju 鞫 "interrogate" is an alternate form for *ju* 鞠 "football."

You 酭 is a loan for *hai* 醢 "pickle/hash."

The unknown graph 雦 should be understood as *zhu* 噈 "taste/sip," which is now read *za* 咂, according to the 1976 editors.

Zhi 止, an error for *fan* 乏, is a loan for *fan* 犯 "violate/disobey," according to the 1980 editors. The *WW* editors transcribed the graph as 正.

慤 is an alternate form for *que* 愨 "frank/sincere."

Qing 頃 "a moment" is an abbreviation of *qing* 傾 "overturn."

Gui jiao 規僥 is a loan and alternate form for *qi yao* 蚑蟯.

The unknown graph 挣 is probably an alternative form for *zheng* 爭 "fight/struggle."

Wu 毋 "do not" is a loan for *wu* 無 "lack."

Shang/cheng/xing 胜 is a loan for *xing* 姓 "surname," according to the 1980 editors. The 1976 editors take it as an alternative form of *xing* 腥 which they interpret as *xing* 姓 "surname."

Miu miu 繆繆 is a loan for *mu mu* 穆穆 "solemn, solemn."

Zhang 章 "chapter" is an abbreviation of *zhang* 彰 "conspicuous/clear."

Fan 反 "in turn" is an abbreviation of *fan* 返 "revolve/turn around."

Ji 幾 "almost" is an abbreviation of *ji* 機 "machine/device."

Huan 環 "ring" is an alternate form for *huan* 還 "return."

Zheng 爭 "fight" is an abbreviation of *jing* 靜 "quiescence."

Nie 涅 "black mud" is a loan for *re* 熱 "heat."

Xi 昔 "old" is an abbreviation of *cuo* 措 "manage/arrange."

Bian 辯 "argue" is an alternate form for *bian* 辨 "differentiate."

Xiang 鄉 "country" is a loan for *xiang* 向 "direction."

Ao 敖 "pride/idle" is an abbreviation of *ao* 傲 "pride."

Ju 居 "dwell" is an abbreviation of *ju* 倨 "arrogance."

Gong 共 "together" is an abbreviation of *gong* 恭 "reverent."

Yan 驗 "investigate" is a loan for *jian* 儉 "moderation/frugality."
Fang 方 "square" is an abbreviation of *fang* 妨 "obstruct/impede."

COMPLETE LAWS

Hua 滑 "smooth" is an alternate form for *hua* 猾 "cunning."
Nian 年 "year/harvest" is a loan for *ning* 佞 "crafty."
You 猷 "plan" is an alternate form for *you* 猶 "still/yet."
虖 is an alternate form of the question marker *hu* 乎.
Zhui 椎 "name of a tree" is an alternate form for *kui* 揆 "manage/administer."
Huai 壞 "damage/harm" is an alternate form for *huai* 懷 "cherish."
Chan 毚 "cunning hare" is an abbreviation of *chan* 讒 "slander."
Jian/xian 减 "moderate" is an alternate form for *xian* 咸 "all."
Fu 枹 "drumstick" is an alternate form for *bao* 抱 "embrace."
Cong 蔥 "scallion" is an alternate form for *zong* 總 "generality."
Kong 空 "empty" is a loan for *kong* 孔 "hole."
Si 寺 "temple" is an abbreviation of *chi* 持 "support."
緫 is an abbreviation of *zong* 總 "generality."

THE THREE PROHIBITIONS

Zeng/ceng 曾 "past" is an abbreviation of *zeng* 增 "add to."
Si 寺 "temple" is an abbreviation for *shi* 恃 "rely on."

THE FUNDAMENTAL TYPES OF ATTACK

Jia 叚 "false" is an abbreviation of *xia* 暇 "leisure."
Wei 唯 "only" is a loan or abbreviation for *sui* 雖 "although."
Gong 玒 is an alternate form of *gong* 攻 "attack."

PUTTING THE DAO FIRST

Yang 羊 "sheep/goat" is an abbreviation of *xiang* 祥 "auspicious."
Sheng 生 "produce/be born" is an abbreviation of *xing* 姓 "surname."

He 荷 "lotus" is an alternate form for *ke* 苛 "harsh."

COMPLIANCE WITH THE DAO

Qian 僉 "all" is an abbreviation of *jian* 儉 "frugal."

Zi 茲 "this" is an abbreviation of *ci* 慈 "kind."

Xu 胥 "petty official/all" is a loan for *dai* 待 "wait for."

Yi 飴 "sweet" should perhaps be read as an alternate form for *dai* 怠 "indolent/lazy."

Wan 宛 "twisting" is an alternate form for *yüan* 怨 "resentful."

Guang 廣 "wide" is an abbreviation of *kuang* 曠 "waste/neglect."

An 案 "tray/seize/limit" is probably an alternate form for *an* 安 "peace/secure."

Cong 從 "follow" is an abbreviation of *zong* 蹤 "footprint/track."

Shi 飾 "ornament" is a loan for *chi* 飭 "order/command/correct."

殸 is an abbreviation of *sheng* 聲 "sound."

THE TEN GREAT PROPOSITIONS

Yi 舵 "a southern tribe" is an abbreviation of *shi* 施 "apply."

DESIGNATIONS

Yi 舵 "a southern tribe" is an abbreviation of *chi* 弛 "lenient."

Bao 葆 "preserve/guarantee" is an alternate form for *bao* 保 "protect."

Yi 義 "righteousness" is an abbreviation of *yi* 儀 "measuring device," later the term used for the armillary sphere.

Tuan/zhuan 剸 "cut/decide" is an alternative form for *zhuan* 專 "monopolize."

Po 泊 "anchor" is a loan for *bo* 薄 "poor/thin/narrow."

Shi 士 "knight/officer" is an abbreviation of *shi* 仕 "serve."

Shu 蜀 "name of a state" is an abbreviation of *du* 獨 "solitary/alone."

Ze 擇 "choose" is an alternate form for *shi* 釋 "loosen."

He 礉 "test/stone" is an alternate graph for *he* 核 "pit/stone."

211

Zeng/ceng 曾 "a particle/add/late" is an abbreviation of *zeng* 憎 "hate."

Mu 母 "mother" is an abbreviation of *wu* 侮 "insult."

Shang que 商闕 is a loan for and alternate form for *chang jue* 猖獗 "savage and wild."

Guo 栝 "carpenter's square" is an alternate form for *huo* 活 "live."

Pi/bi 埤 "accumulate/low ground" is an alternate form for *bei* 卑 "low."

Beng/peng 倗 "friend/assistant" is an alternate form for *beng* 崩 "collapse."

Meng 孟 is an abbreviation of *meng* 猛 "fierce."

Shun/xun 揗 "lay hands on" is a loan for *xun* 馴 "tame."

弐 is an abbreviation of *zai* 哉, a final exclamatory particle.

Can 參 is an alternate form for *san* 三 "three."

Qi 耆 "old" is an abbreviation of *shi* 嗜 "enjoy/indulge."

Ji 籍 "record" is an alternate form for *jie* 藉 "loan."

Liang 量 "measure" is an abbreviation of *liang* 糧 "grain/provisions."

Bi/pi 辟 "ruler/remote" is an abbreviation of *pi* 闢 "open."

Xin 新 "new" is an abbreviation of *xin* 薪 "firewood."

Ji 極 "extreme/pole" is an alternate form for *ji* 亟 "quick."

Gu 古 "old" is an abbreviation of *hu* 怙 "depend on."

Nu 奴 "slave" is an abbreviation of *nu* 駑 "bad (horse)."

Jing 敬 "respect" is an abbreviation of *jing* 警 "quick/be vigilant."

Hua 化 "change/transform" is an abbreviation of *huo* 貨 "cash/wealth."

Qu 取 "take" is an abbreviation of *qu* 娶 "marry."

Xing 性 is an alternate form for *sheng* 生 "give birth/produce."

Hei 黑 "black" is an abbreviation of *mo* 默 "silence."

DAO THE ORIGIN

Mengmeng 夢夢 is an alternate form for *mengmeng* 蒙蒙 "blurred."

Gu 古 "ancient" is an abbreviation of *gu* 故 "therefore."

Liu 流 "flow" is a loan for *you* 游 "swim/wander."

Ze 則 "then" is an abbreviation of *ce* 測 "fathom."

Ou 偶 "even number" is an alternate form for *ou* 耦 "two men or oxen pulling a plow together as a pair/pair."

Chong/zhong 重 "again/heavy" is an abbreviation of *dong* 動 "move."

Jie/xie 解 "loosen" is an abbreviation of *xie* 懈 "idle/lax."

Zheng 政 "rule" is an alternate form for *zheng* 正 "correct."

Ji 畸 "odd/exceptional/singular" is an alternate form for *qi* 奇 "irregular/incorrect."

212

Fang 放 "release" is an alternate form for *fang* 妨 "resist."

Zhe 者 is an abbreviation of *zhu* 諸 "all."

虞 is an alternate form for *yu* 虞 "control/worry."

Bi 蔽 is an alternate form for *bi* 蔽 "hide/cover."

Ling 令 "order" is an alternate form for *ming* 命 "mandate/command."

Mu 洢 is an abbreviation for *hai* 海 "sea."

Zhi 智 "wisdom" is an alternate form for *zhi* 知 "know."

笶 is an alternate form for *ce* 策 "strategy."

Fa 乏 "deficient" is a loan for *fan* 範 "model/mold/form."

Cai 才 "then" is a loan for *zai* 哉 "final particle."

恥 is an abbreviation of *ting* 聽 "listen."

Ji 暨 "reach/end" is an alternate form for *ji* 既 "since/when."

Wang 忘 "forget" is probably an alternate form for *wang* 妄 "rash/ignorant/reckless."

Pian 扁 "small" is an abbreviation of *pian* 偏 "biased/deviant."

Yuan 袁 "robe" is an abbreviation of *yuan* 遠 "distant."

Ji 忌 "fear/envy" is an alternate form for *ji* 己 "self."

Zheng 諍 "remonstrate" is an alternate form for *zheng* 爭 "struggle/conflict."

Jun 君 is a mistake for *Yin* 尹.

Huo 或 "some" should be understood as *you* 又 "also."

Hong 薨 "death (of a feudal lord)" is a loan for *meng* 萌 "sprout."

Qu 詁 "a sound" is an alternate form for *fa* 法 "law."

戭 is an alternate form for *zhuan* 專 "monopolize."

You 酉 "tenth of the twelve branches" is an abbreviation of *you* 猶 "still."

Yu hu 於乎 is an alternate form for *wu hu* 嗚呼 "alas."

Shi 失 "lose" is an abbreviation of *yi* 佚 "idle/profligate."

岛 is an alternate form for *qiu* 仇 "enemy."

懋 is an alternate form for *chou* 讐 "rival."

Shuo 朔 "begin/north" is an alternate form for *su* 愬 "tell."

Cha 差 "error/almost" is an abbreviation of *jie* 嗟 "exclamation of regret."

Wu 吾 "I" is an abbreviation of *wu* 牾 "oppose."

NOTES

PART ONE

1. Li Ling 李零, "Shuo 'HuangLao'" 說黃老, *Daojia wenhua yanjiu* 5 (1994), pp. 142–157.

2. Anne Cheng, "Taoisme, Confucianisme, et Légisme," in Charles Le Blanc and Rémi Mathieu eds., *Mythe et Philosophie à l'Aube de la Chine Impériale: Études sur le Huainan zi* (Montréal: Presses de l'Université de Montréal, 1992), pp. 127–41.

3. Harold D. Roth, "What is Huang-Lao?," paper presented at the Fiftieth Annual Meeting of the Association for Asian Studies, New Orleans, April 13, 1991. See also Roth(1991[a]).

4. John S. Major, *Heaven and Earth in Early Han Thought: Chapters Three, Four, and Five of the Huainanzi* (Albany: State University of New York Press, 1993), p. 12.

5. "The Meaning of Huang-Lao in the *Shiji and Hanshu*," *Études Chinoises* 12.2 (Fall 1993), pp. 161–77.

6. Anna K. Seidel, *La Divinisation de Lao Tseu dans le Taoisme des Han*, Publications de l'École Française d'Extrême–Orient vol. 71 (Paris: École Française d'Extrême–Orient, 1969). The quotation appears on p. 84.

7. "Emulating the Yellow Emperor: The Theory and Practice of HuangLao, 180–141 B.C.E." (Stanford: unpublished Ph.D. dissertation, Stanford University, 1994), p. 9.

8. "*Emulating the Yellow Emperor*," pp. 56–57.

9. Translation by Harold Roth (1991[a]), with minor modifications. *Shi ji* (Beijing: Zhonghua shuju ed., 1985), ch. 130, pp. 3288–92.

215

10. *Shi ji*, ch. 130, pp. 3289–90.

11. *Shi ji*, ch. 1, p. 1.

12. The Yellow Emperor appears in some of the Mawangdui medical texts which are, in part, the source of the *Yellow Emperor's Classic of Internal Medicine*, the *Shi Wen (Ten Questions)*, see Ma Jixing, *Mawangdui guyishu kaoshi* (Changsha: Hunankexue jishu chuban she, 1992), pp. 867–917. See also Donald J. Harper, *The "Wu Shih Erh Ping Fang": Translation and Commentary*, unpublished Ph.D. dissertation (Berkeley: University of California, 1982).

13. Douglas Wile, *Art of the Bedchamber: The Chinese Sexual Yoga Classics Including Women's Solo Meditation Texts* (Albany: State University of New York Press, 1992).

14. Roger T. Ames, *Sun-tzu: The Art of Warfare, the First English Translation Incorporating the Recently Discovered Yin-ch'üeh-shan Texts* (New York: Ballantine Books, 1993), pp. 182–184.

15. See also Mori Yasutaro, *Huangdi de chuanshuo* (Taibei: Shibao wenhua chuban qiye youxian gongsi, 1988); Peerenboom (1993); Norman Girardot, *Myth and Meaning in Early Taoism: The Theme of Chaos (hun-tun)* (Berkeley: University of California Press, 1983).

16. Sarah Allan argues forcefully that the Yellow Emperor was "originally the lord of the underworld or Yellow Springs and thus closely associated with the Xia," the earliest, possibly mythical, Chinese dynasty before the Shang (*The Shape of the Turtle*, Albany: State University of New York Press, 1991, p. 73), so the myths may be of extremely ancient origin.

17. Hu Jiacong, "Yin Wen HuangLao sixiang yu Jixia 'Baijia zhengming,'" *Daojia wenhua yanjiu* 4 (1994), pp. 118–127; Shi Huaci (Benjamin I. Schwartz), "HuangLao xueshuo: Song Xing he Shen Dao lunping," *Daojia wenhua yanjiu* 4 (1994), pp. 128–146. For a valuable and comprehensive collection of materials on the scholars who attended the Jixia Academy, including the Confucians Mencius and Xunzi, see Zhang Bingnan, *Jixia gouchen* (Shanghai: Shanghai guji chuban she, 1991).

18. Another of these essays is an important pre-Mencian Confucian text which has been studied by two Chinese scholars, Pang Pu (1980) and Wei Qipeng (1991).

19. W. K. Liao trans., *The Complete Works of Han Fei Tzu: A Classic of Chinese Political Science*, vol. 1 (London: Arthur Probsthain, 1959), pp. 30–31.

20. Quoted in Herrlee G. Creel, "The Meaning of 刑名 *Hsing-ming*," in *What is Taoism? And Other Studies in Chinese Cultural History*

(Chicago: University of Chicago Press, 1970), pp. 80, 86 (romanization changed).

21. Herrlee G. Creel, "The Meaning of *Hsing-ming*"; "The *Fa-chia*: 'Legalists' or 'Administrators'?," in *What is Taoism?*, pp. 92–120; *Shen Pu-hai: A Chinese Political Philosopher of the Fourth Century B.C.* (Chicago: University of Chicago Press, 1974).

22. "The Meaning of *Hsing-ming*," p. 86.

23. For analysis of the philosophical dimensions of this doctrine, see John Makeham, *Name and Actuality in Early Chinese Thought* (Albany: State University of New York Press, 1994).

24. For detailed studies of Chi You and the mythology of violence, see Mark Edward Lewis, *Sanctioned Violence in Early China* (Albany: State University of New York Press, 1990), and Derk Bodde, *Festivals in Classical China* (Princeton: Princeton University Press, 1975).

25. D. C. Lau trans., *Lao Tzu: Tao Te Ching* (Harmondsworth: Penguin, 1963 [1982]), p. 103.

26. Ames, *Sun-tzu*, ch. 10, "The Terrain," p. 149.

27. Ames, *Sun-tzu*, ch. 11, "The Nine Kinds of Terrain," p. 159.

28. Ames, *Sun-tzu*, ch. 9, "Deploying the Army," p. 144.

29. *Disputers of the Tao: Philosophical Argument in Ancient China*, La Salle: Open Court, 1989.

30. *The World of Thought in Ancient China*, Cambridge: Harvard University Press, 1985.

31. W. Allyn Rickett, *Guanzi: Political, Economic, and Philosophical Essays from Early China*, vol. 1 (Princeton: Princeton University Press, 1985), p. 216. This first aphorism may originally have been written on a single bamboo slip, for it contains exactly forty-four graphs, which we know was one of the numbers regularly used in ancient times.

32. This is a famous quotation from the *Analects* of Confucius, Book 13 "Zilu," subsection 3.

PART TWO

1. THE CANON: LAW

1. There was a difference drawn between *fan* 犯 and *fei* 廢 in the Qin legal documents discovered in Hubei province in 1975, dating from the last half of the third century B.C.E. Hulsewé (1985) D 120, p. 160, translates: [142] What is "to transgress *(fan)* the Ordinances" and "to set aside *(fei)* the Ordinances"? What the Statute means is that when an Ordinance says "do no[t] do this" and yet to do it—that is what is meant by "to transgress the Ordinances." When an Ordinance says "do this," then not to do it—this is what is meant by "to set aside the Ordinances." It is the practice of the court that both are sentenced as "transgressing the Ordinances."

2. *Jian zhi* 見知 "to see and know" is a technical legal term, referring to complete cognizance of a situation.

3. I.e., the Dao. *Guanzi* 管子 (hereafter *GZ*) *pian* 36, "Xinshu shang" 心術上 (Techniques of the Heart A), ch. 13, p. 219, makes the same point: Rickett (1965: 174): "What is vacuous and formless we call the Way." *GZ pian* 49, "Neiye" 內業 (Inner Training), ch. 16, p. 269, also states (Rickett 1965: 160), "It is ever so that the Way has neither roots, nor stalks, Leaves nor flowers. Yet what gives life to all things and brings them to perfection Is termed the Way."

4. *Laozi* 老子 (Fudan daxue zhexuexi 1977: 73), Book One (section 32), states, "He who knows sufficiency is rich"; Book Two (section 46), p. 22, states:

> "There is no crime greater than being capable of desire;
> There is no misfortune greater than not knowing sufficiency;
> There is nothing more painful than desiring to acquire;
> Therefore to know the sufficiency of sufficiency is the constant
>   sufficiency."

5. *Huainanzi* 淮南子 (hereafter *HNZ*) "Yuan Dao Xun" 元道訓 (The Original Dao) ch. 1, p. 4a, states, "The Heavenly (human) nature *(xing)* is that Man is born and then is quiescent; Harm to (human) nature results when he moves after he has been affected by emotion. When things come and the spirit *(shen)* responds, it is the movement of knowledge, knowledge and things join, and love and hatred are born from this union. Love and hatred bring forms to completion, and knowl-

edge is enticed by externals such that one cannot return to oneself, and the Heavenly Principles *(tianli)* are obliterated."

6. "Xingshou" 行守 (Rules for Conduct) below defines "self-promotion" as "to have a word and not to have a (corresponding) action." In other words, to say you can do something, but be unable or unwilling to carry it out.

7. *HNZ* "Renjian xun" 人間訓 (In the World of Men) ch. 18, p. 2b, states, "Now as for the origin of disaster, men produce it themselves. As for the origin of good fortune, men themselves bring it to completion. Disaster and good fortune share (the same) gate. Benefit and harm are neighbors; no one who is not a sage is able to separate them."

8. An autumn hair was considered to be the smallest of the small. The Daoist classic *Zhuangzi* 莊子 states, *pian* 17, "Qiushui" 秋水 (Autumn Floods), (*Zhuangzi jishi* 莊子集釋 ce 3, p. 568 (Watson, trans., 1968: 177), "'Well then,' said the Lord of the River, 'If I recognize the hugeness of heaven and earth and the smallness of the tip of a hair, will that do?'" Another passage is found in *pian* 2, "Qiwu lun" 齊物論 (The Sorting which Evens Things Out), ce 1, ch. 1B, p. 79 (Graham, trans., 1981: 56), "Nothing in the world is bigger than the tip of an autumn hair, and Mount T'ai is small . . ." Zhuangzi is turning ordinary perceptions on their head in this second passage.

9. The difference between black and white was considered to be one of the stock examples of quintessential differences by early Chinese philosophers. We read in the *Mozi* 墨子, for example, ch. 19, "Feigong xia" 非攻下 (Condemnation of Offensive Warfare, Part 3), Mei 1973: 107), "Now the feudal lords in the empire still attack and assault each other. This is to praise the principle without understanding its real meaning. They resemble the blind man who uses with others the names of black and white but cannot discriminate between such objects. Can this be said to be real discrimination?"

10. *Hanfeizi* 韓非子(hereafter *HFZ*) (*Hanfeizi jijie* 韓非子集解, *pian* 5, "Zhu Dao" 主道 (The Dao of the Ruler) (1956: 17–18, ce 1), likewise argues (W. K. Liao, vol. 1, 1959: 31), that, "Therefore, by virtue of resting empty and reposed, he [the ruler] waits for the course of nature to enforce itself so that all names will be defined of themselves and all affairs will be settled of themselves. Empty, he knows the essence of fullness: reposed, he becomes the corrector of motion. Who utters a word creates himself a name; who has an affair creates himself a form. Compare forms and names and see if they are identical. Then the ruler

will find nothing to worry about as everything is reduced to its reality." A similar notion is presented in chapter 8 of the same book "Yangquan" 揚權 (Wielding the Sceptre). Liao, vol. 1, p. 53, translates, "The way to assume oneness starts from the study of terminology. When names are rectified, things will be settled; when names are distorted, things will shift around. Therefore the sage holds oneness in the hand and rests in tranquillity, letting names appoint themselves to tasks and affairs settle themselves."

11. See McLeod and Yates (1981: 130, note 54). In legalist theory, the ruler alone should cover his tracks, but he should be able to track down those of everything and everybody else.

12. Yu Mingguang (1993[a]) interprets *ji* 稽 as *kai* 楷 "model." Chapter 65 of the *Laozi* reads, "He who understands these two (knowledge and ignorance being used to run the state), also understands the model and the system; To understand constantly the model and the system, This is called Profound Potency."

13. *Mozi* "Canons" 經 A 57. *Can* 參 is the standard term in Chinese astronomy for aligning two gnomons with the observed heavenly bodies (see Graham 1978: 307). See also below "The Four Measures," "When both outside and inside are compliant, it is called 'Correspondence with Heaven.'"

14. The 1976 editors take *zhi* 直 as a verb, "Affairs are like straightening a piece of wood."

15. This seems to refer to an object's own innate spirituality or essence.

16. A military text found at Yinqueshan, Shandong, in 1972, in a tomb of early Western Han date, but probably itself of Warring States date and given the title "Qi Zheng" 奇正 (The Unorthodox and the Orthodox) by the editors (Wu Jiulong, 1985) states (# 0146), "When form is used to respond to form, it is orthodox *(zheng)*; to lack form and yet control form is unorthodox *(qi)*."

17. The missing graph is either *xing* 刑 "form" or *shi* 實 "reality."

18. "Dao the Origin" states below,
The One was its appellation;
The Void was its dwelling;
Nonaction was its original constitution;
Harmony was its use.

19. The 1976 editors explain that *ban* 半 "half" should be understood as *pan* 畔 "bank, side"; in other words a "limit/difference" or "division/separation" (Yu Mingguang 1993[a]). A similar usage of *pan*

as "separation" is to be found in the *Mozi*, ch. 14, p. 9a, where the gangs of fifty souls digging each countermine in a siege were to consist of both men and women inhabitants, but they were to be separated from each other *(nannü xiangban* 男女相半*)* (cf. Yates1980: 276). "In the middle" refers to the realm of man between Heaven and Earth.

20. The graph *fu* 富 "wealth" should probably be excised according to the 1976 and 1980 editors. It may, however, be a mistake for *dang* 當 "ought/must."

21. The altars of soil and grain were among the most important ritual sites of the ancient Chinese state and were a symbol of its existence. If its altars were destroyed, the state was considered to exist no longer. The 1976 editors interpret *kuang* 匡 as *kuisun* 虧損 "lose." Guo Yuanxing (1979), p.131, suggests taking it as it appears in the *Li Ji* 禮記 "Li Qi" 禮器 (Ritual Vessels) *pian* 10 *(Li Ji zhengyi* 禮記正義, *Shisanjing zhusu* 十三經注疏 ed., *pian* 23, p. 203a [p. 1431a]), where Zheng Xuan 鄭玄 comments that *kuang* is like *kong* 恐 "fear." Here, Guo argues, it should be understood as *konghuang* 恐慌 "panic." If there is panic, there must be chaos or rebellion: the sentence is like saying, "The world is in great disorder," he declares. It is not, however, a matter of the world being in chaos, but rather that the altars of soil and grain, the center and symbol of the state, are in danger of being destroyed. *Guoyu* 國語 (hereafter *GY*) "Yue Yu xia" 越語下 (Discourses of the State of Yue, B), ch. 21, p. 5a, reads, "Fan Li said, 'Yang reaches its limit and then there is Yin; Yin reaches its limit and then there is Yang. The sun is in difficulties (i.e., in an eclipse) and then it returns; the moon is full and then it wanes.'" The 1980 editors suggest that the graph might possibly be read as *wang* 枉 "crooked/wronged." This seems the most reasonable interpretation.

22. This statement is reiterated in two of the later chapters, "The Features of Warfare" and "The Practice of Defense." The 1976 editors think the "giving" refers to enfeoffing the worthy as feudal lords within the state, but this seems irrelevant to the context, which is rather concerned about the fate of the entire state: Heaven gives life to the state or takes it away. Cf. *GY* "Yue Yu xia," ch. 21, p. 5a, "Fan Li said, 'When you gain the opportune time, do not be lazy, for the time will not come back again. When Heaven gives and you do not take, (Heaven) will in turn *(fan)* create a disaster for it (your nonaction).'"

23. A similar clause appears in the *GY* "Yue Yu xia," ch. 2l, p. 5a: "Fan Li said, 'Your subject has heard that those of the ancients who were expert in warfare used the surplus and the shortage to make the

constant (rules), and used the four seasons to make the main thread *(ji)* (i.e., laws). They did not go beyond the limit of Heaven *(tian ji)*, and inquired into numbers and then stopped.'"

24. In other words, if you attempt to punish another state, issuing prohibitions against its immoral behavior, although in fact it has not behaved poorly, your admonitions will not correspond with the reality of the situation and your punishments will be inappropriate, and you will yourself suffer calamity.

25. I.e., conquer it successfully.

26. The enemy state.

27. In other words, treat it fairly and honestly and act with the welfare of the people in mind.

28. Presumably this is the Heavenly Correspondence mentioned elsewhere.

29. I.e., an enemy.

30. I.e., with Heaven. If you march with Heaven to attack another state, you will conquer it. A similar statement is found in the *GY* "Yue Yu xia," ch. 21, p. 5b, "Therefore those of the ancients who were expert at warfare relied on the constant (rules) of Heaven and Earth and marched together with them."

31. The pair of terms "bending" and "stretching" are found frequently in Warring States texts and refer to the flexibility of one who is attuned to the world. Zhuangzi, in a conversation between Confucius and his favorite disciple, Yan Hui, rejects this approach to action. "'In that case,' said Hui, 'inwardly I shall be straight but outwardly I shall bend, I shall mature my own judgment yet conform to my betters. In being "inwardly straight" I shall be of Heaven's party. In "outwardly bending" I shall be of man's party'." To which Confucius replies, "'Oh no, that's no good at all! Too much organizing'" (ce 1, ch. 4, "Renjian shi 人間世, pp. 143–45) (Graham, 1981, ch. 4, "Worldly Business among Men," p. 68).

32. This is defined below.

33. *Lang miao* 廊廟 refers to a palace or court buildings with long exterior passageways or columned terraces. Cf. *GY* "Yue Yu xia," ch. 21, p. 5a. The sentence means that they build excessively extravagant palatial structures, such as those that were constructed by the First Emperor of China.

34. Bells and drums were used to send signals on campaign and in battle. The sentence means that they mobilize their armies for battle.

35. Cf. *GY* "Yue Yu xia," ch. 21, pp. 1ab, "Fan Li advanced and

remonstrated, 'Now with regard to the affairs of a state, there is "Protecting Fullness," there is "Stabilizing the Collapsing," there is "Controlling Affairs."' The King (Gou Jian) said, 'How does one do these three?' He replied, 'To protect fullness is to share with Heaven; to stabilize the collapsing is to share with Man; to control affairs is to share with Earth.'"

36. Probably a sentence about wasting the royal palaces has dropped out.

37. *Lie* is the same word that is used in the legalist *Book of Lord Shang* to refer to the tearing down of the old field boundaries before the establishment of the new land system that Lord Shang proposed for Qin. The same process must be what is meant here. Lord Shang, however, did not advocate enfeoffing the worthy with the seized land.

38. Literally, *qie* 竊 means "steal." There are two other passages parallel to these difficult sentences. In the second part of "Guan" (Observation) below, the first *qie* is written as *cha* 察 "examine into, see, know, distinguish," which is also the graph in the *GY* "Yue Yu xia," ch. 21, p. 5b. The second *qie* in "Observation" is given as *bi* 敝 "poor," which is probably an abbreviation of *bi* 蔽 "hide/conceal/cover over," for that is the graph used in the "Yue Yu" passage. I believe that the author is saying that one should not have either too much Yang or too much Yin. The first *qie* should therefore be understood as a loan for *cha* and the second *qie* is most likely a mistake for "hide." I.e., "do not be too hidden by Yin."

39. The 1976 editors note that the term *tu bi* 土敝 also appears in the *Lüshi chunqiu* 呂氏春秋 (hereafter *LSCQ*), ch. 6, no. 3 "Yin Chu" 音初 (How Tunes Began), p. 6b, "If the earth is covered over, then the grasses and trees will not grow" (the text has *bi* 弊 for *bi* 敝 (蔽). This same sentence is found in the *Li Ji, pian* 19, "Yue Ji" (Record of Music), ch. 38, p. 307c (p.1535c), with the graph as *bi* 敝 (Legge 1885, vol. 28, p. 109). They state that *tu bi* means to exhaust the strength of the soil beyond its limits so that the plants cannot grow.

40. Guo Yuanxing, p. 131, interprets *gu* 古 "ancient" as *hu* 怙 "rely on" and *yi* 埶 as *shi* 勢 "positional advantage." The graph for *yi* in "Observation" is the same as here, but it is written 藝 in the "Yue Yu xia." The 1976 editors take *yi* as an abbreviation for *nie* 槷 "post (set up as a gnomon to align the buildings of a palace)" according to the *Zhou Li* 周禮 "Kaogong ji" 考工記 "Jiangren" 匠人 (Carpenters), *Zhou Li zhengyi* 周禮正義 (hereafter *ZLZY*), ch. 82, ce 23, p. 84; Biot (1969), vol. 2, p. 554. The word for *gu* in the other two passages is *ren* 人 "others": *ren* also appears below, so quite probably *gu* is an error for *ren*. The grammar of

the sentence indicates that *gu* is the object of the verb *yi*. Guo's interpretation should, therefore, be rejected. *Yi* probably should be understood not as an abbreviation for *nie*, but as an alternate form of *yi* 藝, which means "art, skill, standard." The latter meaning seems perfectly reasonable in all three contexts, here, in "Observation," and in the "Yue Yu xia" passages.

41. The subject of the next sentences is the ruler.

42. *Zhou Li*, "Si Shi" 司士 *ZLZY*, ce 5, ch. 59, p. 2a, Zheng Xuan comments and defines *de* 德 as "the worthy" *xian zhe* 賢者. Cf. Biot (1969) vol. 2, p. 213.

43. Cf. *Lun Yu* 論語, Book 13, "Zilu" 子路 no. 29 (Cheng Shude 程樹德 ed., *Lun Yu jishi* 論語集釋 (hereafter *LYJS*), ce 3, ch. 27, p. 943, D. C. Lau trans. (1979), p. 123: "The Master said, 'After a good man has trained the common people for seven years, they should be ready to take up arms.'"

44. The taxes would appear to be imposts levied at the barriers and markets (see below).

45. Perhaps this means that the people will not be lucky enough to escape punishments for their crimes. Alternatively, it may mean that they will not trust to luck in their everyday dealings, but will abide by the law. The *WW* and 1980 editors read *xing* 幸 as an abbreviation of *xing* 倖 by which they perhaps mean that the sentence should be understood as "the people will not act as/have favorites." This interpretation is followed by Yu Mingguang (1993[a]).

46. Or, "love to make them work hard."

47. The editors read *fa* 發 "promulgate," i.e., "promulgate the prohibitions." I believe the graph is an abbreviation for *fei* 廢 "do away with." The prohibitions would be laws against taking the products of the mountains, woods, streams, marshes, and seas, which would normally all belong to the ruler himself. The people should be allowed to gather them without penalty.

48. For this system, see Robin D. S. Yates (1987), pp. 219–231.

49. For *she* 赦 "remit (crimes)/pardon/amnesty," see McLeod and Yates, p. 136, note 67.

50. The term *si jie* 死節 "die out of a sense of duty" also appears in the *HFZ* and the *HNZ*. The former reference appears in *pian* 26, "Shou Dao" 守道 (The Way of Defence), ce 2, p. 67, Liao trans., vol. I, p. 268, "As the ruler knows how to honour ranks and make rewards definite, he can make people apply their strength to the observance of the yard and weight, die in the cause of their official duties, understand the real desire of Pen and Yu not to choose the death penalty before a peaceful

life, and scrutinize the covetous acts of Robber Che so as not to ruin their characters for the sake of money." The latter reference is translated by Roger T. Ames (1983) pp. 185–186, "Even so King Wu with only three thousand armor-clad soldiers captured him [Zhou, last ruler of the Shang dynasty], at Muye. This was certainly not because the Zhou people died out of a sense of duty while the Yin people turned against their master. It was because their ruler was bountiful and righteous and his orders were carried out."

51. The 1976 editors say this refers to the people being linked into five- and ten-man groups mentioned above.

52. It is unclear what *shang jiu* 上九 means. Possibly *jiu* "nine" is a loan for *jiu* 就 "follow/go to," or for *jiu* 救 "help, rescue, aid." The 1980 editors interpret it as an abbreviation for *jiu* 仇 "harmonize."

53. The 1976 editors interpret *chi* 赿 as *fenlie* 分裂 "separate." Guo Yuanxing takes the graph as *che* 趆, which the *Yu Pian* 玉篇 defines as *qian* 牽 "lead"; this he explains as *qian che* 牽扯 "drag in, involve," i.e., superiors and inferiors do not shirk responsibility for each other or implicate each other in crimes. The 1980 editors take the graph as an alternative form of *chi* 斥 "censure/blame/scold."

54. This sentiment is paralleled in the *Shangjun shu* 商君書 (hereafter *SJS*) (Book of Lord Shang) *pian* 11, "Li Ben" 立本 (The Establishment of Fundamentals), Zhu Shiche (1974), p. 43; J. J. L. Duyvendak (1963), p. 247, "Generally, in the utilizing of soldiers, there are three stages to victory; prior to the outbreak of hostilities, laws should be fixed; laws being fixed, they should become the custom; when they have become customary, supplies should be provided."

55. The people obey the ruler because he allows them to perform their agricultural tasks at the proper season and only employs them in corvée labor projects in the off-season. He does not press them into service at inappropriate times of the year.

56. The ruler's rewards and punishments are appropriate (literally, "match, deserve") to the actions the people have undertaken, either good deeds or crimes.

57. In ancient times, people of different ranks were permitted to wear only those types of clothing deemed appropriate for their station. Sumptuary rules and laws were strictly enforced. *Yu* 逾 is a common legal term for all such transgressions of the laws and customs.

58. *Xing* 刑 means "mutilating punishment" accompanied by hard labor, whereas *fa* 罰 usually means "administrative punishment" in the form of fines, but it can have a more general denotation.

59. *Fan* 反 "turn (back), reversal" is an important concept in these texts, as it is in the *Laozi*. Book Two, ch. 50, reads (D. C. Lau trans. [1982], p. 101,

Turning back is how the way moves;

Weakness is the means the way employs.

The myriad creatures in the world are born from

Something, and Something from Nothing.

60. I.e., in performing agricultural tasks at the proper season and in the proper locations.

61. Tax terminology was highly complicated and changed over time. Nancy Lee Swann (1950), p. 373, suggests that in the *Han Shu fulian* 賦斂 may have been "a general term to cover poll taxes and all other government taxes, but it seems rather to be a term, or expression, to include two specific taxes, both of which went to the imperial treasury for military purposes." As the date of this text is not known for certain, the precise significance of the term *fulian* here is unclear. The authors mean that taxes should not be arbitrarily imposed, but should have rules or measures *(du)* for their application and collection.

62. A graph is probably missing above *ke* 苛 "harsh." The 1976 editors suggest it is *xing* 省 "reduce/economize."

63. I.e., conduct befitting Heaven, Earth, and Man as symbolized by the father and mother.

64. *Jian ai* 兼愛 "universal or inclusive (Ames's translation) love" was one of the fundamental concepts of Mohism. See Mei (1973), pp. 78–97, and Benjamin I. Schwartz (1985), p. 135 ff.

65. Li Xueqin (1993[b]) is probably correct in arguing, on the basis of the similarity of the graphic forms in the silk manuscripts of the words *da* 大 and *liu* 六, that the title is *Da Fen* 大分 "Great Distinctions," not *Liu Fen* 六分 "Six Distinctions," as the 1976 and 1980 editors claimed.

66. This sentence is similar to that in the *GZ pian* 23, "Ba Yan" 霸言 (Conversations of the Lord Protector), ch. 9, p. 144, Rickett (1985), p. 360, "Therefore, when observing a state [the clear-sighted king] observes/ its prince. When observing an army, he observes its generals."

67. The order seems to be wrong: it probably should read, "if you are able to be a ruler, then you are able to act on behalf of a state . . ."

68. From what follows, I suspect that *qi nü nan* 其女男 has been dropped from the text, although the editors do not say so.

69. In other words, they have appointments at the courts of other, possibly enemy, states.

70. The authors believe that the ruler should be the basis or foun-

dation of the state and the ministers should also be its roots. If the ministers below the ruler do not lose their posts, while the ruler loses his position, then they alone will be the roots of the state, usurping the ruler's power. For this reason, they maintain that, in such a situation, the state will be in jeopardy, but it will survive.

71. The editors interpret the graph 頯 as *pan* 頖 "name of a school," an alternate form of *pan* 泮 "dispersed, scattered." The editors believe that another situation has been dropped by the copyist below: the situation in which the ruler is disorderly and the ministers rebellious.

72. This refers to a situation in which a queen or some other female favorite gains equal prestige and power at the court. *HFZ*, *pian* 15, "Wang Zheng" 王徵 (Portents of Ruin), ce 2, ch. 5, p. 3, W. K. Liao trans., vol. 1, p. 139, states, "If the queen is adulterous, the sovereign's mother is corrupt, attendants inside and outside the court intercommunicate, and male and female have no distinction, such a regime is called 'bi-regal.' Any country having two rulers is liable to ruin."

73. The 1976 editors interpret *fei/fu* 曊, an alternate form of 怫 "light, bleached and dried object," as *fu* 拂 "oppose, contradict, defy." The 1980 editors suspect it should be read as *bei* 悖 "go against."

74. This interpretation follows that of the editors, who take *lin* 閵 "trample" as a loan for *lin* 鄰 "close/neighbor." "Trample" may, however, be correct, and the sentence might be translated "and (the state) will share in misfortune and will be trampled upon."

75. In other words, there will be internal rebellion and civil war and enemy states will also attack from the outside.

76. See "A Lord's Government," note 53 above.

77. I.e., manages or controls the rules and regulations.

78. The *WW* and 1976 editors read *bi* 楅 "wooden piece (put on the horns of an ox to prevent it from harming people)" as *fu* 輻 "spokes of a wheel." The 1976 editors interpret *shu* 屬 "belong/attach" as *cou* 湊 "collect, come together," as in the *HNZ* "Zhu Shu Xun" 主術訓 (The Art of Rulership), ch. 9, p. 7a and ch. 9, p. 8a. Ames translates the first passage, p. 178, "As a result, the various ministers will converge on him (the ruler), side by side like spokes at the hub" . . . The second passage is translated somewhat differently.

79. This perhaps should be interpreted as "the superior type of ruler" in contrast to "he who knows the art of true kingship," "he who does not know the art of true kingship," and "he who rules the world as a true king" below. Alternatively, *shang* 上 "above" is an interpolation from the phrase *zhu shang* 主上 below. This would be reasonable if the

silk manuscript copyist was transcribing from a bamboo or wooden slip version of the text, for the words are separated by approximately 96+ graphs. This would constitute a separation of three slips of 32 graphs each: in ancient times to have 30–33 graphs per slip was very common (see Yates 1979).

80. One graph is indecipherable, which the 1976 editors interpret as *xin* 信 "trustworthy, reliable" on the basis of the *HFZ, pian* 36, "Nan yi" 難一 (Criticisms of the Ancients, series one), ce 3, ch. 15, p. 81, W. K. Liao trans., vol. 2, p. 146, "As bestowal and reward are sure and censure and punishment are definite, the ruler can raise ministers of merit and no crook can join governmental service." This is possible, but the *HFZ* sentence and the present context are not precisely parallel. However, the present sentence could be translated, "to give life to those who are being killed, to reward [the faithful], and (to punish) those who must be attacked (or punished)."

81. The desire for the utopia of "Grand Peace" became increasingly popular in the Han and later dynasties, particularly with Daoist millennarian sects and scholars who followed the New Text school of interpretation of the Confucian Spring and Autumn Annals at the end of the Qing dynasty in the late nineteenth century. See Timoteus Pokora (1961), pp. 448–454, and Kaltenmark (1979).

82. As opposed to the "dark potency" mentioned below.

83. Heaven covers over and Earth upholds. In his person, the true king manifests the capabilities and actions of the three primary constituent parts of the cosmos, Heaven, Earth, and Man.

84. Probably the graph *xia* 下 has dropped out below *tian* 天, according to the 1976 and 1980 editors. The *WW* editors supply the graph without indicating that it is an addition.

85. In other words, they do not keep the ruler in ignorance about matters of state interest or policy, nor do they take the credit themselves for successful initiatives: they allow the ruler's majesty to shine forth brilliantly.

86. The phrase "harmonious and compliant" appears in the *GZ pian* 10, "Wu Fu" 五輔 (The Five Aids), ch. 3, p. 48; Rickett (1985), p. 197, translates, ". . . younger brothers submissive in their respect . . ."

87. This could be interpreted as "ruler and superiors."

88. Possibly, this should be translated, "the world has no enemies" or "he (i.e., the ruler) has no match."

89. I.e., to the lowest orders of society or the general mass of the population.

90. The meaning of the second graph is in doubt: see the note on the term in "The Four Measures," note 111.

91. There is a direct parallel to this sentence in *GY* "Yue Yu xia," ch. 21, p. 4b, "A true king, in the galloping of his horses and hunting with stringed arrows, does not go so far as the beast-infested wastelands, and, in the entertainment in his palaces, does not go so far as to be debauched in his drink." Of course, the "beast-infested wastelands" should be interpreted both physically and figuratively: the ruler never for one moment forgets government business. The "entertainment" would primarily be music played by nubile girls, for the graph for "music" is the same as that for "pleasure or entertainment."

92. This term appears in the *Laozi* Book One, section 10; D. C. Lau trans., p. 66:

It gives life to them and rears them.
It gives them life yet claims no possession;
It benefits them yet exacts no gratitude;
It is the steward yet exercises no authority.
Such is called the mysterious virtue *(xuande)*.

93. It is unclear whether *xian/xuan guo* 縣國 should be understood as a single term "appended kingdoms" or as two terms, as the present translation renders it.

94. Heaven covers over and Earth upholds: the true king forms a triad with Heaven and Earth and does what they do.

95. This statement is similar to those in the *Yi Jing* 易經, "Xi Ci shang" 繫辭上 (Gao Heng 1979) p. 513, "It (the *Yi*, according to Gao, but possibly the Great Man or sage, the subject of the previous verses) completes all the myriad phenomena, and makes no omissions," and *Xunzi* 荀子(hereafter *XZ*) "Chen Dao" 臣道 (The Dao of a Minister) *pian* 13 *(Xunzijijie* 荀子集解, *Guoxue jiben congshu* ed.), ce 3, p. 13.

96. These "measures" are the four related pairs "lord and subject," "worthy and worthless," "movement and rest," and "life and death."

97. Cf. *HNZ* "Bing Lüe Xun" 兵略訓 (Planning Warfare) ch. 15, p. 7b, "Those who move and are active all around, are long and short, bend and stretch, and can be crafty and deceitful, none of them are experts (at warfare)."

98. Possibly this means "It enters and takes up position; it exits and reverts."

99. In other words, to accord with the appropriate seasons of Heaven and the proper benefits of Earth, as the 1976 editors comment.

100. The 1976 editors have reconstructed the two indecipherable

graphs as *shigua* 實寡 on the basis of the occurrence of the clause *shenghua shigua* 聲華實寡 "when (a ruler's) reputation is magnificent, but the reality is slight (our metaphor is "hollow reputation")" in "Assessing Destruction" below. However, an opposite meaning is required here. Hu Xintian (1984) reconstructs the phrase as *shun zheng* 順正 "compliance is correct."

101. The meaning of *yong* 用 "use" is obscure as a result of the lacuna.

102. The 1976 editors take *da* 達 as a loan for *tuo* 脫 "lenient." This phrase also appears in "Wang Lun" (Assessing Destruction) and "Bing Rong" (The Features of Warfare) below. Guo Yuanxing also finds examples in early texts such as the *Shi Jing* 詩經 "Zheng Feng" 鄭風 and the *Yi Jing* where *da* has the sense of "relax, be lenient." The 1980 editors take *da* as a loan for *tai* 汰 "eliminate/remove." *Wang Lun* (Assessing Destruction), however, defines *da xing* 達刑 as "to attack those who deserve to be held guilty of a crime, to see profit and to bring it back"; in other words, not only to inflict the deserved punishment, but to pillage the enemy also, an act which is inappropriate and immoral. *Da* must mean "extend."

103. The 1976 editors interpret this clause as "If you go against opposition in harmonizing with the Matching of Heaven."

104. Because Yang is associated with life and Yin is associated with death.

105. As above, "inside" means "inside the state," and "outside" means "outside the state's borders/abroad."

106. Presumably Yang should be used on the inside and Yin on the outside. Both should be used, but only at the appropriate seasons and under the appropriate circumstances.

107. According to the 1976 and 1980 editors, the graph *shang* 上 "on top of" has probably been inadvertently omitted. The latter also suggest that the words "between the marking-line is called straight" *sheng zhi zhong yue zhi* 繩之中曰直, on the basis of a quotation found at the beginning of the *Mozi* ch. 1 *pian* 4, "Fa Yi" 法儀: "The hundred artisans make squares by means of set-squares; they make circles by means of compasses; they make straight (lines) by means of marking-lines; they level by means of suspending (weights)." This interpretation is possible, see note 108 below.

108. In actual fact, as the 1976 editors point out, only seven measures have been mentioned: one has obviously dropped from the list.

109. This could be interpreted "the true king publicly . . ."

110. The 1976 editors suggest that they are those mentioned above "who deserve being held guilty of a crime and deserve destruction."

111. The 1976 editors state that the graph *ren* 刃 is confused with 刃 in the silk manuscripts, and that 刃, is the same as *chuang* 創 "start." Another opinion is that *ren* should be read as *ren* 牣 "fill up." I.e., "you use martiality to the full." See "Great Distinctions," note 90 above.

112. The 1976 editors quote Jia Yi 賈誼, *Xin Shu* 新書 "Da Zheng shang" 大政上 (Great Government A) (*Sibu congkan* ed.), ch. 9, p. 2b, where madness is defined as knowing the good but not carrying it out, and folly as knowing one is being spiritually ugly but not changing. The 1976 and 1980 editors suggest that the second *chu* 處 "place/ locate" is a mistake for *er* 而 "and."

113. The graph for *qi* 六 "his, its, hers" is close in shape to that of *shi* 失 "lose" in the silk manuscripts. The 1976 editors believe that here "his" is a mistake for "lose."

114. The difference between the ideas of this text and that of the *Laozi* should be noted here: the *Laozi* advocates that the ruler adhere to the "soft and weak" in order to gain ultimate control, power, and victory. This belief is not shared by the authors of the *Jing Fa*.

115. The 1976 editors read *fancai* 燔材 "burning talent" as *fanzai* 蕃載 "luxurious activities." The 1980 editors interpret it as *fanzai* 繁載, with the same meaning. Guo Yuanxing, however, p. 132, argues that *fan* is the same as *fen* 焚 "burn," and *cai* is the same graph as *cai* 財 "wealth": thus, "wasting wealth . . ." This latter interpretation seems more reasonable in the context, and in the light of similar sentiments in "Ming Li" (Names and Principles).

116. In other words, it will not be able to stave off defeat at the hands of either internal or external enemies.

117. Elsewhere, it is said that the ruler "forms a triad" *can* 參 = *san* 三 with Heaven and Earth, but it is impossible to tell whether this is the missing word or not.

118. According to the 1980 editors, the "Eight Regulators" are the positions of inner and outer, the transformations of movement and quiescence, and the regularities of the four seasons.

119. The One is probably the Dao, the Two are Yin and Yang, and the Three are Heaven, Earth, and Man.

120. *Qi Fa* is also the title of *pian* 7 of the *Guanzi* (Rickett 1985, pp. 125–135, translates the term "The Seven Standards"), but they are not the same as in this text.

121. These same phrases occur in the *HNZ* ch. 1, "Yuan Dao Xun"

元道訓 (The Original Dao), and "Shu Zhen Xun" 俶眞訓 (Beauty and Truth) ch. 2, p. 1b, in reverse order.

122. The One must be the Dao, and the Three refers to the sun, the moon, and the stars, according to the 1976 editors.

123. Our metaphor would be "rises and sets." These statements also appear in the *He Guanzi* 鶡冠子 (hereafter *HGZ*) *pian* 10, "Tai Hong" 太鴻 (Grand Vastness) (*SBBY* ed.), ch. B, p. 16a.

124. Our metaphor would be "waxes and wanes."

125. This passage is very similar to one in the *HGZ, pian* 10, "Tai Hong" (Grand Vastness).

126. The 1976 editors interpret the Two as brightness, i.e., day, and darkness, i.e., night. Yang and Yin are the names of the two cosmic forces that manifest themselves as lightness and darkness.

127. The 1976 editors understand "Heaven" (*tian* 天) as "nature" or "the self-so," "the natural" (*ziran* 自然) and "measure" as the "norm/standard" (*zhunze* 准則). They state that the meaning is that the changes and development of nature have definite rules and this logic is only natural.

128. The 1976 editors state that the Seven Models are: to brighten in order to correct, appropriateness, faithfulness, to go to the pole (limit) and then turn back, necessity, and two items lost in the lacuna.

129. These definitions are similar to those found in *GZ pian* 30, "Jun Chen shang" 君臣上 (Ruler and Subject A), ch. 10, p. 165: "For this reason, to separate what is connected and to correct distinctions is called 'Principle'; to follow principle without fail is called 'Dao'."

130. Possibly *ming* 命 "mandate" should be understood here as *ming* 名 "name."

131. The five graphs missing have been supplied by the 1976 editors on the basis of the same utterance found in the *SJS* (Book of Lord Shang) *pian* 4 (The Elimination of Strength) (Zhu Shiche [1974], ch. 1, p. 19). Duyvendak (1963), p. 204, translates the passage, "Punishment produces force, force produces strength, strength produces awe, awe produces kindness. Kindness has its origin in force." The 1976 editors also suggest that *hui* 惠 "kindness" is a loan for *hui* 慧 "cleverness," but this is not necessary.

132. The *WW* editors considered that one graph was indecipherable and added the graph *jian* 見 "seeing." The 1976 editors, on the other hand, read the indecipherable graph as *ji* 極 "limit/pole," without comment, and supplied *jian* also. Just possibly the sentence should be translated, "The utmost spirituality reaches the limit, and sees and knows

without being confused." This sentence is practically the same as a passage in *HGZ*, ch. A, *pian* 6, "Dao Duan" 道端 (The Principles of the Dao), pp. 16ab: "The utmost limit of spirituality is seeing without being confused."

133. In other words, the four compass points.

134. Revolution in its original, not its modern, technical, sense. See below.

135. These states are those that are about to perish and those that will continue to survive.

136. The silk manuscript has a reduplicated *yi yue* 一曰 below *zheng ming* 正名 "correction of names." The 1976 editors interpret *yan* 偃 "stop/cease" as a loan for *an* 安 "stabilize/fix," but this is unnecessary. They interpret this in a strictly political way, that lord and minister, superior and inferior each keep to their position. The "correction of names" certainly includes this aspect, but probably should be understood more broadly, in an almost cosmic ontological sense, that all things, all phenomena in the world, are to keep to their respective positions to which they have been assigned by their names.

137. Possibly, "the models/laws and names are perverted." The 1976 editors read *yi* 倚 "incline to one side" as *qi* 欹 "incorrect," which is possible. The passage is similar to the *GZ, pian* 12, "Shu Yan" 樞言 (Cardinal Sayings), ch. 4, p. 66. Rickett (1985), p. 223, translates, "When these terms are correctly adhered to, there is good order; when they are distorted, disorder prevails. If there is no terminology at all, death ensues. Therefore the former kings valued terminology." *GZ, pian* 38, "Bai Xin" 白心 (Purifying the Heart-mind), ch. 13, p. 224, also states, "Correct names put themselves in order; perverted names destroy themselves; when names are correct and laws prepared, then the sage has no business to attend to" (i.e., the world is in good order and so the sage ruler has nothing to do). Shen Buhai 申不害 ("Da Ti" 大體 [The Main Substance]), further states, "In ancient times, Yao ruled the world by means of names; Shun also ruled the world by means of names: if their names had been perverted, the world would have been in chaos." Later, *HFZ* elaborated in *pian* 8, "Yang Quan" 揚權 (Wielding the Sceptre), ce 1, ch. 2 (cf. Liao, vol. 1, p. 53), "If you use the Dao of the One, consider names first. If names are correct, things are fixed; if names are perverted, things are shifted."

138. The 1980 editors suggest that the two words *siguo* 死國 "dead state" should probably be reduplicated on the basis of the reduplication of *shengguo* 生國 "living state" below.

139. There appears to be a problem in the text in the last two lines, as the recommendations seem to be in conflict with the ideas expressed immediately below, that "affairs settle themselves." The 1976 editors are probably right in thinking that the last word *jing* 靜 "quiescent" is a mistake. They take it as *zheng* 爭 "fight," but it may be another graph entirely, for the copyist may have been distracted by the *jing* appearing at the end of the previous sentence. If their interpretation is not correct, then *bu* 不 "not" above the second "correspond" should possibly be excised and *jing* might be correct: "If names and realities correspond, then be quiet."

140. The *Shizi* 尸子 "Fen" 分 (Distinctions) states, "Grasp the One by means of quiescence; let names correct themselves, let affairs settle themselves." Many other texts, such as the *HFZ*, the *GZ*, and the work of Shen Buhai have similar sentiments.

141. The term "Eliminating Principles" is defined below as "to start great earth(-moving) projects in the summer," when agricultural work is at its busiest.

142. For the definition of the Six Dangers, see below.

143. For the definition of the Three Crimes against the Innocent, see below.

144. Possibly *zhi jun* 之君 "ruler of" should be excised from the text.

145. For the Three Blockages, see below.

146. The Three Evils are explained below.

147. The 1976 editors say that "superiors" means "rulers," which is a possible interpretation.

148. Normally *xing* 刑 means "mutilating punishment." The "inferiors" are officials according to the 1976 editors, but usually mutilating punishments were only applied to ordinary commoners, not to officials with rank and position. It is probably better to take the terms in their normal senses, and take "superiors" as officials and "inferiors" as the lower orders of society.

149. The 1976 editors interpret this as "military accomplishments," but it is not necessary to be so specific.

150. The 1976 editors understand *ming* 名 "fame" as the "system of ranking" and *jin* 禁 as "prohibit," but do not state how the whole clause is to be interpreted. They also state that *wang* 王 "to be a true king, rule" is an abbreviation for *wang* 旺, which they define as *xingwang* 興旺 "flourishing." The precise meaning of the sentence is unclear.

151. The 1976 editors suggest that *ru* 襦 "jacket" is a loan for *ru* 繻.

The latter term appears in the *Han Shu,* ch. 64B, p. 7b, "Biography of Zhong Jun" 終軍 where Zhang Yan 張晏 comments that "*ru* means to match as a tally (*fu* 符). You write on silk, rip it, and divide it in two like a contract (*quan* 券) or bond (*qi* 契)." Su Lin 蘇林, on the other hand, defines *ru* as "border of silk," but again specifies that the silk is ripped and used as a contract or passport for entering or leaving the control points at the frontiers. The term *ru* also appears in *Observation* below. The 1976 editors interpret the phrase to mean that such people easily abandon the promises they have made in good faith. It appears to me that the authors of the text are skeptical about those who insist on trusting to written promises and contracts: if they were *really* trustworthy, they would not need such outward signs of faithfulness. Cf. *Laozi,* Book 2, section 63 (Lau, p. 124), "One who makes promises rashly rarely keeps good faith."

152. This term is defined below.

153. The 1976 editors argue that *yongguo* 用國 is the opposite of *shouguo* 守國 and refers to a state that uses arms and therefore is a state that engages in offensive warfare, whereas the opposite type of state merely adopts a defensive strategy.

154. Literally, "conduct opposing the regulations." The phrase occurs in both the *GY* "Yue Yu xia" and in the *GZ* "Shi" 勢 (Positional Advantage).

155. In other words, Heaven will terminate the life of a ruler who engages in or permits illicit behavior, and will not let him live out the time-span which he was originally allotted.

156. On the basis of virtually the same phrase in the *Shuo Yuan jiao-zheng* 說苑校證, ch. 16, "Tan Cong" 談叢 (Collection of Conversations), p. 388, the 1976 editors correctly suggest that *huo* 禍 "misfortune" is a mistake for *fu* 福 "good fortune."

157. The 1976 editors explain this clause as "having no real ability"; presumably "a ruler" is the implied subject. The same terms can be found in "The Four Measures" above.

158. The summer is, of course, the busiest season of the agricultural year for peasants. They would be unable to complete their tasks if they were conscripted by the state for large construction projects at that time. The prohibition is also to be found in the "Yue Ling" 月令 (Monthly Ordinances) of the *LSCQ* and *Li Ji.* A similar stricture is recommended in the Yinqueshan text *Jin* 禁 (Prohibitions) (Wu Jiulong [1985], slip 0348) (see Yates 1994[a]).

159. This statement occurs at the beginning of the chapter. Perhaps

it is a mistaken reduplication, but it could be conceived of as a summary of the previous discussion. Alternatively, the following section is a later commentary or explication of the ideas expressed in the previous passage.

160. This appears in the section "Great Distinctions" above.

161. One graph missing, possibly *li* 離 "abandon," on the basis of the similar statement in "Great Distinctions" above. There, however, the text reads *qun* 群 "massed/assembled," rather than *mou* 謀 "plan." I suspect that *qun* is probably correct. The second and third of the Six Dangers were called the "Blocking Obstruction" in the earlier chapter.

162. The feudal lords are subordinate to the ruler: he should take complete responsibility for appointments in their territories and not delegate responsibility to them. The right to make such appointments was an extremely sensitive political issue in the early Han dynasty, and the central government was only able to insist upon its rights of appointment after crushing the Revolt of the Seven Kingdoms in 154 B.C.E.

163. The term *bizhou* 比周 also appears in the *HFZ, pian* 11, "Gu Fen" 孤憤 (Solitary Indignation), ce 1, ch. 4, p. 54. Liao, vol. I, p. 100, translates the passage, "However friends and partisans who form juntas on purpose to delude the sovereign and twist their words so as to benefit themselves, always win the confidence of the heavyhanded men (i.e., important people)." It also appears in *XZ, pian* 13, "Chen Dao" (The Way of a Minister), ce 3, p. 13, and as *zhou bi* in *HNZ*, ch. 9, p. 10a. The cabal not only restricts information reaching the ruler, but also prevents his orders from being carried out.

164. *HFZ, pian* 9, "Ba Jian" 八姦 (Eight Villainies), ce 1, ch. 2, p. 36, Liao, vol. 1, p. 63, translates rather loosely, "What is meant by 'through the entertainment of uncles and brothers'? In reply I say: Sons by concubines are much loved by the sovereign; prime ministers and court officials are consulted by the sovereign." As Liao points out, the "elder brothers" are likely to be the ruler's half brothers. The text's *fei* (?) 僙 an otherwise unknown graph, should be understood as an alternate form for *fu* 咈, i.e., *fu* 拂/曊 "oppose/contradict/defy." In "Great Distinctions," the graph used was *fei/fu* 曊 (see note 73 above).

165. The clause, "to murder the three types of innocent people" also occurs in the *LSCQ*, ch. 16, "Xian Shi Lan" 先識覽 (Prefigurations), no. 1 "Xian Shi," p. 1b.

166. In other words, the empress and the retinue of concubines, eunuchs, etc.

167. In other words, the courtiers, officials, etc.

168. See note 164 above.

169. The missing graph quite probably is *zei* 賊 "wanton murder, treason" as the 1976 editors suggest, for practically the same words appear in the *Shi Ji* 史記 "Li Si liezhuan" 李斯列傳 (Biography of Li Si) (Zhonghua shuju ed., 1985), ch. 87, p. 2250; Bodde (1967), p. 30.

170. The editors correctly interpret *sui* 遂 "follow" as *zhu* 逐 "pursue," for this is the way *sui* is written in the silk manuscript of the *Yi Jing*. The second graph is unclear: the *WW* and 1976 editors interpret it as *zheng* 諍 "expostulate with," the 1980 editors interpret it as *jing* 靜 "quiescent." All understand it as a loan for *zheng* 爭 "struggle, compete with, fight." The term *zhu zheng* appears in the *Han Shu* "Shi Huo Zhi" 食貨志 (Treatise on Food and Money) ch. 24B, p. 6b, cf. Nancy Lee Swann (1950), p. 239.

171. I.e., other than the ruler.

172. The 1976 and 1980 editors are correct to point out that the graph *zhu* 主 between *ren* 人 and *shan* 擅 is a mistaken reduplication. *Shan* 擅 "on one's own authority" is a technical legal term which appears frequently in the Qin laws and passages in the Mohist military chapters concerned with legal matters.

173. A similar sentiment is expressed in the *HFZ, pian* 30, "Nei Chu Shuo shang 內儲說上, Qi Shu 七術" (Inner Congeries of Sayings, The Upper Series: Seven Tracts), ce 2, ch. 9, p. 77; Liao, vol. 1, p. 286, "Indeed, the sun shines upon everything under the heaven while nothing can cover it; the ruler of men reigns over all the country while nobody can delude him. Accordingly, who sees the lord of men in dreaming, dreams the sun. In the case of a cooking stove, however, if one person stands before it, then nobody from behind can see. Now supposing someone were standing before Your Highness, would it not be possible for thy servant to dream of a cooking stove?"

174. As above, the inner is the inner court, composed of the empress, etc. The outer refers to the officials, etc. When the two courts collude against the ruler, he will be deposed and another will be placed on the throne.

175. These are weapons. The term appears in the *GY* "Yue Yu xia," ch. 21, p. 1b. The *Laozi* (Book One, section 31), p. 71 (Lau, p. 89), calls weapons "instruments of ill-omen."

176. *GY* "Yue Yu xia," ch. 21, p. 1b, defines *yong* 勇 "courage" as the "oppositional virtue": one should let things follow their course, not try to force changes through acts of courage contrary to the natural processes.

177. In other words, the attacker not only carries out the justified

punishment on the guilty party, here probably a state, but proceeds to plunder it as well, bringing the proceeds ("profit") back home, compounding or "extending" the punishment.

178. *Fu* 父, literally family members in the father's generation, including the father; *xiong* 兄 means elders in one's own generation.

179. *Yue* 約 basically means "to tie" and by extension "to bind by agreement." Graham (1980: 485), translates the name of an allegorical figure called "Wu Yue" "Nowhere committed."

180. *Wen* 文 is defined in "The Four Measures" above as "to move and be quiescent, forming a triad with Heaven and Earth." *Wu* 武 is defined as "to punish . . . in a timely fashion." In "A Lord's Government," on the other hand, *wen* is defined as "to rely on Heaven's (season of) life to nourish the living"; *wu* is defined as "to rely on Heaven's (season of) killing to attack the dying."

181. The 1976 editors state that the three seasons are spring, summer, and autumn, and the one season is winter. This statement is similar to one in the *HGZ*, ch. B, p. 16a, *pian* 10, "Taihong" (Grand Vastness), p. 16a.

182. The 1976 editors state that this means that the four seasons change according to the season and *ding* 定 "fix" means to be precise and accurate.

183. *Te* 忒 means "err by excess, by going too far"; *shuang* 爽 means "err by shortage, by not going far enough."

184. Possibly *gu* 故 "therefore, in consequence" should be interpreted as an alternate form for *gu* 固 "assuredly, definitely."

185. In other words, to engage in excessive construction projects exhausting the strength of the people in corvée labor exactions.

186. The 1976 editors interpret *di* 氐 as an abbreviation of *di* 抵 "oppose/make good," which they define as "match/deserve." Guo Yuanxing (p. 132), however, argues that *di* is an abbreviation of *di* 底, which means *zhi* 致 "cause to arrive/bring about." The latter interpretation seems more appropriate. "Criminal conduct" is, literally, "the tally of opposition," which appears in "Rules for Conduct" note 389 below. A similar idea is expressed in *GZ pian* 42, "Shi" (Positional Advantage), ch. 15, p. 252: "When the sprouts of criminal conduct arise and Heaven and Earth have not yet punished it, first prepare a policy (to deal with it), and then the affair will not succeed. Errors will receive punishment."

187. The *sangong* (literally, "three dukes") were the titles given the chief ministers of the state: either the *sima* 司馬 (Chief of Horse), *situ* 司徒 (Chief of Foot-soldiers), and *sikong* 司空 (Chief of Workers), or *taishi* 太師 (Grand Army Chief), *taifu* 太傅 (Grand Teacher), and *taibao*

太保 (Grand Protector). At the beginning of "The Nine Rulers" below, Yi Yin is given the position of *sangong* by Tang, the first ruler of the Shang dynasty, which implies a single position.

188. The 1976 editors interpret this clause to mean, "the world receives their transformative instruction."

189. The same statement can be found in the *Guiguzi* 鬼谷子 "Wai Pian" 外篇 "Ben Jing Yin Fu qi pian" 本經陰符七篇 (Basic Canon: Seven Sections on the Hidden Tally) (Xiao Dengfu 1990, p. 247), "Now Dao is the source of spirituality and brightness." Where "Names and Principles" writes the graph *yuan* 原, the *Guiguzi* adds the "water" radical: 源. The *HGZ, pian* 10, ch. B, p. 15a, states that "Heaven is what spirituality and brightness are rooted in." Graham (1981) translates *shenming* 神明 as "daemonic and illumined."

190. Here, the 1976 editors interpret *du* as *fadu* "moral standards/laws."

191. The 1976 and 1980 editors state that the first two graphs *dong er* 動而 are perhaps redundant and the sentence should read, "It is quiescent, but does not shift." This is possible.

192. A similar passage in *GZ pian* 49, "Nei Ye" 內業 (Inner Training), ch. 16, p. 270, reads, "For this reason, the sage changes with the times, but does not transform; he follows things but does not shift. He is able to be correct, he is able to be quiescent: after that he is able to be firm/stable (*ding*)." Cf. Rickett (1965), p. 160.

193. I.e., a material object or phenomenon. The 1976 editors and Yu Mingguang (1993[a]) say that *you wu* 有物 refers to the Dao, but this does not fit with the following argument.

194. In "Assessing Essentials" above, the "Completion of Opposition" was defined as "to nourish the dying and to attack the living."

195. In these texts, it is usually a ruler who is the object of discussion, but this could refer to any individual. What the text seems to be saying is that by the nature of things, the ordinary ruler is not able to penetrate the Dao. As a result, things in a general ontological sense, and troubles in a particular sense start to arise. As the ruler then is in opposition to the Dao, he is punished by Heaven or the Dao.

196. This is a difficult sentence, and reads, literally, "as though heated, as though quenched . . . as though submissive, as though conceited . . ." The 1980 editors interpret *zu* 卒 "complete/soldier" as an abbreviation of *cui* 淬 "quench"; Yu Mingguang (1993[a]) takes *shi* 事 "affairs" as a loan for *si* 死 "death," to parallel *sheng* 生 "life" below. *You/yao* 繇 literally means "forced labor." The 1980 editors interpret the graph as an alternate

form of *you* 由 "follow," a usage common in Qin and Han excavated texts. Yu Mingguang (1993[a]) takes it as an alternate form of *yao* 繇 "happy." The 1980 editors interpret *jiao* 驕 "arrogant/proud" as an alternate form of *jiao* 矯 "strong/pretend/rectify."

197. The 1976 editors read *cai* 財 "goods, wealth" as *cai* 材 "talents/materials."

198. The editors interpret *tiao* 絩 "skein of silk thread" as *tiao/diao* 佻 "quick/provoke/frivolous." The phrase *tiao chang* 佻長 appears in the *HNZ* "Zhu Shu Xun," ch. 9, p. 15a; Ames (1983), p. 193, translates it as "good appearance."

199. The 1976 editors say that this clause means, "as their lives are very quick, so will their deaths be also." I suspect that this paragraph, which consists of 31 graphs, is an ancient commentary, one bamboo slip long, that has been incorporated into the text. Essentially the meaning is that humans as well as all living things are not quiescent and are separated from the constant Dao. They die because they behave in utterly contradictory ways, first blowing hot, then blowing cold, following their own desires in a vain attempt to gain satisfaction. By participating in the endless flow of reversal *(fan)* of phenomenal things, they bring about their own destruction.

200. The three probably refer to the types of individuals described in the previous paragraph but one.

201. The editors interpret *gua* 桰 "carpenter's frame" as an alternate form for *huo* 活 "live." Guo Yuanxing, however, reaffirms the correctness of the original graph, saying it should be understood as *yingua* 檃桰, the bevel used by carpenters. To bend straight wood is called *yin*, to straighten bent wood is called *gua*. This sentence refers to something being hard and then it is steamed to become soft; although it is curved, it can be straightened, although it is bent, it necessarily will be stretched like a curved piece of wood that can be bevelled and made straight. This is possible, but too complicated and unnecessary, for the parallel verb is *fa* "be attacked": the authors seem to prefer the position of softness, a preference also found in the *Laozi*.

202. *Fu* "tallies" were used to give official authority or permission for a person to act. Made out of two matching pieces, the ruler or higher official kept one half, the individual being given the permission, the other. When the two pieces were placed together, the individual could proceed to carry out his task.

203. The 1976 and 1980 editors suspect that the second *ming* 名 "names" is redundant. If they are correct, the sentence would read, "To

fully investigate and examine the beginnings and ends of the principles and names . . ."

204. See "The Four Measures" above.

205. A similar statement is to be found in *HFZ pian* 8, "Yang Quan," ce 1, ch. 2, p. 32 (cf. Liao, vol. 1, p. 58), "When you blend and harmonize forms and names, the people will then hold fast to their occupations"; *HFZ*'s *zhou* 周 is probably an abbreviation of this text's *diao* 調, according to the 1980 editors.

206. The 1976 editors suggest that *zai* 災 "disaster" is a mistake for *fu* 福 "good fortune," but, if they are correct, the words "abandon their (stands=) positions" makes little sense. The point is that no misfortune or calamity will strike one who truly understands the correct application of forms and names.

207. Cf. *HNZ,* ch. 9, p. 2b, where the graph is also *jing* (Ames, 1983, p. 171).

208. Interpreting with the editors on the basis of *HNZ,* ch. 13, "Fan Lun Xun" 氾論訓, p. 9b, and other texts. The *WW* editors punctuate differently.

209. *Nize* 逆則, literally "oppositional rules," is the same as *nijie* 逆節 "criminal conduct" in "Assessing Destruction" and "Assessing Essentials" above.

210. In other words, when the ruler and the elite engage in conduct opposed to the Dao.

211. The 1976 editors offer two alternative interpretations: either *guo ju* 國舉 should be inverted and the sentence should read, "If you take up a state . . . ," or that *ju* means *ce hua* 策劃 "plan/scheme."

212. I.e., gain a reputation.

2. THE CANON

213. As in the previous texts, the title appears at the end, in column 80A.

214. *Huangzong* 黃宗 (Yellow Ancestral Model) is an alternative title for the Yellow Emperor, Huangdi. The 1976 editors observe that the clause "for this reason he is able to be the ancestral model (*zong* 宗) for the world" appears below; the 1980 editors interpret *huangzong* as the ancestral temple (*miao* 廟) of the Yellow Emperor. They point out that the description below of the Yellow Emperor facing in four directions is similar to the ritual structure known as the Bright Hall (*mingtang*

明堂). It is well known, however, that there was a popular belief that the Yellow Emperor did indeed possess four faces, each facing in a different direction, so it is not necessary to equate *zong* with the actual physical structure of the ancestral temple. The author(s) of these texts do seem to have believed that the Yellow Emperor was a kind of primal originator of things, so it would have been natural to think of him as possessing and, in some senses, inhabiting his own ancestral temple.

215. The 1976 and 1980 editors suggest that perhaps *zhi* 質 "essential substance" is a loan for *shi* 實 "truly." Yu Mingguang (1993[a]) is probably right in keeping the original word: "essentially," i.e., according to his original basic nature.

216. The 1980 editors interpret *xin* 信 "trustworthiness" as *xun* 訊 "investigate/ask questions," but there seems to be no real justification for reading the graph in this way. He wished to be trusted so that he could act as a model for the world.

217. The 1976 and 1980 editors interpret *zuo* 作 as *shi* 始 "begin/start." *Zuo* in the texts has the meaning of initiating conscious action, as opposed to *jing* 靜, which means "quiescence."

218. Yu Mingguang (1993[a]) interprets *zi* 自 "self" as *ziran* 自然 "naturally," but this is not necessary: it is the direct object of "make."

219. It was believed that the Yellow Emperor possessed four faces so that he was able to see and hear everything that was happening in all directions. The *Shizi* states "Zigong (a disciple of Confucius) said, 'Of old, the Yellow Emperor was four-faced: is that believable?'"; *LSCQ*, ch. 14, no. 2 "Ben Wei" 本味 (Original Flavors), p. 4a, says, "Therefore the Yellow Emperor established four faces (for himself)."

220. The 1976 editors suggest that *fu* 傅 "teach" is an alternate form for *fu* 輔 "assist/add to/be close to" or a loan for *fu* 附 "add/attach." Yu Mingguang (1993[a]) interprets it as an alternate form for *fu* 敷 "spread/publish."

221. Both the 1976 and 1980 editors believe that *cen/shen/can* 參 is to be understood as *san* 三 "three," a common usage, and that the sentence is referring to the twelve points of the compass. This is possible, but it seems better to take the word as *can*, for this explains how he "supplemented his heart-mind" in understanding the conditions pertaining in all directions.

222. The 1976 editors interpret *lü* 履 as "move around, following the directions," in other words the four directions that the Yellow Emperor faced. Yu Mingguang (1993[a]) interprets *lü* as a loan for *li* 禮 "ritual practice" and *can* 參 as *san* 三 "three," explaining that it means

that he was modest time and time again, strictly following ritual practice. These interpretations are unnecessarily complex.

223. Probably the copyist dropped the words *Huangzong yue* 黃宗曰 or *Huangdi yue* 黃帝曰 from the text. Quite possibly he was working from a text written on bamboo slips that had 44 graphs to the slip. These words would have been located at the end of the first slip and so missed his attention.

224. Literally, "name." The 1980 editors observe the similarity of this statement with that of the *HGZ* ch. C, *pian* 12, "Shi Bing" 世兵 (Modern Warfare), p. 3b, "(He who obtains the Dao of being excellent in warfare) receives numbers from Heaven, establishes his position on Earth, and gains his reputation from Man."

225. The kings would be heads of the controlling dynasty, and the *Sangong* their principal assistants; the states would be the polities subordinate to those kings, and the three noble ministers the chief assistants to the rulers of those states.

226. *HNZ*, "Lan Ming Xun" 覽冥訓 (Examining the Obscure), ch. 6, p. 6b, states, "In former times, the Yellow Emperor ruled all-under-Heaven and Li Mu and Tai Shan Ji assisted him. He used them to control the movements of the sun and moon, to regulate the qi of Yin and Yang, to measure the regularities of the four seasons, correct the numbers of the pitch-pipes and calendar, separate men and women, distinguish male and female, clarify superiors and inferiors, and rank the noble and the mean . . ."

227. The 1976 and 1980 editors suggest that *yun* 允 "permit" is a loan for *xun* 循 "follow." Yu Mingguang (1993[a]) accepts *yun* as the correct reading with the extended meaning of "pattern/model" (myself on).

228. *Li Ji, pian* 19 "Yue Ji" 樂記 (Record of Music), ch. 38, p. 308b (p. 1536b), states in a similar vein, "For this reason, the pure and bright are modeled on Heaven, the broad and the great are modeled on Earth." Cf. Legge (1885), vol. 28, p. 111.

229. The editors have correctly transcribed the silk manuscript's *shou* 受 "receive" as an abbreviation of *ai* 愛 "love" in the following passage, except for the graph before the lacuna. This latter graph should also be read as *ai*.

230. Confucius said (*Lun Yu*, "Ji shi" 季氏 [Master Ji], *LYJS*, ce 4, ch. 33, p. 1156), "The gentleman is in awe of three things: he is in awe of Heaven's mandate, he is in awe of great men, and he is in awe of the words of the sages."

231. The editors have transcribed the graph *yan* 言 "speech," which does not appear to have a radical in the original photograph, as *xin* 信 "trustworthiness/good faith," which is the way it appears below. The 1976 editors believe that *xu* 虛 "emptiness" here means the Dao, on the basis of *LSCQ*, ch. 25, no. 2, "You Du" 有道 (Possessing Measures), p. 5a, "If one is correct, then one is quiescent; if quiescent, then one is pure and bright; if pure and bright, then one is empty; if empty, then one is without action *(wuwei)* and everything is done," where the commentator Gao You defines "empty" as the "Dao." Cf. Jia Yi, *Xin Shu* "Dao Shu" 道術 (Techniques of the Dao), ch. 8, p. 30b, where the basis of the Dao is defined as "the Empty."

232. The graph that appears in the original text is clearly *shou* 受 = *ai* 愛: all the editors have changed it to *qin* 親 "be intimate with" without comment. They may be correct in believing the copyist made an error.

233. Cf. *HGZ*, ch. B, *pian* 11 "Tai Lu" 泰錄 (Record of the Grand), p. 21a, "Now the supreme sage august Heaven is what the former sages relied on for their awesome majesty: it established (them) as possessing the mandate."

234. Li Hei 力黑 is the same as Li Mu 力牧, one of the Yellow Emperor's assistants. He appears as Li Mo 力墨 in a Han slip found at Dunhuang (Luo Zhenyu and Wang Guowei, *Liusha zhuijian*, p. 4b).

235. The 1976 and 1980 editors think that *jin* 浸 "soak" should be read as *qian* 潛 "secret/hidden."

236. The 1980 editors interpret *liu* 留 "stay" as a loan for *liu* 流 "wander round/flow." The 1976 editors record only the latter graph. Guo Yuanxing, p. 132, thinks it should be read as *you* 游 "travel/wander."

237. The 1976 editors punctuate and interpret this sentence as "in order to observe the inconstant and make excellent laws and rules for them." The 1980 editors read *ze* 則 with the following sentence as "then," and interpret *guan* 觀 as *guanhua* 觀化 "observe and transform," quoting a passage from the *HNZ*, ch.12, "Dao Ying Xun" 道應訓 (Response to the Dao), p. 15b–16a, where Jizi (Mi Zijian) had ruled Danfu for three years when Wu Maqi (one of Confucius' disciples) went to see him to transform him *(guanhua yan* 觀化焉); this story also occurs in the *LSCQ*, ch. 18, no. 8, "Ju Bei" 具備 (Preparations), p. 17a ff., which concludes with the statement, "Therefore Laozi said, 'Put away that and take this.'" This is similar to the passage here, the 1980 editors argue. They present an alternative translation, "Because they observed (and transformed?) no definitely effective methods."

238. The 1976 editors interpret the clause as "investigated the appearance of things."

239. The 1980 editors interpret *shi* 視 "see" as *shi* 示 "show/instruct" and the unknown graph 堯 as *jing* 鏡 "mirror." The *WW* editors do not place a period after *e* and interpret 堯 as *jing* 競 "compete": "If (something or someone) hates man, then he shows (them how) to compete." The 1976 editors retain *shi* as "see": "If it is man, then he sees the mirror." None of these explanations seem particularly satisfactory.

240. *Xing* 刑 "punishment" is an abbreviation of *xing* 型 "model/pattern" according to the 1980 editors. The phrase "the actions of virtue and tyranny" occurs in the *GY*, ch. 21, "Yue Yu xia," p. 3a, which, Fan Li states, he better understands than the *dafu* Zhong.

241. The 1980 editors state that *jun* 囷 "round granary" sounded in the archaic language similar to *quan* 圈 "circular enclosure" and that the fragmentary sentence describes the chaotic state of affairs when Yin and Yang had not yet been differentiated. For a similar sentence see *HNZ*, ch. 2, "Shu Zhen Xun" (The Reality in the Beginning), p. 6a, "Looking at them from the point of view of sameness, the ten thousand things are in a single pen." In other words, everything was crowded together without rank or order, as in a single round granary or animal pen.

242. *HGZ*, ch. C, *pian* 12, "Shi Bing," p. 3b, also contains the clause, "The bright are models, but it is the minute Dao that is to be carried out." *GY* (Shanghai ed., p. 653) "Yue Yu xia" proclaims, "The Heavenly Dao is august; the sun and moon act as (its) constants. When they are bright, they act as models, but it is the minute that is to be followed." Wei Zhao explains that "bright" refers to the time when the sun and moon are at their fullest and most resplendent, and "minute" when they are diminished and in eclipse. Generally speaking, the Daoists and, following them, the Legalists argued that the bright could be used as models for the whole phenomenal world, but the man of Dao and therefore the ruler should cleave to the dark and minute so as to be inconspicuous, for the Dao was dark and mysterious. The sun and moon must be the "constants" of the Heavenly Dao ("its") which is lost in the lacuna.

243. *HNZ*, ch. 7, "Jing Shen Xun" 精神訓 (Quintessential Spirituality), p. 1a, states, "Thereupon it was then divided (*bie* 別) and became Yin and Yang; separated and became the Eight Extremities. The hard and the soft completed each other, and the ten thousand things then were formed." The 1980 editors point out that the silk manuscript's *ruo*

若 should be interpreted as *nai* 乃 "then," a usage that appears frequently below.

244. The term *gui gui* 規規 appears in *Zhuangzi pian* 23, "Geng Sangchu" 庚桑楚 (Geng Sangchu), ce 4, ch. 8A, p. 782, where the *Jingdian shiwen* 經典釋文 defines it as the "appearance of smallness." The graphs are written 睍睍 in *HZ pian* 6, "Fei Shier zi" 非十二子 (Against Twelve Philosophers), ce 2, p. 21, where the same definition is given by the commentators.

245. The graph in the manuscript is clearly *ren* 人 "man," but the editors offer no explanation. Yu Mingguang (1993[a]) interprets the sentence as "If they did not eat, they would not be able to nourish humans."

246. Presumably the author of the passage means that there is a part of Heaven and a part of Earth in Man. To live and grow, man must incorporate them into his basic activities.

247. The 1980 editors point out that Yin begins to grow at the point when Yang is at its fullest, and, similarly, Yang begins to move when Yin is at its height. Therefore the text proposes that one should perform an essentially Yang act "spreading virtue/accretion" when Yin is full, and perform an essentially Yin act "overhauling punishments" when Yang is at its peak (literally, "long").

248. The editors transcribe the very obscure second graph as *mi* or *mei* 麋. The 1976 and 1980 editors consider that it is a loan for *mei* 徽 and that *hei* 黑 is an alternate form of *mo* 纆. *Mei mo* were two different types of string or rope, the former possessing three strands of thread, the latter two, which appear in the *Yi Jing* under the hexagram *Kan* 坎. The 1980 editors quote the *GZ pian* 12, "Shu Yan" (Cardinal Sayings), ch. 4, p. 64: "The former kings did not tie and did not knot. If one ties, then one has to free; if one knots, then one has to cut loose." Cf. Rickett (1985), p. 219, "The former kings did not restrain [people by treaties] or bind them [through oaths]. They released those restrained [by treaties]/ and dissolved the bonds of those bound [by oaths]." So here the meaning is the same, they argue. It is unclear what the subject of the verbs *mi/mei* and *hei* are; the editors clearly take it to be the sage ruler. The subject of the two previous clauses *bu hui, bu ji* and *bu shi, bu ren* was, however, the people. I believe "the people" are also the subject here. Darkness and nonexistence are associated with the Dao and if the people are dissolved in the Dao, the ruler will not be able to control them. It is the ruler who should be associated with the Dao, whereas the people should be evident and part of the phenomenal world.

249. *HFZ*, ce 1, ch. 2, *pian* 7, "Er Bing" 二柄 (The Two Handles),

p. 26, states, "What is meant by virtue and punishment? I say, killing and murdering are punishment, congratulation and reward are virtue." (cf. Liao, vol. 1, p. 46). *Zhuangzi, pian* 30, "Shuo Jian" 說劍 (Discussing Swords), ce 4, ch. 10A, p. 1020, states, "As for the sword of the Son of Heaven, he controls (the world) by means of the Five Phases and makes decisions using punishment and virtue." Zheng Xuanying comments, "The Five Phases are metal, wood, water, fire, and earth; *xing* is punishment and penalty, *de* is virtue and transformation. He uses these Five Phases to control the world and makes decisions using punishment and virtue to rule all living things."

250. *GZ pian* 40, "Si Shi" 四時 (The Four Seasons), ch. 14, p. 241, states, "Virtue begins in spring and grows up in summer; punishment begins in autumn and flows away in winter. When punishment and virtue are not lost, the four seasons are as one. If punishment and virtue were to leave their places, the seasons would then act in opposition (to what is natural and disastrous anomalies would occur)." *HNZ*, ch. 3, "Tian Wen Xun" 天文訓 (Patterns of Heaven), p. 5b, states that at the winter solstice, when the sun is at the center of the northern dipper, Yin qi is at its height, but Yang qi begins to sprout, and so that winter season is called "Virtue" (*de*); similarly in summer, at the summer solstice, the sun reaches the center of the southern dipper, and Yang qi is at its zenith, but Yin qi begins to sprout, and so it is called "Punishment" *(xing)*. See Major (1987).

251. The same idea appears in *GZ pian* 42, "Shi" (Positional Advantage), ch. 15, p. 253: "Therefore do not offend against Heaven's seasons; do not disorder the people's work; adhere to the (proper) seasons to nourish men; put virtue first and punishment last; follow Heaven, and carefully measure Man."

252. *Zuo Zhuan* Duke Yin year 8 states, "The Son of Heaven establishes virtue and bestows surnames on the basis of livelihoods." In other words, he gives surnames on the basis of rank, title, or occupation.

253. For this passage, see "Priorities for a State" above. The 1976 editors take *chuang* 摐 as a loan for *zong* 縱 "indulge," i.e., "will indulge in warfare." The 1980 editors quote the *Guang Ya* "Shi Yan," Zhou Fagao (1977), p. 221, where *chuang* is defined as *chuang* 撞 "strike"; Yan Shigu 顏師古 also defines the word in this way in *HS* "Sima Xiangru liezhuan shang" 司馬相如列傳上. Given the parallel in "Priorities for a State," "Heaven will bring warfare to those who cover over the soil," the latter interpretation is preferable.

254. The three seasons are spring, summer, and autumn. Man was

supposed to rest in winter. Literally, "the three enjoyments." Wei Zhao explains that they are the work of the three seasons because one makes the people labor at their work and enjoy their tasks.

255. Cf. note 251 above.

256. The passage from "at the appropriate season" to "achieve their ambitions" also appears in the *GY*, ch. 21, "Yue Yu xia," pp. 2b–3a, with approximately the same wording. For *zhi* 搳, the *GY* reads *jie* 節 "regulate/control": the 1980 editors therefore think that the silk manuscript's 搳 is another form of *zhi* 挃, which can be read as *zhi* 窒, which is close in sound to *jie* 節. For the silk manuscript's *liu* 溜, the *GY* writes *lu* 稑, which the *Shuo Wen* defines as "ripen quickly." So *liu* should be understood as *lu*.

257. Fullness and insufficiency or deficiency are also found as contradictions in the *Laozi* Book 2 "De Jing," section 45, "Great fullness is like insufficiency." The *HNZ*, ch. 5, "Shi Ze Xun" 時則訓 (Regulations of the Seasons), p. 17b, states that fullness begins in the first month of spring and insufficiency begins in the first month of autumn. Essentially, the text is arguing that men's affairs must be in harmony with the seasons: if they are not, then Yin or Yang will return at the wrong time and disasters will result. Here, the season is full, i.e., it is spring.

258. Overhauling and applying punishments should be done only in autumn.

259. Practically the same sentence appears in the *GY*, ch. 21, "Yue Yu xia," p. 3b, "Fan Li replied, 'Not yet! Li has heard that Shangdi is not crafty (where *kao* 考 is probably an error for *qiao* 巧), the alternation of the seasons is what he preserves.'" *HS* "Sima Xiangru liezhuan" also states, "The sage is not crafty; the change of the seasons is what he preserves."

260. "Assessing Destruction" above defined untrustworthiness as "to make agreements and then to repudiate them."

261. The text never specifies what "The Five Regulators" are. *HGZ*, ch.B *pian* 8, "Du Wan" 度萬, pp. 5ab, defines them as "Transformation by the Spirit" (*shenhua* 神化), "Ordering by Office" (*guan zhi* 管治), "Ordering by Instruction" (*jiao zhi* 教治), "Ordering by Reliance" (*yin zhi* 因治), and "Ordering by Affairs" (*shi zhi* 事治). He explains these as follows: "Transformation by the Spirit" is "being settled by Heaven and Earth, prepared by the four seasons, instructed by Yin and Yang, moved by cold and hot . . ."; "Ordering by Office" is "taking Yin and Yang as one's master, responding to what is going to be so, Earth is at peace, Heaven is pure, everything is beautiful and returns to

him"; "Ordering by Instruction" is "making the work of the four seasons follow the Dao"; "Ordering by Reliance" is "summoning the wise sages and talking about the Techniques of the Heart, respecting life and harmony of affairs"; "Ordering by Affairs" is "summoning the benevolent sages and talking about wisdom with them." The Five Regulators could also be the Five Phases or their presiding spirits. The 1976 editors take *zheng* 正 "correct" as *zheng* 政 "rules" and explain that they are the rules for controlling the people in the four seasons.

262. The Five Brightnesses, according to Lu Dian's 陸佃 comment on the *HGZ*, ch. B, *pian* 8, "Du Wan" (SBBY ed.), p. 3b, are the same as the Five Names (*wu ming* 五名): the emperor with qi (*qihuang* 氣皇), the spiritually illumined (*shenming* 神明), the worthies and sages (*xian-sheng* 賢聖), the lords and kings (*houwang* 后王), and the dukes and overlords (*gongbo* 公伯). These are the individuals who rule the world under the aegis of the Yellow Emperor.

263. These were the forces of Chi You, later deified as the God of War, whose battles with the Yellow Emperor are recounted below.

264. The 1976 and 1980 editors interpret *xing* 刑 "punishment" as an abbreviation for *xing* 型 "law/pattern," which the former understand as "rules" (*faze* 法則), referring to the phrase "knowing myself" above, i.e., "know the laws within yourself." I suspect it may be the alternative form for *xing* 形 "form."

265. The 1976 and 1980 editors suggest that the unknown expression *jin lin* 浸廩 is the same as *jin yin* 浸淫 and other similar phrases which mean "slowly spread about."

266. The 1976 editors suggest the "four" are blood, qi, fat, and grease.

267. Possibly located in modern Anhui province.

268. *Tan* 談 "talk" is probably a loan for *tian* 恬 "calm/quiet." *Deng-xizi* 鄧析子, "Wu Hou" 無厚 *pian* ("No Friendship"), states (Sibu congkan ed., p. 6a), "Calmly rest and let work complete itself." Guo Yuanxing, p. 132, argues that *tan* is simply an alternate form for *dan* 淡, which is the same as *dan* 澹 and *dan* 憺, which the *Shuo Wen* defines as "peaceful/calm" (*an* 安).

269. The 1976 and 1980 editors wish to read *dan cai* 單才, literally, "simple talent" as *zhan zai* 戰哉 "He battled!" The sentence appears in a slightly extended form in "Correcting the Rebellious" below as "The battle will be intense!" Probably *ying* 盈, literally "full," has been inadvertently omitted in the present context.

270. Guo Tong is the name of one of the Yellow Emperor's assistants.

271. The term "Four Assistants" appears in one of the lost books following the *Zhou Yi* in the Mawangdui manuscripts, the *Ersanzi Wen* 二三子問 (Chen Songchang and Liao Mingchun [1993], p. 428, line 35), so the 1976 and 1980 editors suggest that the two missing graphs in the lacuna are *wen si* 問四. The Four Assistants also appear in the sixth section of the Yin-Yang texts from Yinqueshan, which has been given the title *Orders of the Four Seasons* (*Sishi ling* 四時令). In this latter text each of the assistants is correlated with the four directions (east, south, west, and north) and receives in turn the order from the Son of Heaven. He is then in charge of managing the appropriate seasonal activities (Yates 1994 [a]). Kong Yingda's 孔穎達 (574–648) commentary on the *Li Ji, pian* 8, "Wen Wang shizi" 文王世子 (King Wen as Son and Heir), ch. 20, p. 179a (p. 1407a), quotes the *Shang Shu dazhuan* 尚書大傳 as saying that in ancient times the assistants stood on the left of the Son of Heaven and were in charge of knowing what was correct and what was incorrect.

272. Guo Yuanxing, p. 132, understands it as an alternate form for *jian* 儉 "thrifty/economical"; others take the graph *xian* 險 without change, i.e., "do not endanger yourself/take dangerous risks."

273. The 1976 editors interpret *ji* 稽 as "take your model from"; Guo Yuanxing, p. 133, interprets the word as *kao* 考 "investigate/examine": this seems better. The correct relations and distinctions between men and women were considered to epitomize the correct distinctions between all things, great and small, in the entire universe. Guo Tong is urging the Yellow Emperor to examine carefully the three realms of Heaven, Earth, and Man.

274. The 1976 and 1980 editors suggest that *su* 俗 "vulgar" is a loan for *yu* 育 "educate/inculcate," for the term "inculcate virtue" appears in the *Zhou Yi* under the hexagram "Meng" 蒙. This explanation is possible. The graph, however, is very obscure in the photograph, so the editors may have made a mistake in its identification. Guo Yuanxing, p. 133, interprets the word as an alternate form for *yu* 裕 "abundant," which appears in "Establishing the Mandate" above as Earth's special potency *(de)*. Another possibility is that it might be another way of writing *yu* 欲 "desire/want."

275. Yu Mingguang (1993[a]) interprets *de* 德 "potency" as a loan for *zhi* 殖 "multiply."

276. The 1976 editors quote *HNZ*, ch. 9, "Zhu Shu Xun," p. 12b, "Men have their talents; things have their forms; when one person assumes responsibility (for something), it is too heavy, but when a hun-

dred take responsibility (for it), then it is still light." The fragmented sentence here seems to have a similar meaning, they suggest. If they are correct, as seems likely, then the missing graphs probably are *ren yi ze* 任一則.

277. Probably the text's *zhong* 中 "centrality" is a mistake for *cai* 才 "talent," for this is the term in the *HNZ* quoted in note 276 above.

278. *GZ pian* 41, "Wu Xing" 五行 (Five Phases), ch. 14, p. 242, contains the same sentence and *HGZ*, ch. B, *pian* 10, "Tai Hong," p. 19a, states, "Therefore the sages set up Heaven as the father and established Earth as the mother."

279. The 1976 editors believe the missing graphs are *ruo de zheng* 若得正. I.e., "If you are trustworthy, then you will be able to correct."

280. The 1980 editors believe that *kan* 諶 "trustworthy" should be read as *kan* 勘 "investigate," which they interpret as "carefully examine again and again."

281. The 1980 editors take *yuan* 員 as an abbreviation of *sun* 損 "cut off/destroy"; the 1976 editors take it as *yun* 隕 "lose." Yu Mingguang (1993[a]) interprets the word as a loan for *yuan* 緣 with the sense of "follow." The meaning of the two sentences is obscure. Possibly *fa* 法 is a loan for *fa* 罰 "punish": "As for the older generation, punish it"?

282. The 1976 editors interpret *luan* 巒 "low but steep hill" as *liian* 攣, which they interpret as "bent over like a hunchback." The 1980 editors suspect that it is an alternate form for *luan* 孿, which the *Shuo Wen* defines as "water leaking": "carrying a leaky water-bottle" or "carrying a water-bottle in such a way that it leaks out"? The former interpretation seems better.

283. Yu Mingguang (1993[a]) interprets *ying* 營 "manage/arrange" as a loan for *qiong* 煢 "solitary": "He traveled about by himself."

284. Gao Yang was, according to *Shi Ji* "Wudi benji" 五帝本紀 (Basic Annals of the Five Emperors), ch. 1, p. 10, the grandson of the Yellow Emperor, also known as Zhuan Xu 顓頊, who was set on the throne on the Yellow Emperor's death.

285. The Peak of Tai Shan, together with Li Hei (Li Mu), is said in *HNZ*, ch. 6, "Lan Ming Xun," p. 6b, to be one of the Yellow Emperor's assistants.

286. The 1980 editors have mistakenly inverted *fu jiu* 弗救. The *LSCQ*, ch. 20, section 6, "Xing Lun" 行論 (Assessing Behavior), p. 14a, states, "If you wish to destroy something, you must tie it tightly; if you wish to kill someone, you must (first) elevate him." It is easier to destroy something when it is first tied up and it is easier to eliminate

251

someone when he is exposed. The passage in the text is not at all easy to understand because of the lacunae.

287. Possibly this refers to Chi You who fought the Yellow Emperor for control of the world, but ultimately lost.

288. The 1980 editors quote the *Xin Xu* 新序 in which Liu Xiang 劉向 states that Zhuan Xu took over the throne when he was only twelve years old; and the *Mizi* 鬻子 claims that he assisted his grandfather, the Yellow Emperor, when he was fifteen years old. The *Diwang shiji* 帝王世紀, on the other hand, believed that he assisted Shao Hao 少昊 when he was ten years old and ascended the throne when he was twenty.

289. The 1976 and 1980 editors excise *guan* 官 "office" between "Heaven" and "Earth" as a mistaken reduplication of *Di* 地 "Earth." They do not, however, offer an explanation of this obscure sentence.

290. The 1976 and 1980 editors read *si* 寺 as *zhi* 志 "ambition" and say that the sentence means that the Peak of Tai Shan will satisfy him (presumably Chi You) to make him arrogant and self-satisfied so that he will be easier to defeat and kill. Yu Mingguang (1993[a]) interprets the graph as abbreviation for *zhi* 庤 "prepare."

291. The 1976 and 1980 editors interpret 斜 as an abbreviation of *fu* 軵 "push/thrust out." Cf. *HNZ*, ch. 13, "Fan Lun Xun," p. 20b, where Tai Zu (Liu Bang, the founder of the Han dynasty) thrust out his elbow when engaged in swordplay with bare blades.

292. Dai was a general term for the far northern regions. Yu Mingguang (1993[a]) interprets the word as a loan for *te* 慝 "evil," i.e., "throw him into a vile abyss."

293. Cf. *Laozi* "De Jing," ch. 39, Henricks (1989), p. 100, states, "Marquises and kings, by attaining the One[,] made the whole land ordered and secure." *LSCQ*, ch. 17, section 8, "Zhi Yi" 執一 (Grasping the One), p. 16b, states, "The true king grasps the one and makes the myriad phenomena correct."

294. Yu Mingguang (1993[a]), following Guo Yuanxing, interprets the text's *xing* 刑 "punishment" as a loan for *xing* 行 "behavior/activity."

295. The 1976 and 1980 editors believe that the graph 拲 may be an alternative form of *bei* 悖 "disorder/disarray." Guo Yuanxing believes it is an alternate form of 捧 or 拲, which appears in the *Zhou Li* as an ancient form of *bai* 拜 "bend." The graph 拲 also appears on slip 4099 in the Yinqueshan materials in a chart of the Eight Winds, but its significance there is not known. I am grateful to Edmund Ryden for pointing out the connection and different interpretations of the graph, and for suggesting that this passage is rhymed.

296. The 1976 and 1980 editors take *shi* 是 as an abbreviation for *shi* 寔, which they interpret as "full," understanding the sentence as "I will make his evil behavior really full and then I will kill him." I believe that *sui* 遂 "then/follow" is an alternate form of *zhu* 逐 "pursue," a usage which occurs elsewhere in the Mawangdui texts, and that *shi* should be interpreted in its ordinary sense of "correct/right."

297. The 1976 and 1980 editors suggest that *zhi* 直 "direct" is an error for *xiang* 相, for the *GZ pian* 41, "Wu Xing," ch. 14, p. 242, states, "The Yellow Emperor acquired the Six Ministers and Heaven and Earth was well ordered and spiritual illumination arrived."

298. The 1976 and 1980 editors suggest that *xu* 胥 "servant/moment" is an abbreviation of *xu* 諝 "wise."

299. The 1976 and 1980 editors interpret *duo* 朵 as *dong* 動 "move," but without any supporting evidence. The *WW* editors transcribed the graph as *dong* 東 "east."

300. Possibly *qi* 奇 should be understood as "wonderful (way)."

301. The 1980 editors interpret *xi* 戲 as a loan for *ju* 豦 "fight."

302. *Huo* 或 "perhaps/in some cases" should probably be understood as *you* 又 "also" with the 1980 editors.

303. Later on, Chi You's banner was interpreted as a particular variety of inauspicious comet whose appearance forewarned of imminent warfare (cf. Loewe 1980).

304. *Zhi* 執 "grasp" may be a loan for *ta* 蹋 "kick," which is the usual word associated with football. The game began in the Warring States period and was used to train soldiers.

305. Pickling a criminal or a defeated enemy's flesh and bones and eating it was a not uncommon practice in ancient China (see des Rotours 1963, 1968). The Yellow Emperor is sending round the pickled meat and bones of the rebel Chi You to all the people in the world so that they can see his fate and be warned against rebelling.

306. Gong Gong was another mythic criminal in ancient China who fought with Zhuan Xu for the throne. He was responsible for knocking against one of the pillars holding up the sky in the northwestern corner, Mount Buzhou, thereby cutting the connection between the world of Man and the world of the Gods. As a result, the sun and moon and all the stars and constellations traveled to the northwest and a great flood ensued which almost destroyed the world (cf. Boltz).

307. The 1980 editors interpret this to mean "enslaving them."

308. The 1976 editors suspect that *gan* 甘 "sweet" should be understood as an abbreviation of *qian* 鉗 "fetter/manacle" and 箭 to be an

alternative form of *yu* 俞, which they say means the two cavities on either side of the spine. Yu Mingguang (1993[a]) says that *yu* means to "make a cage for criminals," but this is unlikely for grammatical reasons. Probably they are being tied to some kind of post, hence the reference to the "pillars of the Earth" below.

309. The Yellow Emperor turns them into a different type of being altogether, according to the 1980 editors.

310. The 1976 editors think that *ting* 桯 should perhaps be read as *qing* 巠, which the *SW* defines as a "vein of water," i.e., water beneath the earth. The 1980 editors suggest the word be read as *ying* 楹, meaning a pillar of the Earth, and they argue that the figure holding up the earth in the silk banner from tomb number 1 at Mawangdui is Chi You. The scholarship on this banner painting is extensive (cf. Loewe 1979, ch. 2). Yu Mingguang (1993[a]) interprets the word as a kind of arm or headrest in front of a bed (the chair was introduced to China more than a thousand years after this text was composed).

311. Presumably this is the Yellow Emperor.

312. Gao Yang was an alternate name of Zhuan Xu; see note 284 above.

313. After the unification of the empire in 221 B.C.E., Qin Shihuangdi changed the name of the "people" *min* 民 to the "black-haired (ones)." The term appears occasionally in preunification texts, such as the *Zhanguo Ce* 戰國策 (hereafter *ZGC*), *LSCQ*, and *HFZ*.

314. Presumably by showing inauspicious portents, such as eclipses, which presaged death and destruction in war.

315. *Ji* can be interpreted as the hinge or pivot of a door. *Zhuangzi*, *pian* 18, "Zhi Le" 至樂 (Perfect Happiness), ce 3, ch. 6b, p. 625 (cf. Watson 1968, p. 196), states, "The myriad phenomena all issue from the *ji* and all go back into the *ji*." Basically, *ji* means any kind of mechanism, so I translate the term as "key" because this is a common metaphor in English for such a device.

316. In Chinese military terminology, the atttacker is the "guest" and the defender is the "host." It was usually considered best to be the defender rather than the attacker.

317. It seems to me that the copyist has made an error here and basically reproduced the previous passage. It probably should be excised.

318. Cf. *GZ pian* 42, "Shi," ch. 15, p. 252, "Now as for quiescence and action, sometimes one should act as the host, sometimes as the guest: you should value gaining (the proper) measure."

319. Guo Yuanxing interprets *lu* 僇 as a loan for *lu* 陸, which he says means *ru* 辱 "shame."

320. *Huanghou* 皇后 (the emperor) is probably Huangdi, the Yellow Emperor. That he is not specifically named may indicate that this text did not originally belong to the group that does name him. In other words, it may be a text separate from the others included in this second section.

321. The term *tunmo* 屯磨 is obscure. The 1976 and 1980 editors suggest that it should be read as *dongli* 洞歷, the title of a book mentioned by Wang Chong 王充 in his *Lun Heng* 論衡, ch. 13, *pian* 39, "Chao Qi" 超奇 (On Preeminence) (Beijing Daxue lishi xi *Lun Heng zhushi xiao zu, Lun Heng zhushi* 論衡注釋), p. 790 (Forke 1962, vol. 2, p. 302), which should probably be translated as "*The Deep Record*," for it recounted everything from the time of the Yellow Emperor to the Han dynasty. I suspect that *tun* is a loan for *dun* 敦 "assiduous/hardworking/extensive," a usage that occurs elsewhere (Morohashi Tetsuji, *Daikanwa jiten* 大漢和辭典, [hereafter M.] 13276, definition 14), including the *Shi Jing* "Da Ya" 大雅 ode 263 "Chang Wu" 常武: "Extensively he massed his troops on the Huai-river banks; in ever greater numbers he took crowds of prisoners" (Karlgren 1950, p. 235) and Yang Xiong's 揚雄 *Ganquan fu* 甘泉賦 ("Rhapsody on the Sweet Springs"), according to Li Shan's 李善 commentary (*Wen Xuan* 文選, ch. 7, p.143; David R. Knechtges 1987, p. 23: "Assembling a myriad riders in the central camp"). *Mo* probably is an alternative way of writing *li* "record"; but *mo* "ground out" might be correct.

322. The term "female tally" also appears in the *HNZ*, ch. 1, "Yuan Dao Xun," p. 9b, "For this reason, the sage guards the Pure Dao and embraces/holds the female tally." Cf. *Wenzi yaoquan, pian* 1, "Dao Yuan" 道原 (Dao the Origin), p. 45, "Therefore the sage initiates affairs by following the seasons and establishes his merit by relying on his natural abilities; protects the Pure Dao and holds the female tally. He relies on following and thereby responds to changes; is always behind and not first; is soft and weak in order to be quiescent; is at peace and leisurely in order to be stable. In attacking the mighty and grinding away the hard, one cannot fight with him (i.e., no one can match him)." Cf. Yu Dacheng (1968: 18–19).

323. The 1976 editors suggest that *xian* 憲 "law" is a loan for *an* 岸 "high"; the 1980 editors believe that the word is a loan for *han* 悍 "brazen/outrageous"; Guo Yuanxing and Yu Mingguang (1993[a]) interpret it as *xian* 顯 "clear": any one of these interpretations is possible.

324. *Ying/cheng* 浧 may be an alternate form of 逞, which Wang

Niansun 王念孫 demonstrates is an alternate graph for *ying* 盈 "full/ superfluity." (Cf. Guo Moruo, *Guanzi jijiao*, vol. 1, p. 167, on the passage in *GZ pian* 11, "Zhou He" 宙合 (The All-embracing Unity), ch. 4, p. 60, "This means that the sage's movement and quiescence, opening and closing, bending and stretching, fullness/excess and shortage, giving and taking must depend on the seasons." Cf. Rickett (1985), p. 206. The phrase also occurs in the Yin-Yang texts from Yinqueshan (Wu Jiulong 1985), slip 0684, ". . . the dispersion of Yang is the companion of what dies (?)" Wang Chong states that shamans *wu* 巫 are "the compaions of auspiciousness and inauspiciousness" *ji xiong zhi tu ye* 吉凶之 徒也 ("Ding Gui" 訂鬼 [All about Ghosts]) (*Lun Heng zhushi*, ce 3, p. 1288; Forke [1962], vol. 1, p. 247, translates the phrase, "[sorcerers] are the messengers of fate"). The phrase *si zhi tu shi you san* 死之徒十有三 also appears in section 50 of the *Laozi*, which has been analyzed most recently by Robert G. Henricks (forthcoming) in which he comments on this passage. He notes that *Laozi* section 76 also has the clause *jianqiang si zhi tu ye, rouruo sheng zhi tu ye* 堅強死之徒也柔弱生之徒也, which *HNZ*, ch. 1, p. 8b, quotes as *rouruozhe sheng zhi gan ye, jianqiangzhe si zhi tu ye* 柔弱者生之幹也堅強者死之徒也. *Zhuangzi, pian* 22, "Zhi Bei You" 知北遊 (Knowledge Wandered North), ce 3, ch. 7b, p. 733, has a similar clause *sheng ye si zhi tu; si ye sheng zhi shi* 生也死之徒死 也生之始. Not mentioned by Henricks in the unpublished version of his manuscript is the quotation of *Laozi* in the *Wenzi*, ch. 1 (The ICS Ancient Chinese Text Concordance Series, *A Concordance to the Wenzi*, Taiwan: Commercial Press, 1992, p. 4), of the quote from *Laozi*, *gu rouruozhe sheng zhi gan ye, jianqiangzhe si zhi tu ye* 故柔弱者生之幹也 堅強者死之徒也. A further example is to be found in *Zhuangzi pian* 4, "Ren Jian Shi," ce 1, ch. 2B, p. 143 (Graham 1981, p. 68), where "being of Heaven's party" 與天爲徒 is contrasted with "being of man's party" 與人爲徒. Henricks finds Ma Xulun's 馬敘倫 reading of *tu* 途 "road" for *tu* appealing in the context, but given the other quotations, especially that of the *Lun Heng*, where just above Wang Chong states that shamans belong to the faction or party of Yang, *wu wei yang dang* 巫 爲陽黨, this seems a little unlikely. I prefer to retain the meaning of "companion" or "follower" for *tu* 徒. "Fullness" implies excess.

325. *Jian* 兼 is either an abbreviation of *qian* 謙 "modest/moderation," which Yu Mingguang (1993[a]) prefers, or *qian* 歉 "failure/apology" according to the 1980 editors.

326. The 1976 and 1980 editors suggest that the graph *de* 得 below *bi* 必 "inevitable" is redundant.

327. The 1976 and 1980 editors suggest that *fa* 法 "law/model" is a loan for *fei* 廢 "waste/abandon," a common usage in the bronze inscriptions and in the Qin legal documents from Shuihudi (cf. Hulsewé 1985).

328. Yu Mingguang (1993[a]) reads the text's *ku* 絝 "tie" as *jiang* 絳 "red," an alternate form for *jiang* 降 "send down."

329. The 1976 editors take *xing* 刑 as *xiaofa* 效法 "follow the example of/model oneself on."

330. The 1976 editors suggest that the graph *yin* 因 "rely on" be inserted before *ren* 人 "Man," but this is not necessary: *HGZ*, ch. C, *pian* 14, "Bing Zheng" 兵政 (Governance of an Army), p. 7a, states, "The standard method of using weapons is to model it on Heaven, on Earth, and on Man," literally, "Heaven them, Earth them, and Man them."

331. The 1976 editors interpret *xing* 刑 here as "demonstrate" or "reveal/show" and quote the *GY* "Yue Yu xia," "Life and death rely on the form of Heaven and Earth. Heaven relies on Man, the sage relies on Heaven; Man naturally gives it birth; Heaven and Earth form it, and the sage relies on it and brings it to completion." *GZ pian* 42, "Shi," ch.15, p. 252, has practically the same statement.

332. See "The Four Measures" above.

333. These sentiments have been encountered above. *GY* "Yue Yu xia" states, "If you are not successful in obtaining timeliness, you will in turn receive calamity from it."

334. The precise meaning of this sentence is unclear. *Sui* 遂 could either mean "then/consequently," or a "road"—the three roads would be Heaven, Earth, and Man, or "rely on" (Yu Mingguang 1993[a]). Cf. *HNZ*, ch. 15, "Bing Lüe Xun," pp. 14ab, "A general must possess the three roads (*sui* 隧), the four righteousnesses, the Five Phases, and the ten protections. What is meant by the three roads is: above, he knows the Dao of Heaven; below, he becomes familiar with the form of Earth; and in the middle he investigates into the true conditions of Man."

335. All the editors interpret *xiang* 鄉 as an abbreviation for *xiang* 饗 "enjoy/savor," but in the last sentence below, the 1976 editors interpret it as *dang* 當 "match."

336. Elsewhere, the graph *fan* 反 was used: here *huan* 環 "ring," a loan or alternative form for *huan* 還 "revolve/come back/recompense" is found.

337. The 1976 editors suggest that *fu fu yang yang* 茀茀陽陽 is a loan for *fu fu tang tang* 沸沸湯湯, a phrase that appears in the *Shanhai Jing* 山海經 ch. 2, "Xishan Jing" 西山經 for the appearance of jade-

like oil pouring out of Mi mountain (Yuan Ke 1980, p. 41). The 1980 editors, however, quote a passage from *HNZ*, ch. 5, "Shi Ze Xun," p. 19a, where the term *bo bo yang yang* 勃勃陽陽 occurs, with *bo bo* meaning "the appearance of abundance." Probably the expression is the same in each case, but different graphs have been used to write it.

338. The 1976 editors interpret *xiang* 鄉 as *dang* 當 "match," whereas the 1980 editors take it as an abbreviation of *xiang* 饗, as in note 335 above. Literally, it means "country/district." The meaning of the sentence is that the rewards won by means of the inappropriate extraction of the people's labor power in tasks that contradict the Way of Heaven will not be equal to the costs the tasks have entailed.

339. The 1976 and 1980 editors suspect that *zu* 組 "tie" should be read as *ju* 沮 "block/stop up." I am not sure that this is correct, for below it is clear that "Complete Laws" *(chengfa)* are the answer to the problem. Either an *yi* 以 "by means of" has been dropped between *ke* and *fa*, or Yu Mingguang (1993[a]) is correct in believing that *fa* should be read as *fei* 廢 "destroy/eliminate."

340. The *WW* and 1976 editors transcribe the graph as *qin* 捡. This the 1976 editors interpret should be read as *xia/jia* 洽 "harmonize": the sounds of the two words were too far apart for this to be possible. 捡 probably being *k'i̯əm and 洽 *g'əp. The 1980 editors transcribe the graph as *xuan* 拴, which they believe should be read as *zuan* 纘, which is defined in the *Shuo Wen* dictionary as *ji* 繼 "continue." Guo Yuanxing, followed by Yu Mingguang (1993[a]), interprets the word 捡 as the same as 拎, 攟, and 擒, with the meaning of "support." It is unclear what the correct graph should be and so the translation must remain tentative.

341. *HFZ*, ce 1, ch. 2, *pian* 8, "Yang Quan," p. 30, states, "Use the Dao of the One; take names as the beginning." Cf. Liao, vol. 1, p. 53, "The way to assume oneness starts from the study of terminology."

342. *Feng* 馮 should be read as *feng* 風 "wind" according to the *WW* and 1976 editors, and as *feng* 鳳 "phoenix" according to the 1980 editors. In ancient times, the two graphs were considered to be the same. The phoenix appears as a servant of Shangdi, the Lord-on-High, in the Shang oracle bones.

343. 朳 should be read as *ba* 扒 "split apart/separate": the "hand" and "tree" radicals are often confused in the silk manuscripts as in other early texts such as the *Mozi*. Different lists of the Five Emperors are given in different texts: Shao Hao, Zhuan Xu, Di Gu, Tang Yao, and Yu Shun; Huangdi, Zhuan Xu, Di Gu, Tang Yao, Yu Shun; Da Hao, Yandi,

Huangdi, Shao Hao, Zhuan Xu; Bao Xi, Shen Nong, Huangdi, Yao, Shun; Tai Hao, Yandi, Shao Hao, Zhuan Xu, Huangdi, etc.

344. It is not clear what the "Five Evils" were: the commentators are silent on the topic. In *GZ pian* 57, "Du Di" 度地 (Measuring the Earth), ch. 18, p. 303, Guan Zhong states that the Five Harms (*wu hai* 五害) are floods; droughts; wind, fog, hail, and frost; pestilence; and insects. Cf. Rickett (1965), p. 75.

345. This eight-word sentence has already appeared above. Possibly it is a mistaken reduplication, the result of the copyist looking at the sentence two slips back when he was transcribing the text from the bamboo or wooden slip version he was using: the distance between the passages is approximately 68 graphs long, two slips of 34 graphs each.

346. Cf. *GZ pian* 37, "Xin Shu xia," ch. 13, p. 224; Rickett (1965), p. 172, "For this reason the sage uses the one word to explain it, yet on high it reaches to Heaven and below reaches to [the ends of the earth]." *GZ pian* 49, "Nei Ye," ch. 16, p. 270; Rickett (1965), p. 161:

"Since he (the man of quality, *junzi*) grasps the Unity of Nature
    and does not lose it,
He is able to become prince over all things . . ."
P. 162:
"Through the explanation of the one word,
You may on high reach to Heaven, below touch the ends of
    earth,
And all around fill the nine regions."

Cf. *HNZ*, ch. 1, "Yuan Dao Xun," p. 11b, "For this reason, the principle of the One is applied to (all within) the Four Seas; understanding of the One penetrates to/harmonizes with Heaven and Earth."

347. The graph *xun* 紃 was not decipherable by the *WW* and 1976 editors. *HNZ*, ch. 7 "Jing Shen Xun," p. 5b, states, "When you take the Dao as the string (the commentator interprets this to mean "the model" *[fa]*), then, when you wait for something, it will be naturally so of itself."

348. *Zou* 騶 "drive a horse" is interpreted as *qu/cu* 趣 or *cu* 促 "encourage/promote" by the 1976 editors and as an alternate form of *qu* 趨 "hasten" by the 1980 editors. Guo Yuanxing takes it as *zou* 驟 in the sense of "frequent."

349. The 1976 editors say that this means that the four directions—east, west, north, and south—join each other and rely on each other: i.e., without the west, there could be no east; nor could the north be north without its opposite, the south.

350. This same statement occurs in slip 0463 of the Han texts found at Yinqueshan in 1972, which is part of the lost book *Wu I* 五議 (The Five Deliberations), as the first of the deliberations.

351. *HNZ*, ch. 1, "Yuan Dao Xun," p. 11b, has a similar statement, as does the *Wenzi*. *HNZ* reads, "The general mass of the myriad phenomena all pass through a single hole; all the roots of every affair come out from a single gate."

352. The "Corrected Person" would seem to be the sage *(shengren)* who understands the Dao, the One, and has corrected himself so as to be in accordance with it. "Them" must refer to the myriad phenomena just mentioned.

353. The passage is similar to the *HNZ*, ch. 7, "Jing Shen Xun," p. 3b, "Now Heaven and Earth revolve and communicate with each other; the myriad phenomena are a collectivity, but yet are one."

354. The three prohibitions are those relating to Heaven, Earth, and Man.

355. I.e., their agricultural duties.

356. The 1976 editors quote *Yanzi Chunqiu* 晏子春秋 "Nei Pian Wen Shang" 內篇問上 (Inner Section, Questions A) (Sun Xingyan 孫星衍 and Huang Yizhou 黃以周 eds., ch. 3, p. 23), where the clause "[In ancient times, the former rulers] did not persecute (*bi* 偪) the rivers and marshes" occurs. "Persecute" they interpret as "dam up," and the expressions in this text and in "The Three Prohibitions" are the same. The 1980 editors quote the *GY*, ch. 3, "Zhou Yu xia" 周語下 (Discourses of Zhou B), p. 5a, "The leaders of the people in ancient times did not knock down mountains, did not raise fens, did not block up rivers (*bu fang chuan* 不防川), did not drain marshes." They note that the clauses *bu fu chuan* 不服川 of "The Three Prohibitions" and the *bu fang chuan* of the *GY* have the same meaning and that there is just a variation in the sound of *fu* and *fang*.

357. The three graphs *wu ni tu* 毋逆土 have been mistakenly reduplicated by the copyist, although Yu Mingguang (1993[a]) prefers to retain the original text. The phrase *tu gong* 土功 first appears in the *Shang Shu* 尙書 (*Book of Documents*) "Yi Ji" 益稷 (*Shisan jing zhusu* ed.), *pian* 5, ch. 5, p. 31b (p. 143b), and also occurs in the *Li Ji,* ch. 15, *pian* 6, "Yue Ling" 月令 (Monthly Ordinances) "Meng Xia zhi yue," p. 137b (p. 1365b), Legge (1885) vol. 27, p. 270, "In this month . . . (t)here should be . . . no commencing of works in earth."

358. 俓, an abbreviation of *jing* 徑, is interpreted by Guo Yuanxing as "direct" and *sui* 遂 is understood by him as "advance." The 1976

editors interpret *jing sui* as a "road/path," as in the medical text *Su Wen* 素問 "Tiao Jing Lun" 調經論 (Discussion of Regulating the Paths), "The roads of the Five Visceral Orbs all derive from the paths (*jing sui* 經隧)."The 1980 editors quote *HFZ, pian* 20 "Jie Lao" 解老 (Explaining *Laozi*), ce 2, ch. 6, p. 26; Liao vol. 1, p. 189, "When the crooked mind rules supreme, affairs go straight to a deadlock. When affairs go straight to a deadlock, disasters take place."This *jing* 經 should be read as *jing* 徑 according to Gu Guangqi 顧廣圻. *Jing sui* 徑遂 is the same as *jing jue* 經絕, which means "to initiate movement rashly."

359. Reading *ling* 淩 "pass over" as *ling* 陵 as in the *Li Ji, pian* 18, "Xue Ji" 學記, ch. 36, p. 295a (p. 1523a), Legge (1885), vol. 28, p. 86, "the suitability of the lessons in adaptation to circumstances," literally, "applying (the lessons) by not exceeding the regulations is called humility."

360. *ErYa* 爾雅 "Shi Gu" 釋詁 and *Guang Ya* 廣雅 "Shi Gu" 釋詁 define *qiu* 丘 as *kong* 空 "empty."

361. *Xian* 憲 should be understood like *fa* 法 "imitate/model on," according to the 1976 editors and Yu Mingguang (1993[a]).

362. These are the Confucians according to the 1976 editors.

363. *Yu* 浴 "wash" should be understood as *yu* 欲 "desire/wish." The 1980 editors interpret the word as *gu* 谷 "valley" and Yu Mingguang (1993[a]) takes it as *su* 俗 "vulgar," but they do not seem to be correct.

364. These are the Mohists.

365. The 1976 and 1980 editors interpret *shoushou* 壽壽 "long-lasting" as *youyou* 悠悠 "distant/far-reaching"; Guo Yuanxing takes *shou* as an abbreviation for *tao/dao* 燾 "illuminate by covering over."

366. The 1980 editors take *zhu* 諸 "all" as an abbreviation of *chu* 儲 "accumulate," which is possible.

367. The *Shenzi* 慎子 of Shen Dao 慎到, quoted in the Song encyclopedia *Taiping yulan* 太平御覽, ch. 356, p. 2a (p.1635) has the statement, "States that store armor must possess the Dao of warfare *(bing dao)*. Merchants in the market *(shiren)* can be provoked into a fight, but the warfare that keeps a state secure does not arise from anger." Cf. Paul Thompson (1970), p. 290, fragments 104 and 105.

368. I.e., they are not in harmony with each other.

369. In ancient times, the size of city-states was calculated formulaically by the number of chariots it could put on the field of battle: the ten-thousand chariot state was the largest.

370. I.e., the conquest of the world.

371. The Chinese believed that anger was a type of sickness: if the

anger did not have some means of escape or expression, an individual would fall sick and even, perhaps, die.

372. *Laozi*, Ch. A, section 29, states, D. C. Lau trans. (1982), p. 87, "Whoever takes the empire and wishes to do anything to it I see will have no respite." Section 31 also states, Lau trans., p. 89, "Arms are instruments of ill omen, not the instruments of the gentleman. When one is compelled to use them, it is best to do so without relish." Line 147B below also has practically the same statement.

373. *Zhi* 赾 is possibly an alternate form for *tuo* 拓 "expand." It would be easier to determine the meaning if the previous graph was legible. The final particle *ye* 也 has been supplied by all the editors.

374. The 1976 editors consider *liu* 留 "cease" to be a loan for *liu* 流 "flow" on the basis of the same expression in *HNZ*, ch. 9, "Zhu Shu Xun," p. 5a; cf. Ames (1983), p. 174, "(the scales, the compass, and the set-square) being used for a special purpose, they do not adapt themselves."

375. The title has been supplied by the editors, for the silk in this chapter has been badly damaged and the original title lost. I suspect that this chapter may have a somewhat different origin from the others, for the text speaks of "righteousness" (*yi* 義) and "profit" (*li* 利), two concepts not found elsewhere, and some of the other ideas are not compatible with the other passages.

376. Possibly a word is missing after *min* 民 "people," for the pattern of four-graph clauses is broken here. It may be *li* 理 "principles/patterns," for a similar passage can be found in the *HNZ*, ch. 13, "Fan Lun Xun," p. 4b, "To be in harmony with the affairs of a generation, one has to gain (knowledge of) the principles of men, conform to Heaven and Earth, and be favorable to the ghosts and spirits."

377. Yu Mingguang (1993[a]) interprets *shi* 世 "generation" as *da* 大 "great" without supporting evidence.

378. Because of the lacuna, it is impossible to determine the meaning of this sentence. One or possibly two graphs are missing, and the editors have deciphered a third as *zhi* 執 "hold," after "high reputation." Possibly *yu shi xu* 於士虛 belongs to the next sentence.

379. The referent is unclear: it may be the word lost in the lacuna.

380. This four-graph fragment was found on a small scrap of silk; it probably belongs somewhere in this section and was originally part of line 131B or 132B; but its location cannot be determined for certain.

381. The 1980 editors quote the *Li Ji*, *pian* 31, "Zhong Yong" 中庸 (Doctrine of the Mean), ch. 52, p. 402b (1630b), "As for the Dao, if

you fix (plans) beforehand, it (the Dao) will be limitless." Cf. Legge (1885), vol. 28, p. 316.

382. The 1980 editors quote a similar passage in the *Su Wen* "Qi Jiao Bian Da Lun" 氣交變大論, "The Upper Classic states, 'Now the Man of Dao above knows the patterns of Heaven; below, knows the principles of Earth; and, in the middle, knows human affairs. He can long endure.'" The *Su Wen* "Zhu Zhi Jiao Lun" 著至教論 also states, ". . . and the Man of Dao above knows Heaven's patterns; below, knows the principles of Earth; and, in the middle, knows human affairs."

383. *GZ pian* 8, "You Guan Tu" 幼官圖, ch. 3, p. 45, cf. Rickett (1965), p. 217, and *GZ pian* 17, "Bing Fa" 兵法 (Methods of Warfare), p. 80, ch. 6, p. 95. Cf. Rickett (1965), p. 227, both contain the statement, "Beginning in the endless is the Dao."

384. The 1980 editors suggest that *huan/guan* 萑 is a loan for *huan* 桓, which is the same as *hua* 華 "flower." Ch. 38 of the *Laozi* states that great man "dwells in the fruit and does not dwell in the flower."

385. 涅 is defined by the *Fang Yan* 方言 (*Fang Yan suzheng* 方言疏證, ch. 3, p. 2a [SBBY ed.]) as *hua* 化 "transform."

386. See "The Female and Male Tally" above.

387. The text reads, "*not* perish": I suspect that this is an error and *bu* 不 "not" should be excised.

388. The 1976 editors are probably correct in interpreting *jiang* 將 "lead/will" as a loan for *qiang* 戕 "harm." Yu Mingguang (1993[a]) interprets the word as *jiu* 就 "go to," but this is exactly *not* what should happen.

389. *GY* "Yue Yu xia"; *GZ pian* 42, "Shi," ch. 15, p. 252, see note 186 above; and *Han Shu*, ch. 64A, "Zhufu Yan liezhuan" 主父偃列傳 (Biography of Zhufu Yan), p. 19b, contain a similar phrase. Cf. *HGZ*, ch. A, *pian* 7, "Jin Die," p. 19b, "Where the tally of opposition grows, the worthless encroach on the worthy. That is called 'Oppression.'"

390. The text's *gu* 骨 "bone" is probably an error for *ken* 肯 "be able."

391. In other words, "Who can stop them?"

392. For an interview, seeking employment at a ruler's court.

393. In other words, his words and actions correspond.

394. The 1976 editors take 怡 as a loan for *xi* 嬉 "playful," and the 1980 editors take it as an abbreviation of *xi* 熙, which is defined in the commentary to *HNZ*, ch. 18, "Ren Jian Xun" 人間訓 (In the World of Men), p. 7a, as *xi* 戲 "playful." Guo Yuanxing thinks that *cai* 采 should be understood as the ancient form of *bian* 辨, i.e., *bian* 辯

"dispute" and *xi* should be understood as *zao* 燥 "impatient/arid"; this is possible: "If his speech is sophistic and his actions are rash and hasty."

395. For the *fu* tally, see above note 151.

396. *GY* "Jin Yu," section 11, states, "Now the appearance is the embellishment of the feelings; speech is the extremity of the appearance." *Hanshi waizhuan* 韓氏外傳, ch. 4, states, "The eyes are the tally of the heart; speech is the pointer to behavior."

397. See "Way and the Law" above, note 6.

398. The 1976 and 1980 editors believe that *si* 寺 is an abbreviation of *chi* 持 "support." Another interpretation is that it is a mistake for *zhi* 志 "will/ambition."

399. *Zhuangzi*, ce 3, *pian* 20, "Shan Mu" 山木 (Mountain Tree), p. 680, states, "The straight tree is cut down first; the sweet well is exhausted first." Cf. Watson (1968), p. 213. *Shuo Yuan,* "Tan Cong," states, "He who is straight like an arrow dies."

400. All the editors have transcribed this graph *xian* 先 "put first": "who was born before Heaven and Earth." In the silk manuscripts the form of the graph *wu* 无 "have not/lack" and that of *xian* are virtually indistinguishable. I think that *wu* makes the better sense here. Yu Mingguang (1993[a]) takes the sentence as referring to the Dao: "The Dao lacks a name and lacks form; it was born before Heaven and Earth, and up to now it is not yet complete."

401. The editors interpret the unknown graph 茎 as an alternate form of *ting* 庭. Da Ting was apparently one of the most ancient rulers of China, according to myths current in the Warring States, for his name appears second in a list of such denizens in *Zhuangzi, pian* 10, "Rifling Trunks" (Watson [1968], p. 112) (*Zhuangzi jishi*, ce 2, ch. 4B, p. 357). Another interpretation is that Dating shi was an alternate name for the Divine Husbandman, Shen Nong 神農 (the commentary on Zheng Xuan's *Shi Pu Xu* 詩譜序, quoted in M. 5831.1682.2).

402. The 1976 editors interpret *zhi* 志 "will/ambition" as *zhi* 知 "know," whereas the 1980 editors take the word as a loan for *shi* 識 "recognize." Yu Mingguang (1993[a]) understands the original word as meaning *ji* 記 "record." Any of these interpretations is possible.

403. The "tally of softness" is the same as the "female tally" discussed above. Similar sentences appear in *Liu Tao* 六韜 (Kambun taikei ed.), ch. 1, *pian* 4, "Da Li" 大禮 (Great Ritual), p. 10; *Guiguzi, pian* 12, "Fu Yan" 符言 (Talk about Tallies) (Xiao Dengfu 1990, p. 232) starts with the saying, "Calm, gentle, correct, and quiescent; when you bear the tally, nothing is not settled; be good at giving and not contending;

empty your heart-mind and calm your will in order to wait for collapse and destruction." *GZ, pian* 55, "Jiu Shou" 九守 (Nine Defenses), ch. 18, p. 301 and *pian* 42, "Shi," ch. 15, p. 253, also speak of the "tally of softness" in the same terms as the text here, whereas the first section of *Wenzi* (*Wenzi yaoquan*, p. 45) urges that the one follow the "Pure Dao" and embrace the "female tally," be soft and weak in order to be quiescent and be calm and gentle in order to be settled.

404. The 1980 editors suspect that the unknown graph 兂, indecipherable by the *WW* editors, should be read as an alternate form of *wan* 睕 "sunset," which should be understood as *wan* 宛, with the meaning of "tactful" (*weiwan* 委婉). Yu Mingguang (1993[a]) reads it as *ang* 昂 in the sense of "stop/rest."

405. The 1980 editors take *shi* 濕, literally "damp," as an alternate form of *shi* 溼, which appears in *XZ pian* 2, "Xiu Shen" 修身 (Cultivating Oneself), *ce* 1, ch. 1, p. 16, and is defined in the commentary as "humbling oneself" like low ground which is damp. The *Fang Yan* records this as being a typical expression in the western part of China ("west from the passes in the region of Qin and Jin").

406. The 1980 editors have transcribed this graph as *sheng* 生 "produce," but it is clearly *zhu* 主 "advocate/master."

407. The text's *shi* 失 "lose" is clearly the copyist's error for *xian* 先 "put in front/first," as all the editors claim. The *WW* and 1976 editors read the graph *ti* 膿 (= 體 "body") with the next sentence, but they are probably incorrect and the punctuation of the 1980 editors should be followed. The 1976 editors, followed by Yu Mingguang (1993[a]), state that *ti* should be read as *lü* 履, which they say means "practice/realize." Although this is phonetically possible, the 1980 editors' interpretation is preferable.

408. The 1976 editors think that the silk manuscript's *yong* 勇 is a mistake for *xiang* 象 "model/appearance," the graph that appears in *GZ pian* 42, "Shi," ch. 15, p. 253, where *zheng* 正 is given as *zheng* 政, but, in my opinion, the silk manuscript is superior and should be followed. Guo Yuanxing believes that *xiang* should be added to the text, "He was upright, correct, and appeared brave." Cf. note 410 below.

409. The 1976 editors quote *Laozi*, Ch. B, section 67, D. C. Lau trans., p. 129:

I have three treasures
Which I hold and cherish.
The first is known as compassion,
The second is known as frugality,

The third is known as not daring to take the lead in the
empire . . .

410. The 1976 editors argue that *qing* 請 should be read as *qing* 情
on the basis of *GZ pian* 42, "Shi," ch. 15, p. 253, but the graph in that
text should be read as *jing* 靜 "quiescent," which is the way Yu Mingguang
(1993[a]) reads it. The *GZ* commentary interprets the sentence as meaning, "In his heart he was calm and quiescent."

411. The 1976 and 1980 editors interpret the unknown graph *qiu*(?)
刟 as a loan for *qiu* 絿, which appears in the *Shi Jing* "Shang Song" 商
頌, ode 304 "Chang Fa" 長發 with the meaning of *ji* 急 "quickly/
rashly": "(Tang) received the grace of Heaven; he was not forceful, he
was not pressing" (Karlgren trans., 1950, pp. 264–65). The 1976 editors
interpret the whole line as "he had no impetuous feelings."

412. These sentiments are also repeated in *GZ* "Shi," *Wenzi* "Dao
De" 道德 (The Dao and Potency) and "Dao Yuan," and *HNZ* "Yuan
Dao Xun." The military theorist Sunzi also advocated that you should
deceive your enemy by pretending that you are not capable.

413. The 1980 editors say that *zhi* 執 "hold" should be read as *she*
設 "apply."

414. The text in the *GZ* "Shi" adds the graph *chu* 處 "dwell": "He
firmly dwelled in it."

415. When the male tally has reached the furthest point, the female
must take over, just as when Yang has reached its apogee, Yin begins to
return. Thus the sage is able to win by relying on the rising Yin.

416. *GY* "Yue Yu xia" (ZHSJ ed., p. 645) states, "(Fan Li said)
'Make the work of men and women equal, and get rid of what harms
the people in order to avoid heavenly calamities. When the fields and
wild lands are opened up, the treasuries and granaries are full, and the
people are numerous, do not waste their numbers in order to create a
ladder (i.e., opening) for disorder.'"

417. Similar sentences appear in the *Wenzi* (*Wenzi yaoquan, pian* 5,
"Dao De" [Dao and Potency], p. 103), "Now he who loses the Dao
considers warfare crucial and creates the beginning of disorder." Here
zhu 邾 should be read as *zhu* 主 "main point/crucial," according to the
1976 and 1980 editors. They both interpret *zhu* as "one who starts
military operations or battles," but I do not think this is correct.

418. This means that he waited for his enemy to reach the point
where he (the enemy) was at his most vulnerable, when his "tally of
opposition" to Heaven and Earth was at its uttermost point, and then
he attacked.

419. This sentence also appears in *HNZ*, ch. 15, "Bing Lüe Xun," p. 17b.

420. *GY* "Yue Yu xia" (ZHSJ ed. p. 646) also contains the same phrasing.

421. I follow Li Xueqin (1993b) in taking *Shida* 十大 as the title of the last section only: previously *Shida Jing* 十大經 (Ten Great Canons) or *Shiliu Jing* 十六經 (Sixteen Canons) was taken as the title of the entire second part of the silk manuscripts.

422. The *WW* and 1976 editors, followed by Yu Mingguang (1993[a]) take *qing* 請 in the sense of "please/invite/request," and place a comma between *shi* 失 and *qing*: "If you desire to know about gain and loss, you must please . . ." This does not seem to make as much sense as my rendition, where *qing* is an alternate form of writing or a loan for *qing* 情 "true facts/conditions." However, the 1980 editors' punctuation is to be preferred, for the passage is rhymed: *qing, xing, ding, jing.*

423. This is similar to the *HNZ*, ch. 14, "Quan Yan Xun" 詮言訓 (Illustrations), p. 4b, "The sage does not think or cogitate; he does not arrange or store. What comes, he does not welcome; what goes, he does not lead away."

424. These questions are similar to the *Zhuangzi*, ch. 23 (ce 4, p. 785), "Gengsang Chu," Watson (1968), p. 253, "Lao-tzu said, 'Ah—the basic rule of life-preservation. Can you embrace the One? Can you keep from losing it? Can you, without tortoise shell or divining sticks, foretell fortune and misfortune? Do you know where to stop, do you know where to leave off? Do you know how to disregard it in others and instead look for it in yourself . . .'" The *GZ pian* 49, "Nei Ye," ch. 16, p. 271 (Rickett tr. [1965], pp. 164–65) also states,

> "Can you concentrate?
> Can you adhere to the Unity of Nature?
> Can you know good fortune from bad without resorting to divination?
> Can you halt [at the right place]?
> Can you stop [when you ought to stop]?
> Can you forgo seeking from others but rather obtain fulfillment in yourself?"

Cf. *pian* 37, "Xin Shu xia" (Techniques of the Heart B), ch. 13, p. 222 (Rickett 1965, p. 169).

425. The 1976 editors suggest that 紵 should be understood as *bao* 褓 "swaddling clothes." They do not explain *mao* 毛 "hair/down" or the meaning of this sentence. The 1980 editors give two other inter-

pretations: 紓 should be read as *guo* 裹 "wrap/bind" and *mao* should be read as *biao* 表 "open" as in the *Shi Jing* "Xiao Ya" 小雅, poem 197: "but I am not attached to [the garment's] outside, I am not attached to [the garment's] lining" (Karlgren 1950, pp. 144–45). Yu Mingguang (1993[a]) interprets the first graph as *bao* 褓 "swaddling clothes" and argues that *mao* should be understood as *wu* 无 "not." Alternatively, 紓 could be interpreted as *zi* 孳 "multiply" and *mao* as *hao* 耗 "diminish/reduce": the line means "Life and Death" or "Multiply and Contract." I follow the interpretation of Li Xueqin (1993b: 281), who takes *mao* as a mistake for *tun* 屯 "stockpile/hoard."

426. The 1976 editors suggest that *liu*/*liao* 翏 should be interpreted as an abbreviation of *jiu* 摎 "mix/intermingle." Yu Mingguang (1993[a]) understands it as *jiu* 糾 "entangle/involve."

427. The 1976 editors explain *zhou* 周 as "'continuous/revolving': it means 'without end.'" "I am without end." *Zhou* is, however, the main verb of the relative clause. *Suo* 所 can be either the direct object of *zhou*, or the object of an understood *yu* 於 "I have where I *zhou*." As the meaning is a little unclear to me, I follow Hu Xintian (1984). *Zhou* can also mean "be prudent/careful" or "to be faithful to" or "to come to." Yu Mingguang (1993[a]) understands the word as *tiao* 調 "select." One of these other meanings may be more appropriate here. The 1980 editors quote *Zhuangzi*, *pian* 7, "Ying Di Wang" 應帝王 ce 1, ch. 3b, p. 307, which Watson (1968) translates, p. 97, "The Perfect Man uses his mind like a mirror—going after nothing, welcoming nothing, responding but not storing. Therefore he can win out over things and not hurt himself."

428. Guo Yuanxing points out that this title refers only to the previous passage: it is not the title of the entire 4000+ graph chapter. The 1980 editors, however, argue that *da* 大 "great" should be read as *liu* 六 "six," i.e., "sixteen" and this title refers to the entire book.

3 . DESIGNATIONS

429. Cf. "The Dao and the Law" and "Names and Principles" above.

430. The answer to this riddle is "designation" *cheng* 稱, the title of the section.

431. The *WW* editors supposed the missing graph was *xing* 刑 "punishment." Possibly they are understanding *huan* 環 "promote/further/encircle" in the sense of "refuse," a usage that appears in the Qin legal

documents and the *Zhou Li* (Hulsewé [1985], D 125, pp. 161–162, note 4, i.e., "Refusing to punish harms authority." Yu Mingguang (1993[a]) accepts the reading of *xing*, but takes *huan* in the sense of "multiply." These are possibilities. The 1980 editors believe the missing graph is *si* 私 "private/self-interest": *GZ pian* 31, "Jun Chen xia," ch. 11, p. 176, Rickett (1985), p. 417, "They (subjects close to the sovereign at the center) will have [gained the support of] both their superior (*sic*) and subordinates in order to promote their self-interest on all sides." *GZ pian* 6, "Qi Fa," ch. 2, p. 29, Rickett (1985), p. 130, "Assorted hidden evils are harmful to the majesty of the sovereign." *HFZ, pian* 52, "Ren Zhu" 人主 (The Lord of Men), ce 4, p. 73, Liao (1959), vol. 2, p. 320, "The same is not so in these days. The ministers in power arrogate favourable positions and manage state affairs at random in order to further their private interests," where Wang Xianshen states that *huan*, the graph in the present text, should be understood as *ying* 營 "manage." The 1980 editors' interpretation is better.

432. The 1980 editors suspect that *sui/duo/tuo* 隋 "strips of meat/ fall" should be read as 嫷, which the *Shuo Wen* defines as "destroying one another/mutually destructive." Here this means if there is no objection or opposing opinion, the Dao will not easily develop perfection. This is possible, but reading the graph more simply as an abbreviation of *sui* 隨 "follow" makes good sense.

433. *Ting* 庭 (literally, "court") the editors interpret as *wei* 位 "position." I.e., "They do not have the same position." Literally, the meaning seems to be that the regular and the irregular cannot be present in the same court at the same time. Something is either regular or irregular, it cannot be both at the same time.

434. This is similar to the *Laozi*, ch. B, section 41, Lau trans., p. 102, "The way that leads forward seems to lead backward," and section 48, Lau trans., p. 109, "In pursuit of the way one does less every day."

435. This sentiment is the same as that found in the *HGZ*, ch. C, *pian* 17, "Tian Quan" 天權 (The Authority of Heaven), p. 14a, and *HNZ*, ch. 17, "Shuo Lin Xun" 說林訓 (Forest of Sayings), p. 7a.

436. Possibly *ji* 己 "himself" should be read as *yi* 已 "end." This whole passage appears with slight modifications in *HNZ*, ch. 14, "Quan Yan Xun," p. 4b.

437. The 1976 editors suspect that *di/zhai* 翟 should be read as *chuo* 逴, which they define as "surpass." The 1980 editors suggest that it might be a loan for *di* 敵 "match/oppose." They note that the sentences appear to rhyme, with rhymes being *si*, *di/zhai*, *wei*, and that therefore

the second sentence may have lost a word and that the second "dies" (*si*) should be read as *dai* 殆 "imperiled": "He who cheats his ruler is imperiled." Yu Mingguang (1993[a]) interprets the graph as *di* 狄, which he says is the same as *yi* 易 "make light of/disrespect." Possibly *di/zhai* should be taken as an abbreviation of *yao* 曜 "splendor/glory": in other words, the subordinate is more glorious, has a better reputation than his superior.

438. *HS*, ch. 75, "Yi Feng zhuan" 翼奉傳 (Biography of Yi Feng), p. 16b, appears to quote this aphorism: "It is like nest-dwellers knowing the wind and cave-dwellers knowing about rain." It was believed that in ancient times men lived in nests in trees or in caves dug in the ground.

439. This passage is put into the mouth of Guo Wei 郭隗 in the *Shuo Yuan*, ch. 1, "Jun Dao" 君道 (The Way of a Lord), p. 16. Virtually the same argument can be found in several other Qin and Han texts, including the *HGZ*, ch. A, *pian* 1, "Bo Xuan," p. 2a, "Therefore an emperor dwells with teachers; a true king dwells with friends; a lost ruler dwells with servants." Cf. *ZGC* "Yan Ce" 燕策 (Discourses of Yan), Crump (1970), p. 523; Jia Yi, *Xin Shu*, ch. 8, "Guan Ren" 官人 p. 27a, where the characteristics of the different types of associates of the ruler are exhaustively defined, and the *Hanshi waizhuan*.

440. I suspect that the meaning is that he makes himself more glorious than he really is, i.e., he is a self-flatterer or a self-promoter. The 1976 and 1980 editors interpret *guang* 光 "light/bright/illuminate" as a loan for *guang* 廣 "broaden," but this is not necessary.

441. Possibly there is a period mark at the end of this sentence, for this passage is almost identical with a passage in the *Shenzi* "Yin Xun" 因循 (Relying on and Following). See P. M. Thompson (1970), fragments 30–32, pp. 248–249.

442. These pronouncements are similar to those found in the *GZ pian* 38, "Bai Xin," ch. 13, p. 227, "A flourishing state cannot be served; a flourishing family cannot be married into; an arrogant and rude man cannot be associated with."

443. The 1976 editors read *yi/zhi* 埶 as an abbreviation of *yi* 藝, which is defined by Fu Qian in a comment on *Zuo Zhuan*, Duke Zhao year 23, as *chang* 常 "constant." The 1980 editors interpret it as an abbreviation of *xie* 褻 "slight/disrespect."

444. The *LSCQ* also makes a point of not advocating an entirely pacifist policy, which is implied by the term *yan bing* 偃兵 "ceasing war/arms/weapons": in ch. 7, no. 2, "Dang Bing" 蕩 (Eliminating

Warfare), p. 2b, it proclaims, "The ancient sage kings had righteous arms/warfare *(yibing)*; they did not desist from arms/warfare *(yanbing)*."

445. Cf. *Laozi*, ch. 31, Mawangdui Text A, Henricks, p. 248:

"Weapons are instruments of ill-omen.

When you have no choice but to use them, it's best to remain tranquil and calm."

446. The 1976 and 1980 editors suggest that *milun* 糜論 should be read as *milun* 彌綸, a phrase that appears in the *Yi Jing* "Xi Ci shang" (Gao Heng, p. 511), "Therefore he is able to control extensively the Dao of Heaven and Earth."

447. The 1976 editors suggest that *he* 合 should be understood as "sew up" *fenghe* 縫合, but they do not indicate what they think the object pronoun *zhi* 之 refers to. It could either be "the world," or the people, or the territory under the ruler's control. The following passage is also to be found in the *Shenzi*, section 5, "De Li" 德立 (Establishment of Potency), Thompson (1970), no. 57, p. 264, with some minor variations. Probably this whole text derives from the original *Shenzi* and perhaps the *zhi* "it/them" referred to something or somebody previously mentioned. In the extant text of the *Shenzi*, the second half of the passage appears as the first item in section 5, so there is no context to help identify the object.

448. The 1976 editors read *yi* 疑 "doubt" as *ni* 擬 "liken" in the sense of comparing one's own prerogatives, position, and power to that of a superior, i.e., to encroach upon. The commentator on the *Shenzi*, after defining *yi* as *huo* 惑 "delude," goes on to paraphrase the passage using the word *ni* for *yi*: "The feudal lords do not dare to compare themselves to the Son of Heaven." This is the way the 1980 editors interpret the word.

449. The term *bei/bi* 婢 "female slave" does not appear in the Qin laws, whereas *qie* 妾 does appear in several combinations: *nuqie* 奴妾, *rennuqie* 人奴妾, etc. The precise difference in status between *bei/bi* and *qie* remains obscure. It is also possible to interpret *beiqie* as a single term "slave (unfree) concubine." The 1980 editors consider that *bei* should be read as *bi* 嬖 "favorite." This is also possible.

450. I.e., the social and legal positions of the previous pairs are not to be confused: one should not treat the concubine's son like the legitimate heir.

451. Possibly the missing graph is *zhi* 之 "him," and the order of the sentence should be changed to *li [zhi] wei wang* 立 [之] 為王, to parallel the subsequent sentence *liu zhi si wang* 流之死亡. The subject

of the sentence would probably be Heaven: "Heaven establishes [him] as a true king."

452. Cf. *GY*, ch. 21, p. 3b, "There is taking away, there is giving, and there is not giving." The commentator interprets the subject of the sentences as being Heaven, who has thereby the means to bestow success or destruction.

453. All the editors interpret *huan xing* 環刑 as *huan xing* 還刑, which they define as *fanxing* 反刑 "punishments for transgression (?)/ punishments in retribution (?)." There is an obscure item in the Qin laws, D 85, which throws light on this passage, studied in depth by Hulsewé (1985), pp. 147–148, note 5. "(A man) relieved (from statutory duties because of) age denounces another person because of unfilial behavior and requests that he be killed. Is he warranted (=does he deserve) to be *san huan* 三環or not? He is not warranted (=does not deserve) to be *huan*. He is to be quickly seized and not be lost." The editors of the Shuihudi texts interpret *san* as "three" and *huan* as a loan for *yuan* 原, which they interpret as "forgive/treat indulgently"; other interpretations include *huan* being understood as "mitigating conditions" or something to do with the later system of "three hearings or investigations" of a crime. If *huan* is taken to mean "recompense" in both the silk manuscripts and in the Shuihudi legal text, both passages would make sense. *San* might then be interpreted as a loan for *can* 參 "investigate/examine": "Does he deserve to be examined and recompensed? He does not deserve to be recompensed."

454. The first part of the passage is contradicted by the *GZ*, ce 1, ch. 1, *pian* 2, "Xing Shi" 形勢 (Conditions and Circumstances), p. 5, Rickett (1985), p. 77, translates, "Those who can give without taking [in return] are like Heaven and Earth." The *Explanation* reads, "Heaven produces the four seasons and Earth produces all resources, thereby nourishing all things but not taking anything [in return]. The enlightened ruler is like Heaven and Earth. He instructs the people in accordance with the seasons. He exhorts them to plough and weave in order to enrich their livelihood, /and he does not push his own achievements nor regard his gains as belonging to himself."

455. All the editors punctuate this aphorism differently. The *WW* text reads 世恆不可擇法而川我. 用我不可,是以生禍. This would probably translate as, "According to the constant (way of the) world, one cannot relax the laws and use one's self. If using one's self is not possible, from this disaster is born." This does not seem to be as good as the 1976 and 1980 editors' rendition. It is, however, unusual for this

text to recommend using one's self (literally, the Chinese says "myself") rather than the constant and regular standards and laws. Guo Yuanxing follows the initial punctuation of the *WW* text and interprets the sentence to mean, "It is the constant way of the world that you cannot abandon the old laws and use your own new laws." This is possible.

456. The 1976 editors interpret *cong* 從 "follow" as *zong* 蹤 "track/trace." The sentence seems to mean "hide yourself away again, following the track you did before, not putting yourself ahead of the times, and you will not be removed by someone else."

457. Cf. *GZ pian* 42, "Shi," ch. 15, p. 253, "If you have not yet reached heaven's pole (*tian ji* 天極, i.e., the furthest point you can go, the natural crucial moment), hide yourself in potency. If you have reached heaven's pole, then bring your strength to bear. When your strength is brought to its completion, be acquiescent and preserve the track *(cong)*, and other men will not be able to replace you."

458. The lacuna makes it impossible to determine the precise meaning of the last sentence. Does it mean that vengeance is only to be found among the common people?

459. *XZ*, ce 3, ch. 9, *pian* 14, "Zhi Shi" 致仕 (On Attracting Scholars), p. 20, states, "People who harbor hatred and those who obstruct and conceal, the gentleman does not approach." (The 1980 editors have mistakenly quoted the last graph as *zheng* 正 "correct" instead of *jin* 近 "approach.") *XZ*, ce 4, ch. 19, *pian* 27, "Da Lüe," p. 71, states, "Those who conceal the impartial are called 'blind'; those who hide the good are called 'jealous.' Those who recommend the 'blind' and the 'jealous' are called 'deliverers of craftiness.' 'Deliverers of craftiness' and ministers who are 'blind' and jealous' are the noxious weeds of a state." Here *du mei* 妒妹 is the same as *du mei* 妒昧.

460. "Internal affairs" refers to matters within yourself, family, or state.

461. This aphorism also appears in Liu Xiang's *Shuo Yuan*, ch. 16, p. 390.

462. *HNZ*, ch. 4, "Di Xing Xun" 地形訓 (The Form of the Earth), 7a, also states, "Four-footed (animals) lack wings, (beasts) that bear horns lack upper teeth." The aphorism also appears in the *LSCQ*, ch. 24, no. 5, "Bo Zhi" 博志 (Broad Ambition), *Da Dai Li Ji jinzhu jinyi* 大戴禮記今註今譯, *pian* 81, "Yi Benming" 易本命 (Basic Fate According to the Yi), p. 475, and Dong Zhongshu's 董仲舒 *Chunqiu fanlu* 春秋繁露 *pian* 25, "Du Zhi" 度制 (Measures and Controls), ch. 8, p. 1b. Yu Mingguang (1993[a]) explains that this refers to ruminants such as sheep,

cattle, and deer, who lack the canine teeth of flesh-eating predators. Both horns and teeth are types of weapon, and animals don't possess both types.

463. Cf. Liu Xiang, *Lienü zhuan* 列女傳, ch. 3, "Jin Bozong qi" 晉伯宗妻 (The Wife of Jin Boqi), p. 3a, where the first two statements appear, and *HNZ*, ch. 17, "Shuo Lin Xun," p. 2a, "The best taste is not pleasing; the best words are not refined (*wen*); the best music is not ridiculous; the best sounds are not shouted out." Possibly *yue* 樂 "music" should interpreted as *le* "pleasure."

464. *Er Ya* "Shi Cao" 釋草 states, "Lotus . . . the seed is *lian* 蓮; the root is *ou* 藕; the center (of the stem) is *di* 的; inside the *di* is *yi* 薏." The commentary quotes Lu Ji 陸機 who says that the green pith in the center of the lotus stalk is very bitter and that therefore there is a common saying, "Bitter as the center of the lotus stalk." Here, the author is saying that at the heart of every beautiful and lovely thing there is something bitter. We might say "a rotten heart." He prefers the simple and straightforward to the flowery and ornamented.

465. *GY*, ch. 21, "Yue Yu xia," pp. 5b–6a, states, "In general, the Dao of (military) formations is to establish the right as the female and to increase the left as the male." *HNZ*, ch. 15, "Bing Lüe Xun," p. 12b, states, "What is meant by the advantages of Earth *(di li)* is to have 'live (ground)' behind and 'dead (ground)' in front; to have male on the left and female on the right." "Dead ground" is where one perishes, so it was advisable to try to force the enemy to take up his position there, so that he could be destroyed. The same chapter states, p. 3a, "Have your back to Yin and embrace Yang; have the soft on your left and the hard on your right." See also the Yin-Yang military texts from Yinqueshan, the *Di Dian* 地典 (Yates (1994[a]) and *Male and Female Cities* 雄牝城 (Needham and Yates 1994, p. 259).

466. The 1980 editors suggest that *gao gao* 誥誥 "tell, tell" should be read as *hao hao* 皓皓 "pure and brightly white." Yu Mingguang (1993[a]) thinks it should be understood as *hao hao* 浩浩 meaning "very broad and large."

467. The 1980 editors suggest that the first *long* 隆 is a mistake for *lun* 輪 "wheel" and the second *long* should be understood as *long* 龍 "dragon." The first suggestion should be accepted, the second not. Cf. *HNZ*, ch. 1, "Yuan Dao Xun," p. 3b, "Thunderous are the chariot wheels!"

468. All the editors interpret the unknown graph *ji* (?) 齎 "matériel/means" as a loan for *zi* 資 "materials." This is possible, but not necessary.

469. The 1980 editors interpret the unknown graph 犆 as an alter-

nate form of *xiu* 袖, which they say here is a loan for *you* 由 "follow/ reason." This might be possible. They also suggest that this passage is similar to *HNZ*, ch. 9 "Zhu Shu Xun," p. 7a, Ames (1983), pp. 178–79:

"This is (for the ruler) to mount a chariot, which is the overwhelming support of the people *(ch'e),* and to drive horses which are the intelligence of the people *(ma).* Even on a remote or treacherous stretch of road *(t'u),* there is no fear of his not knowing which way to go *(huo)."*

Yu Mingguang (1993[a]) interprets the last word as similar in meaning to *fu* 福 "good fortune" or *shan* 善 "good." This makes better sense in the semantic and grammatical context, although it does not have textual support.

470. *GZ pian* 40, "Si Shi" 四時, ch. 14, p. 238, reads, "The state will then be *lu* 路." Yin Zhizhang 尹知章 says this means "loses its constant dwelling-place." The 1976 editors say the present sentence means, "Though he may live there, it will not be for long." *Lu* is, however, probably an abbreviation of *lu* 露 "expose," as Wang Niansun 王念孫 believes is true for the graph in the *GZ* (*Guanzi jijiao*, vol. 2, p. 701).

471. The 1980 editors suggest that *yi* 役 "corvée labor" should be read as *yi* 疫 "pestilence," a common practice in the Yinqueshan slips. It was believed that pestilential vapors (qi) and pestilence demons lived in watery places, so opening up the marshlands might permit these to run wild among the population. This is not, however, as good grammatically as Yu Mingguang's (1993[a]) interpretation, which I follow here.

472. *Cong* 蓯 should be read as *cong/can* 藂, also written 菆 (it is the same as 葬, according to M. 31146, definition 9), which means "pile up wood to make coffins [and plaster them]," according to the 1980 editors. This interpretation is based on *Li Ji pian* 3, "Tan Gong shang" 檀弓上, ch. 8, p. 66a (p. 1294a), where the graph is read as *can.* As the products of the woods, marshlands, rivers, and seas were reserved exclusively for the ruler, many texts record prohibitions of the same nature— for example, the Qin laws from Shuihudi, the *Mencius*, the texts from Yinqueshan, and the *Zhou Li.* Yu Mingguang (1993[a]) takes *cong* as an alternate form of *cong* 從 "follow" and says that the sentence means to allow the various weeds and grasses to stifle the growth of young trees.

473. In other words, you should only complete a task at the same time as Heaven completes its tasks.

474. Similar opinions appear in *GY*, ch. 21, "Yue Yu xia," p. 5a, "Fan Li said, 'Your subject has heard that those of the ancients who excelled in warfare considered excess and shortage their constants and

the four seasons their rules. They did not exceed Heaven's limits; they scrutinized numbers and then stopped.'" *GZ pian* 42, "Shi," ch. 15, p. 253, states, "In the Dao of achieving success, excess and shortage are treated as treasures. Do not lose Heaven's limits; scrutinize numbers and then stop."

475. In other words, neither the sons nor the subjects would behave in a fashion becoming their station and would abandon their fathers and rulers respectively: the fathers and rulers would then not be fathers and rulers. The Chinese believed that all relationships were reciprocal and the person in the dominant position, although he had the power and authority on his side, nevertheless had to fulfil the obligation of protecting and nurturing those under him. Needless to say, the obligation was not always fulfilled.

476. The 1976 editors interpret *fa* 伐 "cut" as a loan for *bai* 敗 "be defeated/defeat" with the meaning of "collapse" in the second occurrence of the word below. Although the loan is possible, the meaning is inappropriate for this first occurrence and so their suggestion should be rejected. If there were no lacuna, it would be easier to understand the sentence. Perhaps *fa* is correct after all, and the simile is to a tree being cut in the forest, where in the mountain it falls a long way down the slope, whereas in the valley (?), the timber stays more or less where it was felled. *Fa* may well be a loan for another word, however.

477. *Lian* 連 "link" is a loan for *lie* 烈, according to all the editors. The word *lie* 裂 appears in *LZ*, ch. B, section 39 in the line 天毋以清將恐裂, where the B version of the Mawangdui silk manuscripts has the graph *lian* 蓮 (Henricks [1989]), pp. 100–101, "If Heaven were not by means of it clear, it would, I'm afraid, shatter."

478. *Shuo Yuan*, ch. 16, "Tan Cong," p. 387, contains the second half of this adage with virtually the same wording, except that the silk manuscript's *zhi lien* 之連 is written *yu lie* 餘烈. *Zhi* 之 is probably a mistake for *yu* 餘.

479. This same saying appears with virtually the same wording in the *Shuo Yuan*, ch. 16, "Tan Cong," p. 398.

480. The 1980 editors argue that *guo* 國 "state" should be read as *yu* 域, which the *GuangYa* "Shi Qiu" 釋丘 defines as a "place of tombs/cemetery." Here the spirits of the dead ancestors are meant. Yu Mingguang (1993[a]) accepts the reading of *guo*, i.e., "(This) harms the spirits of the state."

481. In other words, going to war recklessly, in the heat of passion, without taking into consideration the relative strength of one's enemy.

482. A similar proverb is to be found in the *Shuo Yuan*, ch. 17, "Za Yan" 雜言 (Miscellaneous Sayings), p. 420, where it is put into the mouth of Confucius in a conversation with Duke Ai of Lu, and in *Wenzi, pian* 4, "Fu Yan" 符言 (Speaking Reliably), p. 88. Judging from the other passages, the last statement means engaging an enemy on the battlefield who is far more numerous than one's own troops.

483. This graph and the one below are hard to decipher. The *WW* and 1976 editors read the graph as *li* 裏, which the latter understood as *lai* 賚, meaning *yu* 予 "give," according to the *Er Ya* "Shi Gu." The 1980 editors point out that the silk manuscript version of the *Zhou Yi* "Xi Ci xia,'' in a passage where the received text has *yi* 衣 "clothe" ("In burials of the ancients, they clothed them thickly with brushwood") (Gao Heng, p. 566), has the graph *li* 裏 (Chen Songchang [1993(a)], p. 421, line 37A). This they interpret as a loan for *li* 理 "manage/offer."

484. The first part of this passage is an adage that appears in four other texts: *ZGC* "Qin Ce 3" 秦策 in a persuasion by Fan Ju (Li Weiqi [1988], p. 43; Crump (1970), no. 94, p.106); *XZ, ce* 4, ch. 19, *pian* 27, "Da Lüe," p. 80; *Shi Ji*, ch. 79, p. 2409, "Fan Ju lie zhuan" 范雎列傳, and Li Si's letter advising against the expulsion of the aliens, *Shi Ji*, ch. 87, p. 2547. Sentences similar to the last part of the passage are also to be found in *GY*, ch. 21, "Yue Yu xia," p. 5a and *HGZ*, ch. C, *pian* 12, "Shi Bing," p. 3b. The point is that the relative strength of yourself and the enemy will radically alter, shifting the advantage to the enemy.

485. 勮 should be read as *jue* 臄 "palate/skin on the inside of the mouth," according to the 1980 editors. The point of this saying seems to rely on a pun: *fu* 膚 "skin" sounds like *fu* 傅 "be near/close to" and *jue* "skin on the inside of the mouth" sounds like *que* 卻 "rift/be far from." The authors would rather one rely on both Yin and Yang and not just on one alone: you must have skin on the inside and on the outside, and you must prepare for all eventualities. Yu Mingguang (1993[a]) interprets the passage completely differently, saying that *fu* means "(outwardly) beautiful" and *jue* means "to work hard," hence Leo Chang's translation, "A person may appear intimately affectionate, but he in fact be hateful within (*sic*). Such a person is called beautiful in appearance and confused within . . . Conversely, if one perceives beauty as beauty and confusion as confusion . . ." Whichever interpretation is correct, the initial aphorism is still rather obscure, in my opinion.

486. What "it" refers to is unclear. Is "it" the Dao?

487. The *WW* and 1976 editors transcribed this graph as *ai* 艾, in other words *yi* 刈 "mow." The 1980 editors point out that the graph in

the manuscript is written 㓞, with *li* 立 at the top, which is similar to the way in which the upper part of *hua* 華 appears in these texts. Therefore it should be transcribed 刐, with *dao* 刀 "knife" as the radical. This graph should be understood as another form of *yi* "mow." Yu Mingguang (1993[a]) transcribes the graph as *wan* 刓 "chop down."

488. This saying appears in extended form in the *Shenzi*, Thompson (1979), pp. 228–30, section 1.1–4, in which the sage appears as the third of the group: "Heaven possesses brightness and does not grieve that the people are in darkness; Earth has its resources and does not grieve that the people are poor; the sage has his potency and does not grieve that the people are in danger. Although Heaven does not grieve that the people are in darkness, if they close their doors and windows, inevitably taking light from it, Heaven has nothing to do with it. Although Earth does not grieve that the people are poor, if they cut down trees and mow the grasses, inevitably taking their wealth from it, Earth has nothing to do with it. Although the sage does not grieve that the people are in danger, if the hundred surnames take their standard from their superiors and compare themselves with their inferiors, inevitably gaining safety for themselves from this, the sage has nothing to do with it." *Wenzi*, ch. 4, "Fu Yan," p. 93, has an abbreviated version: "Heaven possesses brightness and does not grieve that the people are in darkness; Earth has its resources and does not grieve that the people are poor." *HNZ*, ch. 14, "Quan Yan Xun," p. 8b, has another version, different only in saying, "The hundred surnames bore out (holes for) doors and drill windows and take light from it." Some versions of the *Shenzi* add the graph *kai*, and the commentator also includes it, thus reading, ". . . close their doors and open their windows." It is most likely that the silk manuscript composer abbreviated the original *Shenzi* text and quite probably inadvertently omitted the word *kai* 開.

489. *Liang* 兩, literally, "two/both/double." The author is arguing for a rigid and complete hierarchy to be established in the bureaucracy and in the family.

490. The *WW* editors transcribed this graph here and below as *yi* 曳 "drag." The 1976 and 1980 editors interpret it as *yu* 與 "short time/drag." The 1980 editors suggest that this should be read as a loan for *you* 猶 "still," because this is the word that appears in a passage almost exactly identical to this one in the *Qunshu zhiyao* 群書治要, ch. 37, where it is attributed to Shen Dao. Cf. Thompson (1979), p. 265, section V, pp. 58–59.

491. This adage appears in both *ZGC* "Qin Ce 4" (Li Weiqi [1988],

p. 57; Crump [1970], no. 90, p.96) and in *Shi Ji*, ch. 78, pp. 2387–88, "Chunshen jun liezhuan" 春申君列傳, where the text reads, "(Huang) Xie then sent up a memorial to King Zhao of Qin which stated: 'In the world, no one is as strong as Qin and Chu, but now I have heard your majesty, the Great King, is desiring to attack Chu. This is like two tigers doing battle. When two tigers do battle, bad dogs receive the spoil. It would be better to be on good terms with Chu.'"

492. This may be a particular criticism of rulers and aristocratic elites who stored up ice in underground chambers for their use in the summer and kept themselves warm in heated palaces in the winter, but it should be read as a general rule that one should always be in harmony with the natural order.

493. For "lost states," see *The Canon: Law* above.

494. The 1976 and 1980 editors suspect that 賣, which the *WW* editors transcribed as *mai* 賣 "sell," is an alternate form of *guan* 觀 "observe."

495. *Shu* 樹 literally, "plant (as a tree)." The translation is tentative.

496. Probably this last sentence consisted of pairs of opposites as in *The Canon: Law* "Assessing Destruction" and must have read something like, "to know the seasons when he has misfortune and good fortune, incorrectness and correctness, nobility and meanness, survival and destruction." The term *cheng* 稱 "designate" here is the same as the title to the entire section.

497. Guests are attackers and hosts defenders in Chinese military parlance.

498. Yu Mingguang (1993[a]) takes the pair as "masters" and "disciples." I follow the 1976 editors and Qiu Xigui. There were two forms of service required of the able-bodied: military service and corvée labor.

499. Because of the lacuna, it is not clear what this means.

500. For the "female tally," see "The Female and Male Tally" above.

501. In fact, there are a few more than 1,600 graphs.

4. *DAO THE ORIGIN*

502. The *WW* editors transcribed *wu* 无 "nothing" as *xian* 先 "first": this is followed by Yu Mingguang (1993[a]) and Jan (1977), who translates it as "past."

503. The 1976 and 1980 editors interpret *tong* 迵, which the *Shuo*

Wen defines as *da* 達 "penetrate," as the same as *dong* 洞 "cave/hole/ penetrate." The same expression appears in *HNZ*, ch. 14, "Quan Yan Xun," p. 1a, "Totally the same as Heaven and Earth, Confusedly chaotic it was the uncarved block; though not yet created, it brought phenomena to completion: It was called the Grand Unity." *HNZ*, ch. 10, "Miu Cheng Xun," p. 1a, also states, "Embracing and enveloping the cosmos, yet without appearing to envelop, totally the same it covered over and held up, but nowhere was it blocked."

504. *Zhuangzi, pian* 12, "Tian Di" 天地 (Heaven and Earth), ce 2, ch. 5A, p. 424, states, (Watson [1968] trans., p. 131), "In the Great Beginning, there was non-being; there was no being, no name. Out of it arose One; there was One, but it had no form . . ."

505. The term *shi shi* 濕濕 appears in the *Shi Jing* "Xiao Ya" ode 190 "Wu Yang" 無羊 as the "flapping of an ox's ears": "your cattle come, their ears are flapping" (Karlgren 1950, pp.131–32). *Shi* by itself means "moisture" either in the clouds or rising from the earth and it seems to me this metaphor is more appropriate here. Jan (1977) translates the term as "unsettled."

506. Cf. *GZ pian* 36, "Xin Shu shang" (Techniques of the Heart A), ch. 13, p. 220; Rickett (1965), p. 173, "The Way lies between Heaven and Earth. It is so large that nothing can exist outside it. It is so small that nothing can exist within it." The Mawangdui *Laozi*, ch. 34, Henricks (1989) trans., p. 254,

"It (the Dao) can be named with the things that are small.
The ten thousand things entrust their lives to it, and yet it does
    not act as their master.
It can be named with the things that are great."

507. Cf. *HNZ*, ch. 1, "Yuan Dao Xun," p. 16a, "For this reason, he who acquires the Dao . . . is not scorched in fire, is not soaked in water." The Heshang gong 河上公 commentary on section 25 of the *Laozi* quotes this passage.

508. Cf. *HNZ*, ch. 1, "Yuan Dao Xun," p. 12a, "For this reason, the sage takes One as his measure and follows its standard, and does not change what is appropriate."

509. Cf. *HNZ*, ch. 1, "Yuan Dao Xun," p. 1b, "The mountains were high because of it (the Dao); the abysses were deep because of it; by it, the wild animals ran; by it, the birds flew; the sun and moon were bright because of it . . ."

510. Cf. *GZ pian* 49, "Nei Ye," ch. 16, p. 269, Rickett (1965), p. 160:

"Having lost it (the Dao), men will die;
Having obtained it, they will live.
Having lost it, affairs will fail;
Having obtained it,, they will succeed."
HNZ, ch. 1, "Yuan Dao Xun," p. 10a, "If the myriad phenomena do not acquire it (the Dao), they do not grow; if the numerous affairs do not acquire it, they are not completed."

511. Cf. *GZ pian* 38, "Bai Xin," ch. 13, p. 227, "The Dao . . . is what the people use, but those who understand it are few"; *GZ pian* 49, "Nei Ye," ch. 16, p. 270; Rickett (1965), p. 162:

"The Way fills the world and exists everywhere people are,
Yet people are unable to understand it."

512. Cf. *HFZ*, ce 1, ch. 2, *pian* 8, "Yang Quan" (Wielding the Sceptre), p. 31; Liao (1959), vol. 1, p. 55, "Tao is never a pair. Hence it is called one." *HNZ*, ch. 1, "Yuan Dao Xun," p. 11a, "What is referred to as 'The Formless' means the One."

513. Cf. *HNZ*, ch. 14, "Quan Yan Xun," p. 2b, "The Level is the plainness of the Dao; the Void is the dwelling-place of the Dao." *HNZ*, ch. 2, "Shu Zhen Xun," p. 8b, states, "The Void and Nothingness are the dwelling-place of the Dao; the Level and the Easy are the plainness of the Dao."

514. Cf. *HNZ*, ch. 1, "Yuan Dao Xun," p. 1a, "Now the Dao covers over Heaven and holds up Earth; it extends to the Four Cardinal Points; it opens up the Eight Directions; it is so high it cannot be scrutinized; it is so deep it cannot be fathomed; it embraces and envelops Heaven and Earth, and receives and accepts the Formless."

515. *Wenzi*, *pian* 1, p. 33, states, "In the changes of the hundred affairs, none are not paired." I.e., only the Dao is not paired.

516. As the general pattern for this text consists of four-graph phrases, I suspect that "Dao" should be part of this line. All the editors, however, take "Dao" with the next line, "Dao does not increase or reduce them."

517. "Dao" should be read with the second line. The 1980 editors quote *GZ pian* 38, "Bai Xin," ch. 13, p. 225, "As for the Dao, when one man uses it, it is not heard to have a surplus; when the world puts it into practice, it is not heard to be insufficient: this is what is meant by the Dao."

518. The same line occurs in two other locations, where *Wenzi*, ch. 1, p. 43, writes this text's *gui/kui* 匱 as *gui/kui* 匱 "deficient/short/lacking." *HNZ*, ch. 1, "Yuan Dao Xun," p. 12b, uses the graph *gui* 籟,

which Gao You defines as *zhe* 折 "break," i.e., "It is hard and strong, yet is not broken." Another interpretation is that the graph is an alternate form of *hui* 潰 "overflow." Both interpretations are possible. Generally speaking, the Daoists prefer the soft and the weak to the hard and the strong, believing the latter can be easily destroyed. Therefore *Wenzi, pian* 1, p. 34, states, "Softness is the hardness of the Dao."

519. *Zhuangzi, pian* 12, "Tian Di" (Heaven and Earth), ce 2, ch. 5A, p. 411 (Watson [1968], p. 128), "He (The man of kingly virtue) sees in the darkest dark, hears where there is no sound." *HNZ*, ch. 17, "Shuo Lin Xun," p. 2a, "If you see into the formless, then you will obtain what you are looking for; if you listen to the soundless, then you will obtain what you are listening for." *Dengxizi*, "Zhuan Ci" 轉辭 ("Turning Phrases Round"), p. 7b, states, "If you see into nonexistence, then you will get what you are looking for; if you listen to the soundless, then you will obtain what you are listening for. Therefore the formless is the root of what has form, the soundless is the mother of what has sound."

520. In other words, he becomes entirely at one with Heaven and Earth and the Dao.

521. Cf. *GZ pian* 49, "Nei Ye," ch. 16, p. 268, Rickett (1965), p. 158:

"It is ever so that the essence of things is what gives them life.
Below it gives life to the five grains; above it creates the ranked
    stars.
When floating between Heaven and earth, we call it the spirit.
When stored in the breast [of a person], we call it the sage."

HNZ, ch. 3, "Tian Wen Xun," p. 1a, states, "The harmonious quintessence of Heaven and Earth is Yin and Yang," where the commentary defines "quintessence" as qi, the cosmic ether.

522. Yu Mingguang (1993[a]) interprets *fu* 服 as *de* 得 "acquire." Possibly, however, *fu* should be understood here as "wear," i.e., "a man who wears (the Dao)" as in *Zhuangzi*, ce 3, ch. 7B, *pian* 21, "Tian Zifang," p. 718, Watson (1968) trans., p. 227, (Zhuangzi said to Duke Ai of Lu), "But a gentleman may embrace a doctrine without necessarily wearing the garb *(fu)* that goes with it, and he may wear the garb without necessarily comprehending the doctrine."

523. Cf. *GZ pian* 36, "Xin Shu Shang," ch. 13, p. 221, Rickett (1965), p. 176, "The Way of Heaven is vacuous; the Way of Earth is quiescent. Being vacuous, it is not to be bent. Being quiescent, it does not change. Since it does not change, there are no errors. Therefore it is said: 'There are no miscalculations.'"

524. I.e., are not involved in day-to-day business, have no special interests to respond to. Possibly *shang* 上 here should be translated "superiors," i.e., "If superiors are trustworthy . . ."

525. All the editors take *pian/bian* 扁 "narrow" as an abbreviation of *bian* 遍 "everywhere." It seems better to take it as *bian* 編 "arrange."

526. The *Yinwenzi* "Da Dao Shang," ch. A, p. 4 (Shanghai Guji chuban she ed.), states:

"If names are fixed, then things will not contend;

If divisions are clear, then private interests will not develop."

Shizi, ch. A, "Fa Meng" 發蒙 (SBBY ed.), p. 7b, states, "Now the division of names, the sage fully investigates . . . When he fully investigates the division of names, none of the assembled ministers ventures not to exhaust his strength and tire out his wisdom. That the world can be ordered is because divisions are complete; that the right and wrong can be distinguished is because names are settled/fixed."

527. Cf *Laozi*, ch. B, section 64, D. C. Lau, trans., p. 125:

"Deal with a thing while it is still nothing;

Keep a thing in order before disorder sets in."

528. The title is the same as the first section of the *Wenzi*.

5. THE NINE RULERS

529. Tang was the first ruler of the Shang dynasty.

530. Jie was the wicked last ruler of the Xia dynasty. Li Xueqin (1979) interprets *yi* 以 as *er* 而 "and then."

531. This seems to be an introductory paragraph: the story and conversation between Tang and Yi Yin are related below.

532. This sentence is rather obscure. Li Xueqin (1979) takes the first *wu wu* 吾吾 as a binomial expression meaning "happy": "Tang was very pleased with himself." *Shi* 是 "this" Li understands as *shi* 示 "show" and *da* 達 as *xiao/shao* 曉 "realize." The 1980 editors consider that the first *wu* might be read as *yu* 御 "drive a chariot": "Tang then drove himself . . ." The second *wu* they think might be an alternate form for *wu* 五 "five." In other words, he five times went to Yi Yin. This would be in accord with the story of Tang and Yi Yin related in the *Shi Ji*, ch. 3, "Yin ben ji" 殷本紀 (Basic Annals of the Yin Dynasty), p. 94, where Yi Yin is said to have been a hermit who only left retirement after Tang had sent emissaries to him five times requesting his services. *Shi* the 1980 editors understand as *zhi* 知 "know." I interpret the first *wu* as an

abbreviation for *yu* 語 "speak" and the second and third *wu* as *wu* "five."

533. The 1980 editors interpret *chou* 讎 "respond" as *jiu* 咎 "hate/calamity." Li Xueqin (1979) interprets the word as a loan for *chou* 稠 "many."

534. A similar idea is to be found in *HGZ*, ch. A, *pian* 4, "Tian Ze," p. 7a, "Where subordinates can obstruct, and when superiors can be kept in the dark, this is abandoning proper human activities and losing Heaven's rules." The notion is repeated in *HGZ*, ch. A, *pian* 7, "Jin Die" 近迭, p. 21b, "If a ruler knows that he is not bright (i.e., spiritually illumined), he takes what is noble as the Dao; he takes his own opinions as the law; he fails to follow the seasons and deceives his own generation; controls inferiors and keeps superiors in the dark, and causes affairs to be doubly perverse; nourishes what is wrong and promotes what is lost; considers quiescence a bother and considers peacefulness dangerous; the families of the hundred surnames are in difficulties and the people hate him. What disaster is greater than this?"

535. Li Xueqin (1979) interprets *shi* 適 "appropriate" as *di* 敵 "enemy." The 1980 editors take it as *zhe* 謫 "hold responsible for crime/type of punishment." Li's interpretation is possible—the ministers are behaving like enemies for committing the crimes enumerated by Yi Yin above. Either interpretation is possible.

536. That the word *bang* 邦, the tabooed personal name of the first ruler of the Han dynasty, Liu Bang, appears here suggests that this text was copied prior to the founding of that dynasty.

537. Cf. *GZ pian* 46, "Ming Fa" 明法 (Making Laws Clear), ch. 15, pp. 258–59, "Therefore if a lord and a minister share (the same) Dao, there is disorder; if he bestows his monopoly (of power), he is lost."

538. The ruler who labors is one who works hard himself instead of letting his subordinates exhaust their energies and ruling by non-activity *(wuwei)*.

539. A half-ruler is one who shares his power with another, whether his wife, relative, or close friend. Thus he is equal in authority with a partner, and does not have supreme dominance.

540. Li Xueqin (1979) reads *yu ji yi* 於寄一. A "parasitic ruler" is explained in *GZ pian* 67, "Ming Fa jie" 明法解 (Explanation of *Making Laws Clear*), ch. 21, p. 344, in the following terms: "Therefore, if order and disorder are not decided by the laws, but rather determined by important ministers, and the handles of life and death are not controlled by the ruler, this is a ruler who is a parasite."

541. A "Chart of the Nine Rulers" was also found in the Mawangdui hoard but it was written in a different hand than this manuscript.

542. This must have been an ancient work with authority in the HuangLao tradition that has now been lost.

543. The 1980 editors explain them as Heaven, Earth, the Four Seasons, and the myriad phenomena.

544. *XZ* ce 3, *pian* 17, "Tian Lun," p. 55, states, "Heaven has its constant Dao; Earth has its constant numbers." *HGZ*, ch. C, *pian* 12, "Shi Bing," p. 1a, "The Dao has measures and numbers and therefore the spiritually illumined can communicate (with it)."

545. Cf. *HGZ*, ch. C, *pian* 17, "Tian Quan" 天權 (Heaven's Authority), p. 16b, "Now Heaven gives birth to things, but it is not itself a thing; it may originate Yin and Yang."

546. Birth is spring; growth summer; harvest autumn; and store winter.

547. Li Xueqin (1979) adds the three graphs *fa jun zhi* 法君之 "(assistants) of a ruler who abides by the law."

548. Cf. *GZ pian* 16, "Fa Fa" 法法 (Taking Law as the Model), ch. 6, p. 93, "Loyal ministers do not falsify their abilities to seek emoluments and ranks" (cf. Rickett [1985], p. 264); *HFZ*, *pian* 7, "Er Bing" (Two Handles), Liao trans., vol. 1, p. 50, "If the ruler reveals his likes, ministers will pretend to talent."

549. The unknown graph 彊, deciphered by Li Xueqin (1979) as 彊, an extended form of *qiang* 強 "strong," may be an alternate form of *jian* 薦 "promote," according to the 1980 editors.

550. In other words, their positions are formally and correctly registered with the ruler through use of name and tally described above.

551. Li Xueqin (1979) was not able to decipher the graph 夅. I do not know what this means.

552. In other words, those close to the ruler, not necessarily his relatives.

553. In other words, there is no possibility that the high officials can create factions and gain the allegiance of swarms of members of the lower orders, such as swordsmen, and of officials and leaders of local elites away from the capital, making them serve those higher officials, not the ruler.

554. The 1980 editors quote from *HNZ*, ch. 15, "Bing Lue Xun" (Planning for Warfare), p. 3a, "Heaven is round and has no end; therefore it cannot be observed. Earth is square but has no root; therefore no one can peer into its gate . . . In general, things have external manifes-

tations. Only the Dao lacks external manifestations. The means by which it lacks external manifestations is used as the means for it to be constantly without form or positional advantage." The *Wenzi pian* 8, "Zi Ran" 自然 (Self-So-ness), p. 159, contains the same passage with minor word differences that include writing *zhen* 朕 "external manifestation" as *sheng* 勝 "conquest." *HGZ*, ch. B, *pian* 8, "Du Wan" 度萬 (Measuring the Myriad Things), p. 1b, also states, "What is meant by Heaven is what makes things so of themselves and lacks external manifestations." On the basis of the quotations, the editors believe that our text's *sheng* should be read as *zhen*. In the other silk manuscripts *sheng* is regularly written as *zhen*, so their suggestion is entirely reasonable. Li Xueqin (1979) interprets *yuan* 原 "origin" as "measure" or "examine into."

555. The 1980 editors have identified this graph as *ji* 極. The term *ji bu* 極卜 appears in the *Shang Shu* "Da Gao" 大誥 (Great Proclamation), ch. 13, p. 88a (p. 200a).

556. Cf. *HGZ*, ch. A, *pian* 4, "Tian Ze" (Heaven's Rules), p. 5b, "If Heaven were to abandon the One, it would in turn be a thing"; *GZ pian* 37, "Xin shu xia" (Techniques of the Heart B), ch. 13, p. 223, states, "As for the ruler who grasps the One, when he grasps the One and does not lose it, he is capable of ruling the myriad phenomena; he shares the same light as the sun and moon, and he shares the same principles as Heaven and Earth. The sage regulates things and is not used by them." Cf. Rickett (1965), p. 170.

557. The 1980 editors interpret *cai* 才 "talent" as a loan for *zai* 哉 "a final particle" and omit *zhe* 者, which is clearly visible in the photograph. Li Xueqin's (1979) transcription and punctuation make better sense.

558. Li Xueqin (1979) interprets the graph *hong* 薨 as *zhong* 眾 "numerous" or *duo* 多 "many." The 1980 editors have mistakenly inserted *de zhu zhe* 得主者 from the previous line. The first graph *fu* 夫 (Li) or *wu* 无 (1980 editors) is partially missing, making its identification unsure.

559. Presumably this means the rules of the four seasons.

560. I.e., the ruler will be unimportant, his ministers will be important.

561. The term *renbang* 人邦, literally "man of the state," may be similar to the term *renchen* 人臣 "slave."

562. In other words, the ministers are just as ferocious with their own subordinates as the ruler is with them.

563. The subject of the sentence seems to be the ruler and his

ministers: they are equally fierce and uncompromising in the application of the law. The copyist has mistakenly reduplicated the graph *gong* 共 "together."

564. "Both rulers" refers to the ruler himself and the subject-minister who acts like a ruler.

565. Jie, the infamous last ruler of the Xia whom Tang defeated and replaced, has committed the same crimes as Yi Yin has just enumerated.

566. This was a major concern of HuangLao specialists, for the issue is raised in several other essays in the silk manuscripts.

567. Li Xueqin (1979) suspects that *heng* 橫 "horizontal/sideways/perverse" may be a loan for *heng* 衡 "weigh/horizontal." Both he and the 1980 editors suspect that the text should read 臣橫主危 "that the subject is perverse and the ruler endangered is the height of danger." Although this interpretation is possible, the text can stand as is.

568. I.e., the actual ruler and powerful minister.

569. This twelve-graph passage has appeared above. The copyist seems to have made an error in transcribing the text again here. It might be possible, however, to read the sentence as, "The names of the eight types of offense are complete."

570. Cf. *HFZ pian* 5, "Zhu Dao" (The Dao of the Ruler), "Get rid of likes, get rid of dislikes and then ministers will appear plain"; this Liao, vol. 1, p. 31, paraphrases, "If the like and hate of the ruler be concealed, the true hearts of the ministers will be revealed." The same idea is found in *HFZ pian* 7, "Er Bing" (Two Handles), Liao vol. 1, p. 50.

571. In other words, he secluded his advisor Yi Yin.

1. In fact, the only actual quotation of Fan Li's *Art of War* preserved in ancient texts is a small quote in Zhang Yan's commentary on a passage on trebuchets (a type of ancient Chinese catapult) in the *Shi ji*, which is not found in the *Guoyu* text: see Robin D. S. Yates, "Siege Engines and Late Zhou Military Technology," *Explorations in the History of Science and Technology in China: a Festschrift in Honour of Dr. Joseph Needham*, Li Guohao, Zhang Mengwen, and Cao Tianqin eds. (Shanghai: Shanghai Classics Publishing House, China, 1982), p. 416, note 29. There is no evidence in support of the notion that Fan Li actually wrote this *Art of War*, or that the *Guoyu* "Yue Yu xia" actually preserves his text: many works in ancient China are attributed to famous men or ancient, sometimes mythological, sages. Although it is quite evident that there are considerable parallels between the silk manuscripts and what is preserved in the *Guoyu*, this is flimsy evidence on which to base a hypothesis that Fan Li is the originator of the HuangLao philosophical tradition.

BIBLIOGRAPHY

ABBREVIATIONS

BSOAS   *Bulletin of the School of Oriental and African Studies*
HJAS   *Harvard Journal of Asiatic Studies.*
SBBY   Sibu beiyao
WW   *Wenwu*

Allan, Sarah. 1991. *The Shape of the Turtle: Myth, Art, and Cosmos in Early China.* Albany: State University of New York Press.

Ames, Roger T. 1983. *The Art of Rulership: A Study in Ancient Chinese Political Thought.* Honolulu: University of Hawaii Press.

————. 1993. *Sun-tzu: The Art of War: The First English Translation Incorporating the Recently Discovered Yin-ch'üeh-shan Texts.* New York: Ballantine Books.

Asano Yuichi 淺野裕一. 1992. *Kōrōdō no seiritsu to tenkai* 黃老道の成立と展開. Oriental Studies Library no. 40. Tokyo: Sobunsha.

Beijing Daxue lishi xi *Lun Heng zhushi* xiao zu 北京大學歷史系論衡注釋小組. 1979. *Lun Heng zhushi* 論衡注釋. Beijing: Zhonghua shuju.

Biot, Edouard. 1969 (1851). *Le Tcheou-li, ou Rites des Tcheou.* Rpt. ed. Taipei: Ch'eng-wen.

Bodde, Derk. 1967 (1938). *China's First Unifier: A Study of the Ch'in Dynasty As Seen in the Life of Li Ssu 280?–208 B.C.* Hong Kong: Hong Kong University Press.

289

————. 1975. *Festivals in Classical China: New Year and Other Annual Observances During the Han Dynasty 206 B.C.–A.D. 220.* Princeton: Princeton University Press.

Boltz, William G. 1981. "Kung Kung and the Flood: Reverse Euhemerization in the *Yao Tien.*" *T'oung Pao* 67: 141–53.

Chen Guuying 陳鼓應 ed. 1993(a). *Daojia wenhua yanjiu* 道家文化研究 Vol. 3. Shanghai: Shanghai Guji chuban she.

————. 1993(b). "Guanyu boshu *Huangdi sijing* chengshu niandai deng wenti de yanjiu" 關於帛書黃帝四經成書年代等問題的研究 in Tang Yijie 湯一介 ed., *Guogu xinzhi: Zhongguo chuantong wenhua de zai quan shi* 國故新知中國傳統文化的再詮釋. Beijing: Beijing daxue chuban she: 139–46.

————. 1995. *Huangdi sijing jinzhu jinyi—Mawangdui Hanmu chutu boshu* 黃帝四經今註今譯——馬王堆漢墓出土帛書. Taibei: Taiwan Shangwu yinshu guan.

Chen Ligui 陳麗桂. 1991. *Zhanguo shiqi de HuangLao sixiang* 戰國時期的黃老思想. Taibei: Lianjing chuban shiye gongsi.

Chen Songchang 陳松長. 1993(a). "Boshu *Xi Ci* shiwen" 帛書繫辭釋文, *Daojia wenhua yanjiu* 3: 416–23.

————. 1993(b). "Boshu 'Xing De' lüeshuo" 帛書刑德略說, *Jianbo yanjiu* 簡帛研究 1: 96–107.

Chen Songchang and Liao Mingchun 廖名春. 1993. "Boshu *Ersanzi Wen, Yi zhi Yi, Yao* shiwen" 帛書二三子問易之義要釋文, *Daojia wenhua yanjiu* 3 (1993): 424–35.

Cheng Chung-ying 1983. "Metaphysics of *Tao* and Dialectics of *Fa*: An Evaluation of HTSC in Relations to Lao Tzu and Han Fei and an Analytical Study of Interrelationships of *Tao, Fa, Hsing* and *Ming*," *Journal of Chinese Philosophy* 10: 251–284.

Cheng Shude 程樹德 ed. 1992. *Lun Yu jishi* 論語集釋. Beijing: Zhonghua shuju.

Cheng Wu 程武. 1974. "Hanchu HuangLao sixiang he fajia luxian—Du Changsha Mawangdui sanhao Hanmu chutu boshu zhaji," 漢初黃老思想和法家路線——讀馬王堆三號漢墓出土帛書札記 *WW* 10: 43–47, 64.

Chunqiu fanlu 春秋繁露. By Dong Zhongshu 董仲舒. SBBY ed.

Creel, Herrlee G. 1970(a). "The Meaning of 刑名 *Hsing-ming*," in *What is Taoism? And Other Studies in Chinese Cultural History*. Chicago: University of Chicago Press: 79–91. Originally published in Soren Egerød and Else Glahn eds., *Studia Serica Bernhard Karlgren Dedicata* (Copenhagen, 1959): 199–211.

————. 1970(b). "The *Fa-chia:* "Legalists" or "Administrators?", in *What is Taoism? And Other Studies in Chinese Cultural History*. Chicago: University of Chicago Press: 92–120.

————. 1974. *Shen Pu-hai: A Chinese Political Philosopher of the Fourth Century B.C.* Chicago: University of Chicago Press.

Crump, J. I. 1970. *Chan-kuo Ts'e*. Oxford: Clarendon Press.

Da Dai Liji jinzhu jinyi 大戴禮記今註今譯. 1975. Gao Ming 高明 ed. Taibei: Shangwu yinshu guan.

Decaux, Jacques. 1989. *Les Quatre Livres de l'Empereur Jaune: le Canon Taoique Retrouvé*. Taibei: Ouyu chuban she.

Dengxizi 鄧析子. 1989. Sibu congkan ed. Shanghai: Shanghai shudian.

des Rotours, Robert. 1963. "Quelques Notes sur l'Anthropophagie en Chine," *T'oung Pao* 50: 386–427.

————. 1968. "Encore Quelques Notes sur l'Anthropophagie en Chine," *T'oung Pao* 54.1–3: 1–49.

Dubs, Homer H. trans. 1966. *The Works of Hsüntze*. Reprint ed. Taibei: Ch'eng-wen Publishing Company.

Duyvendak, J. J. L. trans. 1963. *The Book of Lord Shang*. Reprint ed. Chicago: University of Chicago Press.

Fang Yan suzheng 方言疏證. Dai Zhen 戴震 ed. SBBY ed.

Forke, Alfred. 1962. *Lun-Heng: Philosophical Essays of Wang Ch'ung*. 2 vols. New York: Paragon Book Gallery (1907).

Fu Juyou 傅舉有 and Chen Songchang 陳松長. 1992. *Mawangdui Hanmu wenwu* 馬王堆漢墓文物, Changsha: Hunan chuban she.

Fudan daxue zhexuexi *Laozi zhushi* zu 復旦大學哲學系老子注釋組. 1977. *Laozi zhushi* 老子注釋. Shanghai: Renmin chuban she.

Gao Heng 高亨. 1979. *Zhouyi dazhuan jinzhu* 周易大傳今注. Shandong: QiLu shushe.

Gao Heng and Dong Zhian 董治安. 1975. "*Shi Da Jing* chulun" 十大經初論, *Lishi yanjiu* 歷史研究1: 89–97.

Gao Zheng 高正. 1993. "Boshu 'Shisi Jing' zhengming" 帛書十四經正名, *Daojia wenhua yanjiu* 3: 283–84.

Graham, A. C. 1980. "How Much of *Chuang Tzu* did Chuang Tzu Write?," *Journal of the American Academy of Religion* 47.3 Thematic Issue 5: 459–501.

————. 1981. *Chuang Tzu: The Seven Inner Chapters and Other Writings from the Chuang-tzu*. London: George Allen and Unwin.

————. 1978. *Later Mohist Logic, Ethics and Science*. London and Hong Kong: School of Oriental and African Studies and the Chinese University, Hong Kong.

———. 1989(a). *Disputers of the Tao: Philosophical Argument in Ancient China*. La Salle: Open Court.

———. 1989(b). "A Neglected Pre-Han Philosophical Text: *Ho-Kuan-Tzu*," *BSOAS* 52.3: 498–532.

Guanzi jiaozheng 管子校正. 1990 (1954). Dai Wang 戴望 ed. Zhuzi jicheng ed. Beijing: Zhongha shuju.

Guo Moruo 郭沫若, Wen Yiduo 文一多, Xu Weiyu 許維遹 eds. 1956. *Guanzi jijiao* 管子集校. Beijing: Kexue chuban she.

Guo Yuanxing 郭元興. 1979. "Du *Jingfa* 讀經法," *Zhonghua wenshi luncong* 中華文史論叢 2: 125–136.

Guojia wenwuju guwenxian yanjiushi 國家文物局古文獻研究室 ed. 1980. *Mawangdui Hanmu boshu* 馬王堆漢墓帛書 vol.1. Beijing: Wenwu chuban she.

Guoyu 國語. 1968. SBBY ed. Taibei: Zhonghua shuju.

Han Shu buzhu 漢書補注. ca. 1960 (1900). Wang Xianqian 王先謙 ed. Reprint ed. Taibei: Yiwen yinshuguan.

Hanfeizi jijie 韓非子集解. 1956. Wang Xianshen 王先慎 ed. Guoxue jiben congshu ed. Taibei: Shangwu yinshuguan.

Harper, Donald J. 1982. *The "Wu Shih Erh Ping Fang": Translation and Commentary*, unpublished Ph.D. dissertation. Berkeley: University of California.

Heguanzi 鶡冠子. SBBY ed. Shanghai: Zhonghua shuju.

Henricks, Robert G. 1989. *Lao-Tzu: Te-Tao Ching: A New Translation Based on the Recently Discovered Ma-wang-tui Texts*. New York: Ballantine Books.

———. (Forthcoming). "Chapter 50 in the *Laozi*: Is it 'Three out of ten' or 'Thirteen'?" Proceedings of the Internationales Laudse-Symposium, Westerwald, Germany, May, 1993, *Monumenta Serica* Special Issue.

Hu Jiacong 胡家聰. 1993. "Boshu *Dao Yuan* he *Laozi* lun dao di bijiao" 帛書道原和老子論道的比較, *Daojia wenhua yanjiu* 3: 260–64.

———. 1994. "Yin Wen HuangLao sixiang yu Jixia 'Baijia zhengming'," 尹文黃老思想與稷下百家爭鳴 *Daojia wenhua yanjiu* 4: 118–127.

Hu Xintian 胡信田. 1984. Li Zongtang 李宗唐 ed. *Huangdijing tongshi* 黃帝四經通釋. Taibei: Tiangong shuju.

———. 1992. *Huangdi Dadao jing* 黃帝大道經. Taibei: Dingyuan wenhua shiye youxian gongsi.

Huainanzi 淮南子. 1966. SBBY ed. Taibei: Zhonghua shuju.

Hulsewé, A. F. P. 1985. *Remnants of Ch'in Law*. Leiden: E. J. Brill.

Hunan sheng bowuguan 湖南省博物館. 1979. *Mawangdui Hanmu yanjiu* 馬王堆漢墓研究. Changsha: Hunan renmin chuban she.

ICS Ancient Chinese Text Concordance Series. 1992. *A Concordance to the Wenzi*. Taiwan: Commercial Press.

Jan Yün-hua. 1980. "*Tao Yüan* Or *Tao: The Origin*," *Journal of Chinese Philosophy* 7: 195–204.

———. 1983. "Political Philosophy of the *Shih Liu Ching* Attributed to the Yellow Emperor Taoism," *Journal of Chinese Philosophy* 10: 205–228.

Jia Yi 賈誼. *Xinshu* 新書. Sibu congkan ed.

Jochim, Christian. 1990. "Flowers, Fruit, and Incense Only: Elite versus Popular in Taiwan's Religion of the Yellow Emperor," *Modern China* 16.1: 3–38.

Kaltenmark, Max. 1979. "The Ideology of the T'ai-p'ing ching," in Holmes Welch and Anna Seidel eds., *Facets of Taoism: Essays in Chinese Religion*. New Haven: Yale University Press: 19–52.

Karlgren, Bernhard. 1950. *The Book of Odes: Chinese Text, Transcription and Translation*. Stockholm: Museum of Far Eastern Antiquities.

Knechtges, David R., trans. 1987. *Wen xuan or Selections of Refined Literature by Xiao Tong*. Vol. 2. Princeton: Princeton University Press.

Laozi 老子. 1976. SBBY ed. Taibei: Zhonghua shuju.

Lau, D. C. trans. 1979. *Confucius: The Analects*. Harmondsworth: Penguin.

———. 1982 (1963). *Lao Tzu: Tao Te Ching*. Harmondsworth: Penguin.

Lau, D. C. and Roger T. Ames trans. 1996. *Sun Pin: The Art of Warfare*. New York: Ballantine Books.

Le Blanc, Charles. 1985/1986. "A Re-Examination of the Myth of Huang-ti," *Journal of Chinese Religions* 13, 14: 45–63.

Le Blanc, Charles and Rémi Mathieu eds. 1992. *Mythe et Philosophie à l'Aube de la Chine Impériale: Études sur le Huainan zi*. Montréal: Presses de l'Université de Montréal.

Legge, James. 1885. *The Li Ki. The Sacred Books of the East*. F. Max Müller ed. Vols. 27 and 28. Oxford: Clarendon Press.

Lewis, Mark Edward. 1990. *Sanctioned Violence in Early China*. Albany: State University of New York Press.

Li Ling 李零. 1993. "Daojia yu 'Boshu'" 道家與帛書, *Daojia wenhua yanjiu* 3: 386–94.

———. 1994. "Shuo HuangLao" 說黃老, *Daojia wenhua yanjiu* 5: 142–157.

Li Weiqi 李維琦 ed. 1988. *Guo Yu Zhanguo Ce* 國語戰國策. Changsha: Yuelu shushe.

Li Xueqin 李學勤. 1979 (1974). "Shilun Mawangdui Hanmu boshu 'Yi Yin, Jiu Zhu'" 試論馬王堆漢墓帛書伊尹九主, in Hunan sheng bowuguan (1979): 110–19.

———. 1990. "Fan Li sixiang yu boshu *Huangdi shu*" 范蠡思想與帛書黃帝書, *Zhejiang xuekan* 浙江學刊 1: 97–99, 90.

———. 1993(a). "*Cheng* pian yu *Zhouzhu*" 稱篇與周祝, *Daojia wenhua yanjiu* 3: 241–48.

———. 1993(b). "Mawangdui boshu *Jing Fa Da Fen* ji qi ta" 馬王堆帛書經法大分及其他, *Daojia wenhua yanjiu* 3: 274–82.

Liao, W. K., trans. 1959 (1939). *The Complete Works of Han Fei Tzu.* 2 vols. London: Arthur Probsthain.

Lienü zhuan 列女傳. 1987(1979). By Liu Xiang 劉向. Taibei: Guangwen shuju.

Liji zhengyi 禮記正義. 1987(1980). *Shisanjing zhusu* 十三經注疏 Ruan Yuan 阮元 ed. Beijing: Zhonghua shuju.

Liu Tao 六韜. Kambun taikei ed.

Liu Weihua 劉蔚華 and Miao Runtian 苗潤田 1986. "HuangLao sixiang yuanliu" 黃老思想源流, *Zhongguo zhexue shi* 中國哲學史 2: 49–58.

Loewe, Michael. 1979. *Ways to Paradise: The Chinese Quest for Immortality.* London: George Allen and Unwin.

Loewe, Michael A.N. 1980. "The Han View of Comets," *Bulletin of the Museum of Far Eastern Antiquities* 52: 1–31.

Long Hui 龍晦. 1975. "Mawangdui chutu 'Laozi' yibenqian guyishu tanyuan" 馬王堆出土老子乙本前古佚書探原, *Kaogu xuebao* 考古學報: 23–32.

Luo Zhenyu 羅振玉 and Wang Guowei 王國維. 1934. *Liusha zhuijian kaoshi* 流沙墜簡考釋. Shanyu: Privately published.

Lüshi chunqiu 呂氏春秋. 1975. SBBY ed. Taibei: Zhonghua shuju.

Ma Jixing 馬繼興. 1992. *Mawangdui guyishu kaoshi* 馬王堆古醫書考釋. Changsha: Hunan kexue jishu chuban she.

Major, John S. 1987. "The Meaning of Hsing-te," in Charles Le Blanc and Susan Blader eds., *Chinese Ideas about Nature and Society.* Hong Kong: Hong Kong University Press: 281–291.

———. 1993. *Heaven and Earth in Early Han Thought: Chapters Three, Four, and Five of the Huainanzi.* Albany: State University Press of New York.

Makeham, John. 1994. *Name and Actuality in Early Chinese Thought.* Albany: State University of New York Press.

Mawangdui Hanmu boshu zhengli xiaozu 馬王堆漢墓帛書整理小
組. 1974. "Changsha Mawangdui Hanmu chutu *Laozi* yiben juanqian guyishu shiwen 長沙馬王堆漢墓出土老子乙本前古佚
書," *WW* 10: 30–42.

Mawangdui Hanmu boshu zhengli xiaozu. 1976. *Jing Fa* 經法. Beijing:
Wenwu chuban she.

McLeod, Katrina C. D. and Robin D. S. Yates. 1981. "Forms of Ch'in
Law: An Annotated Translation of the *Feng-chen shih*," *HJAS* 41.1:
111–163.

Mei Yipao, trans. 1973 (1929). *The Ethical and Political Works of Motse*.
Westport, CT.: Hyperion Press.

Mori Yasutaro 森安太郎. 1988. *Huangdi de chuanshuo: Zhongguo gu-
dai shenhua yanjiu* 黃帝的傳說: 中國古代神話研究. Wang Xiao-
lian 王孝廉 trans. Taibei: Shibao wenhua chuban qiye youxian gongsi.

Morohashi Tetsuji 諸橋轍次. 1977. *Daikanwa jiten* 大漢和辭典. Tokyo:
Daishukan shoten.

Mozi 墨子. *Daozang* 道藏 ed.

Needham, Joseph. 1956. *Science and Civilisation in China* Vol. 2 "History
of Scientific Thought," Cambridge: Cambridge University Press.

Needham, Joseph and Robin D. S. Yates. 1994. *Science and Civilisation
in China* Vol. 5, part 6. Cambridge: Cambridge University Press.

Pang Pu 龐樸. 1980. *Boshu Wuxing pian yanjiu* 帛書五行篇研究.
Shandong: QiLu shushe.

Pang Pu. 1993. "Huangdi yu Hundun—Zhonghua wenming de qidian"
黃帝與混沌——中華文明的起點 in Tang Yijie ed., *Guogu
xinzhi: Zhongguo chuantong wenhua de zai quanshi*. Beijing: Beijing
daxue chuban she: 96–109.

Peerenboom, R. P. 1990. "Natural Law in the *Huang-Lao Boshu*," *Philosophy East and West* 40.3: 309–330.

———. 1991. "*Heguanzi* and Huang-Lao Thought," *Early China* 16:
169–86.

———. 1993. *Law and Morality in Ancient China: The Silk Manuscripts of
Huang-Lao*. Albany: State University of New York Press.

Pokora, Timoteus. 1961. "On the Origins of the Notions T'ai-p'ing and
Ta-t'ung in Chinese Philosophy," *Archiv Orientalni* 29.3: 448–454.

Qiu Xigui 裘錫圭. 1980. "Mawangdui *Laozi* jiayi ben juan qianhou
yishu yu 'Daofa jia'" 馬王堆老子甲乙本前後佚書與道法家,
Zhongguo zhexue 中國哲學 2: 68–84.

———. 1993. "Mawangdui boshu *Laozi* yiben juanqian guyishu bing fei *Huangdi sijing*" 馬王堆帛書老子乙本前古佚書幷非黃帝四經, *Daojia wenhua yanjiu* 3: 249–55.

Queen, Sarah. 1993. "Dong Zhongshu he HuangLao sixiang" 董仲舒和黃老思想, *Daojia wenhua yanjiu* 3: 285–96.

Rao Zongyi 饒宗頤. 1993(a). "Chu Boshu yu *Dao Yuan Pian*" 楚帛書與道原篇, *Daojia wenhua yanjiu* 3: 256–59.

———. 1993(b). "Mawangdui 'Xing De' yiben jiugong tu zhushen shi—jian lun chutu wenxianzhong de Zhuan Xu yu She Ti" 馬王堆刑德乙本九宮圖諸神釋——兼論出土文獻中的顓頊與攝提, *Jianbo yanjiu* 1: 89–95.

Rickett, W. Allyn. 1965. *Kuan-tzu: A Repository of Early Chinese Thought*. Vol. 1. Hong Kong: Hong Kong University Press.

———. 1985. *Guanzi: Political, Economic, and Philosophical Essays from Early China. A Study and Translation*. Volume One. Princeton: Princeton University Press.

Roth, Harold. 1991(a). "Psychology and Self-Cultivation in Early Taoistic Thought," *HJAS* 51.2: 599–650.

———. 1991(b). "What is Huang-Lao?" Unpublished paper presented at the Annual Meeting of the Association for Asian Studies.

Schwartz, Benjamin I. 1985. *The World of Thought in Ancient China*. Cambridge, MA: Belknap Press of Harvard University Press.

Seidel, Anna K. 1969. *La Divinisation de Lao Tseu dans le Taoisme des Han*. Publications de l'École Française d'Extrême-Orient vol. 71. Paris: École Française d'Extrême-Orient.

Shi Huaci 史華慈 (Benjamin I. Schwartz). 1994. "HuangLao xueshuo: Song Xing he Shen Dao lunping 黃老學說: 宋鈃和慎到論評," *Daojia wenhua yanjiu* 4: 128–146.

Shiji 史記. 1985. Composed by Sima Qian 司馬遷. Beijing: Zhonghua shuju (1959).

Shizi 尸子. SBBY ed.

Shuo Yuan jiaozheng 說苑校證. 1991 (1987). Composed by Liu Xiang; Xiang Zonglu 向宗魯 ed. Beijing: Zhonghua shuju.

Swann, Nancy Lee. 1950. *Food and Money in Ancient China*. Princeton: Princeton University Press.

Taiping yulan 太平御覽. 1985 (1960). Li Fang 李昉 ed. Beijing: Zhonghua shuju.

Tang Lan 唐蘭. 1974. "*Huangdi sijing* chutan" 黃帝四經初探, *WW* 10: 48–52.

Thompson, Paul M. 1979. *The Shen Tzu Fragments*. Oxford: Oxford University Press.

Tu Wei-ming. 1979–80. "The 'Thought of Huang-Lao': A Reflection on the Lao Tzu and Huang Ti Texts in the Silk Manuscripts of Ma-wang-tui," *Journal of Asian Studies* 39: 95–110.

Turner, Karen. 1989. "The Theory of Law in the *Ching-Fa*," *Early China* 14: 55–76.

———. 1993. "War, Punishment, and the Law of Nature in Early Chinese Concepts of the State," *HJAS* 53.2: 285–324.

Wang Bo 王博. 1992. "*Huangdi sijing* he *Guanzi* sipian" 黃帝四經和管子四篇, *Daojia wenhua yanjiu* 1: 198–213.

———. 1993. "Lun *Huangdi sijing* chansheng de diyu" 論黃帝四經產生的地域, in *Daojia wenhua yanjiu* 3: 223–240.

Watson, Burton, trans. 1968. *The Complete Works of Chuang Tzu*. New York: Columbia University Press.

Wei Qipeng 魏啓鵬. 1980. *Huangdi sijing* sixiang tanyuan" 黃帝四經思想探源, *Zhongguo zhexue* 4: 179–91.

———. 1991. *De Xing jiaoshi* 德行校釋. Chengdu: BaShu shushe.

———. 1993. "Qian HuangLao xingming zhi xue de zhengui yipian—du Mawangdui Hanmu boshu 'YiYin, Jiu Zhu'" 前黃老形名之學的珍貴佚篇——讀馬王堆漢墓帛書伊尹九主, *Daojia wenhua yanjiu* 3: 330–39.

Wen xuan 文選. 1978. Compiled by Xiao Tong 蕭統. 2 Vols. Hong Kong: Shangwu yinshu guan (1936).

Wenzi yaoquan 文子要詮. 1988. Li Dingsheng 李定生 and Xu Huijun 徐慧君 eds. Shanghai: Fudan daxue chuban she.

Wile, Douglas. 1992. *Art of the Bedchamber: The Chinese Sexual Yoga Classics Including Women's Solo Meditation Texts*. Albany: State University of New York Press.

Wu Guang 吳光. 1985. *HuangLao zhi xue tonglun* 黃老之學通論. Hang-chou: Zhejiang renmin chuban she.

Wu Jiulong 吳九龍. 1985. *Yinqueshan Hanjian shiwen* 銀雀山漢簡釋文. Beijing: Wenwu chuban she.

Xiao Dengfu 蕭登福. 1990. *Guiguzi yanjiu* 鬼谷子研究. Taibei: Wenjin chuban she.

Xiao Shafu 蕭萐父. 1993. "HuangLao boshu zhexue qianyi" 黃老帛書哲學淺議, *Daojia wenhua yanjiu* 3: 265–73.

Xu Kangsheng 許抗生. 1979. "Lüe shuo HuangLao xuepai de chan-sheng he yanbian" 略說黃老學派的產生和演變, *Wenshizhe* 文史哲 3: 71–76.

Xunzi jijie 荀子集解. 1929. Wang Xianqian ed., Wanyou wenku ed. Shanghai: Shangwu yinshuguan.

Yanzi chunqiu 晏子春秋. 1991. Sun Xingyan 孫星衍 and Huang Yizhou 黃以周 eds. Shanghai: Guji chuban she.

Yates, Robin D. S. 1979. "The Mohists on Warfare: Technology, Technique and Justification," *Journal of the American Academy of Religion*, Thematic Supplement 47.3S (Studies in Classical Chinese Thought): 549–603.

———. 1980. "The City under Siege: Technology and Organization in the Military Chapters of Mo-tzu." Unpublished Ph.D. dissertation. Cambridge, MA: Harvard University.

———. 1982. "Siege Engines and Late Zhou Military Technology," in Li Guohua et al. eds, *Explorations in the History of Science and Technology in China: a Festschrift in Honour of Dr. Joseph Needham*, Li Guohao, Zhang Mengwen, and Cao Tianqin eds., Shanghai: Shanghai Classics Publishing House, China, 1982: 409–452.

———. 1987. "Social Status in the Ch'in: Evidence from the Yünmeng Legal Documents. Part One: Commoners," *HJAS* 47.1: 197–237.

———. 1988. "New Light on Ancient Chinese Military Texts: Notes on their Nature and Evolution, and the Development of Military Specialization in Warring States China," *T'oung Pao* 74: 211–248.

———. 1994(a). "The Yin Yang Texts from Yinqueshan: An Introduction and Partial Reconstruction, with Notes on their Significance in Relation to Huang-Lao Daoism," *Early China* 19: 74–144.

———. 1994(b). "Dui Handai Mawangdui HuangLao boshu xingzhi de jidian kanfa" 對漢代馬王堆黃老帛書性質的幾點看法, *Mawangdui Hanmu yanjiu wenji—1992-nian Mawangdui Hanmu guoji xueshu taolun hui lunwen xuan* 馬王堆漢墓研究文集——1992-年馬王堆漢墓國際學術討論會論文選 Proceedings of the International Symposium on the Mawangdui Han Tombs. Changsha: Hunan Provincial Museum: 16–26.

———. forthcoming (a). "Purity and Pollution in Early China," in 歷史語言研究所 ed., *Lishi yu kaogu zhenghe zhi yanjiu* 歷史與考古整合之研究, Taipei.

Yinwenzi 尹文子. 1990. Zhong Changtong 仲長統 ed. Shanghai: Shanghai guji chuban she.

Yu Dacheng 于大成. 1968. "Wenzi jiaobu" 文子斠補, *Zhongshan xueshu wenhua jikan* 中山學術文化集刊, no. 2: 637–729.

Yu Mingguang 余明光. 1989. *Huangdi Sijing yu HuangLao Sixiang* 黃帝四經與黃老思想. Harbin: Heilongjiang renmin chuban she.

———. 1993(a). *Huangdi sijing jinzhu jinyi* 黃帝四經今注今譯. Changsha: Yuelu shushe.

———. 1993(b). "Boshu *Yi Yin Jiuzhu* yu HuangLao zhi xue" 帛書伊尹九主與黃老之學, *Daojia wenhua yanjiu* 3: 340–48.

Yuan Ke 袁珂. 1980. *Shanhai Jing jiaozhu* 山海經校注. Shanghai: Shanghai guji chuban she.

Zhang Bingnan 寂秉南. 1991. *Jixia gouchen* 稷下鉤沈沉. Shanghai: Shanghai guji chuban she.

Zhou Fagao 周法稿. 1977. *Guang Ya yinde* 廣雅引得. Hong Kong: Zhongwen daxue chuban she.

Zhouli zhengyi 周禮正義. Sun Yirang 孫詒讓 ed. SBBY ed.

Zhu Shiche 朱師轍. 1974. *Shangjunshu jiegu dingben* 商君書解詁定本. Hong Kong: Zhonghua shuju.

Zhuangzi jishi 莊子集釋. 1961. Guo Qingfan 郭慶藩 ed. 4 vols. Beijing: Zhonghua shuju.

ROBIN D. S. YATES is the chairman of the department of East Asian studies and director of the Centre for East Asian Studies at McGill University. Professor Yates, who holds an M.A. from both Oxford University and the University of California, Berkeley, and a Ph.D. from Harvard, has published widely on Chinese military technology, law, and the history of Chinese philosophy. His most recent acclaimed work is his collaboration with Dr. Joseph Needham on Vol. 5.6 of Cambridge University Press's *Science and Civilisation in China*. Professor Yates and his wife, Professor Grace Fong, live in Montreal, Canada.